Family Upheaval

EASA Series

Published in Association with the European Association of Social Anthropologists (EASA)

Series Editor: James G. Carrier, Senior Research Associate, Oxford Brookes University

Social anthropology in Europe is growing, and the variety of work being done is expanding. This series is intended to present the best of the work produced by members of the EASA, both in monographs and in edited collections. The studies in this series describe societies, processes, and institutions around the world and are intended for both scholarly and student readership.

FAMILY UPHEAVAL

Generation, Mobility and Relatedness among Pakistani Migrants in Denmark

Mikkel Rytter

berghahn
NEW YORK · OXFORD
www.berghahnbooks.com

Published in 2013 by

Berghahn Books

www.berghahnbooks.com

©2013 Mikkel Rytter

Library of Congress Cataloging-in-Publication Data

Rytter, Mikkel.
 Family upheaval : generation, mobility and relatedness among Pakistani
migrants in Denmark / Mikkel Rytter. -- First edition.
    pages cm. -- (EASA series ; 21)
 Includes bibliographical references.
 ISBN 978-0-85745-939-8 (hardback : acid-free paper) -- ISBN (invalid)
978-0-85745-940-4 (ebook)
1. Pakistanis--Denmark--Social conditions. 2. Immigrant
families--Denmark. 3. Immigrants--Denmark--Social conditions. 4.
Intergenerational relations--Denmark. 5. Marriage--Denmark. 6. Social
mobility--Denmark. 7. Pakistanis--Denmark--Ethnic identity. 8.
Transnationalism. 9. Denmark--Ethnic relations. 10. Denmark--Social
conditions--1945- I. Title.
 DL142.P34R97 2013
 305.891'412204895--dc23

2012032928

British Library Cataloguing in Publication Data
A catalogue record for this book is available from the British Library
Printed in the United States on acid-free paper.

ISBN: 978-0-85745-939-8 (hardback)
ISBN: 978-0-85745-940-4 (ebook)

Contents

List of figures

Preface

On 15 September 2001, I met Tahir at Nørrebro community centre in order to conduct my first ethnographic interview ever. Like millions of others around the world, both of us had four days earlier watched in disbelief as airplanes crashed into the World Trade Centre in New York. As I had just started doing the fieldwork for my anthropology MA, focusing on arranged marriages among Pakistani immigrants in Denmark, the topic of our conversation that afternoon was Tahir's upcoming wedding. After a long interview, he checked his mobile phone and giggled. 'I've just received a text message from one of my friends: "Dear Tahir, I need a place to sleep tonight, can I stay at your house? – Osama Bin Laden."' Tahir confirmed that there were numerous sarcastic jokes like this circulating among his friends. The text message shows not just how Tahir and I – both of us university students, both of us products of the Danish welfare state – were so unfamiliar with terror that we could hardly relate to the gravity of the event. It also illustrates how, even though we both sensed that September 11 would have an impact in the future, neither Tahir nor I – nor any of us, perhaps – could imagine what consequences the terror attacks would soon have on international relations, nor how the massive focus on security and securitisation that followed in numerous nation-states would affect the everyday lives of ordinary people – including the Pakistani immigrant families that have lived in greater Copenhagen since the late 1960s.

In Denmark, September 11 was followed in November by a national election that brought to power a new Liberal-Conservative government, based on the support of the right-wing Danish People's Party. This constellation of parties had an absolute majority in the Folketing from 2001 to September 2011 – a mandate used to set a new trajectory for the development of Danish society. Like many other countries, Denmark responded to the global threat of Islamist terrorism. It did this not just by sending troops to Iraq and Afghanistan, but also with a strict immigration regime and far-reaching anti-terror legislation. Since 2001, several Islamist terror attacks have been prevented by the secret service, Denmark became the centre of the cartoons controversy, and endless debates have been ongoing about Muslim immigrants and their place in Danish society. In general, the decade succeeding September 11 was characterised by intense securitisation and a rising ethno-nationalism that stressed differences between indigenous Danes and Muslim minorities.

However, as this book goes to press, al-Qaeda leader Osama Bin Laden is dead, killed by American special forces at his residence in Abbottabad, and US president Barack Obama has ended a decade of global 'war on terror'. The book has therefore become a study of how a relatively small group – of approximately 25,000 immigrants connected to Pakistan – was affected by these turbulent times: partly because the upcoming young generation of Danish Pakistanis in various ways challenge their parents' ideas of what it means to be and to do family, of who they are and of who they want to be in the future; and partly because these critical renegotiations of family relatedness, identity and belonging take place within a specific social and political context where, since September 11, public denigration, suspicion and securitisation have been the order of the day. Even though the main object of this book is to analyse the dynamics, impacts and outcomes of the current process of family upheaval among Pakistani migrants, it can also to some extent therefore be read as a study of extraordinary and previously unimaginable developments in Danish society over the last decade. In other words, the book attempts to answer some of the questions concerning the future of Pakistani migrant families, the position of Muslim minorities and the changing Danish welfare state that neither Tahir nor I could have foreseen that afternoon in 2001.

Several research projects have contributed to the material presented in the book. When I did the fieldwork for my MA in 2001–2, the main arena for the recruitment of interlocutors was the Organisation of Pakistani Students and Academics (OPSA), a student organisation which at that time had lots of semi-public political, cultural and religious activities and an internet site (*desi*-debate) with many animated discussions. Most of the young Danish Pakistanis I got to know through OPSA were not married at the time, but were preoccupied with discussing the topic, both among themselves and in their families. The organisation became my entry into the well-educated rising middle class within the migrant community. Today, my interlocutors from that period have finished their education and started working. Many got engaged, got married (some even divorced), became parents and established their own households, and some have had to deal with problems related to aging and sick parents, or have had to bury them. In this respect, my friends became adults, in the process being confronted with a new moral landscape of the obligations and expectations that constitute the Pakistani migrant family. Following these life-phase transitions and the many conflicts they have generated has formed my perspective of family life.

In 2003, I became research assistant at the Danish Folklore Archives, where I was responsible for a study of how Pakistani families were coping with the transformations of family relations and obligations due to the growing number of marriages being contracted between Pakistani families living in Denmark.[1] In 2004, I went to Islamabad and the villages around Kharian in the

---

1. At the Danish Folklore Archives, I was responsible for the projects 'Gift med intention' (Married with intention) and 'Pakistanske Danmarkshistorier' (Pakistani narratives of Denmark).

Gujrat district in order to interview Pakistanis who had returned, after decades in Denmark, about their lives in Denmark and about the troubles they faced settling and being reintegrated in their families. In the autumn of 2007, I returned for another month to the same area of Pakistan to continue collecting data from returnee families.

In 2005–6, working in a cross-disciplinary project on transnational marriages at the Academy of Migration Studies in Denmark,[2] I carried out a study of how the Danish legislation of 2002 on family reunification was affecting Pakistani marriage practices and family life. As a result of the strict new immigration regime, hundreds of newly-wed transnational couples have had to settle in Sweden in order to achieve family reunification. Besides interviewing relevant Swedish and Danish actors in the field, I also conducted interviews with eighteen couples (one or both spouses) in either Sweden or Denmark.

In 2006, I initiated the research for my PhD dissertation at the Department of Anthropology, University of Copenhagen, which focused on the dynamics of Pakistani migrant families in Denmark.[3] The study was based on life-story interviews and semi-structured thematic interviews both with older, first-generation Pakistanis and with their adult children. The research also included case studies on responses in the Pakistani community to the Kashmir earthquake in 2005, and on suspicions and anxieties about *kala jaddu* (sorcery) in local and transnational families. Part of this latter research was carried out in Pakistan in 2007.

This long-term engagement, from 2001 to 2008, has enabled insights into life-phase transitions and shifting ideas about what it means to be and to do family for Pakistani migrants embedded in a transnational social field. It has also enabled me to address the complexity and uncertainty resulting from change in the institution of the family in a post-September 11 context: change that can slip from analytical view in the course of short-term study.

Any ethnographic study is dependent on the goodwill of the people it involves. I am therefore above all indebted to the numerous Pakistanis, Danes, Britons and Swedes with a Pakistani background who, over the years, have let me into their lives and families. They not only shared family occasions and activities with me, but also involved me in their pasts, presents and future lives, as they related their wishes and worries, hopes and fears, dreams and nightmares. Thank you all. It has been a wonderful journey. I hope this book redeems the trust you have shown me.

---

2. The MiMa project (Migration and Marriage) formed part of the Academy of Migration Studies i Denmark (AMID). The MiMa research group was headed by Professor Garbi Schmidt and also included Camilla Elg and Vibeke Jakobsen.
3. The project was called 'Familien som integrerende institution: flygtninge og indvandrere i Danmark' (FiiD) (The Family as an Institution of Integration among Immigrants and Refugees in Denmark). The FiiD research group was headed by Professor Karen Fog Olwig, and also included Birgitte Romme Larsen.

A major part of the material presented in the book stems from my affiliation with the research programme, 'The Family as an institution of integration among immigrants and refugees in Denmark' (FiiD), generously funded by the Danish Research Council for Culture and Communication (FKK) and hosted by the Department of Anthropology, University of Copenhagen. I thank the administration for helping me with practical matters, especially PhD secretary Jorgen Pedersen, librarian Jan Starcke and the IT support staff for helping me with various issues concerning money, books and computers. Thanks to Anders Rytter for providing illustrations, and to Iram Nisa Asif and Zubair Butt Hussain for reading selected passages and helping me with Urdu and Punjabi concepts. Warm thanks go to Robert Parkin, Lenore Messick and Lucy Seton-Watson for carefully correcting my English in different parts and versions of the book.

The parts of the fieldwork conducted in Pakistan were only possible due to the economic support of external funders and sponsors. I therefore thank the Knud Højgaards Fond, Christian og Ottilia Brorson's Rejselegat til yngre Videnskabsmænd og -kvinder, and the Danish Institute in Damascus's Rejselegat, as I gratefully acknowledge the support of the Danish Folklore Archives. I thank everyone who contributed to making my travelling in Pakistan rewarding, both for me personally and for my collection of data. I am especially grateful for the hospitality, help and company of Mazhar Hussain and his family and of the entire Sharif family, and to the families of Urfan Zahoor Ahmad and Imran Hussain.

During the long and difficult journey of turning raw ethnographic data into anthropological writings, I have benefited from the readings, comments and discussions provided by numerous people. Here, I thank the students, colleagues and participants at conferences, seminars and workshops at which I have presented parts of my material for providing invaluable suggestions on how to improve my analysis and lines of argumentation. I am especially grateful for comments provided by Birgitte Romme Larsen, Line Bøgsted, Maria Ventegodt Liisberg, Jonathan Schwartz, Marita Eastmond, Lisa Åkesson, Mette Ringsted, Bo Wagner Sørensen, Kirsten Rønne, Sally Andersson, Palle Ove Christiansen, Karsten Pærregaard, Karen Valentin, Laura Gilliam, Roger Ballard, Nils Bubandt, Ann Benwell, Susan Reynolds Whyte, Bjarke Oxlund, Morten Nielsen, Jonas Østergaard Nielsen, Garbi Schmidt, Vibeke Jakobsen, Camilla Elg, Jørgen Bæk Simonsen, Heiko Henkel, Cecilie Rubow, Lotte Meinert, Marta Erdal Bivand, Katharine Charsley, Marta Bolognani, Peggy Levitt and Bruce Kapferer. I am also grateful for inspiring discussions with the committee for my doctoral thesis, consisting of Helle Bundgaard, Filippo Osella and Pnina Werbner. The final manuscript benefited from the comments and suggestions of three anonymous reviewers, and from the generous help of James Carrier, editor of the EASA series along with Ann Przyzycki DeVita and Megan Palmer from the Berghahn editorial team.

My initial interest in questions related to Muslim minorities in general and Pakistani migrant families in particular is indebted to the teaching of Professor Peter Hervik. My colleague Marianne Holm Pedersen has been a deeply appreciated reader and discussant throughout. Finally, the help and support of Professor Karen Fog Olwig has been invaluable. Thank you for your inspiring and productive cooperation over the years.

Last but not least, I thank Helene, who has encouraged and supported me all along, regardless of how distant and unreasonable I was when writing up the material; and Anton and Gustav, both born during the project, who have always been able to turn my attention towards more important matters than 'writing books'.

Mikkel Rytter, May 2012

Acknowledgements

Portions of this book are partial revisions of papers published previously in which I developed my understanding of the people and processes described here. I want to acknowledge the permission for this granted to me by the copyright holders, and express my gratitude to the anonymous reviewers who commented on earlier versions. Chapter 2 is an extended version of the article, 'Money or education? Strategies of improvement among Pakistani families in Denmark', *Journal of Ethnic and Migration Studies* 2011, 37(3): 197–215. Chapter 3 is based on the article 'Between preferences: marriage and mobility among Danish Pakistani youth', *Journal of the Royal Anthropological Institute* 2012, 18(3): 572–90. Chapter 4 is based on 'The semi-legal family life: Pakistani couples in the borderlands between Denmark and Sweden', *Global Networks* 2012, 12(1): 98–117. Chapter 5 is a shortened version of '"The Family of Denmark" and "the Aliens": kinship images in Danish integration politics', *Ethnos* 2010, 75(3): 301–22. Chapter 6 is a revised version of the article 'Pakistan tur/retur: forhandlinger af hjem og tilhørsforhold inden for flergenerationsfamilien', published in *Tidsskriftet Antropologi* 2006, 111–28. Chapter 7 is based on the article '*A Sunbeam of Hope*: negotiations of identity and belonging among Pakistanis in Denmark', *Journal of Ethnic and Migration Studies* 2010, 36(4): 599–618. Chapter 8 is based on the article 'Events and effects: intensive transnationalism among Pakistanis in Denmark', *Social Analysis* 2010, 54(3): 90–106. Chapter 9 is based on the article 'In-laws and outlaws: black magic among Pakistani migrants in Denmark', *Journal of the Royal Anthropological Institute* 2010, 16(1): 46–63. Finally, Chapter 10 is an extended version of the chapter 'Demonic migrations: re-enchantment of middle class life among Danish-Pakistani Muslims', from the edited volume, *Mobile Bodies, Mobile Souls: Family, Religion and Migration in a Global World* (Aarhus University Press, 2011), 53–76.

Introduction

This book is about Pakistani migrant families who have been living more or less permanently in Denmark since the late 1960s or early 1970s. After four decades in Denmark, many families have achieved levels of material prosperity, economic security and social mobility that the first generation could only dream of before they left Pakistan; however, their success has come at a price.

In general, the approximately 25,000 people in Denmark who have a family history related to Pakistan have done extremely well as hard-working breadwinners, whether successfully self-employed in 'ethnic' businesses such as corner shops, taxis or travel agencies, or working for the state as, for instance, bus drivers, cleaners, teachers and interpreters. Since the 1990s, a significant number of second-generation Pakistanis have entered higher education, and an impressive number have become doctors, engineers, dentists or the like. Many families have also left the cramped apartments of the inner city and moved into the suburbs, where they aspire to a middle-class life-style. Generally speaking, therefore, in many respects the Pakistanis of Denmark constitute a successful migrant community. Today the pioneers in most families are growing old and have started having various health problems. Others have already passed away and been buried in Pakistan or Denmark. Meanwhile, the second generation has married and become parents themselves. Due to life-course transitions and family cycles, however, Pakistani families are currently in a period of unrest and upheaval, with authority and priorities within households and families being renegotiated. The Danish-born second generation is in different ways challenging the organisation, meaning and content of local and transnational family life that their elders tend to cling on to. In this respect the cherished family institution, which often was the main reason for leaving Pakistan in the first place, has gone through some radical changes in the wake of demographic developments, upward social mobility and economic success. Significant sites for this transformation are marriage and household organisation. The traditions of arranged endogamous marriage, which are basic to the reproduction of family values, relations and obligations, and of patrilocal households, in which sons and daughters-in-law take care of aging parents, are eroding and are gradually being replaced by the widespread practice of 'love marriage' and of newly-wed couples moving out and establishing independent households. These trends have been supplemented by a strict national immigration regime that, since 2002, has made family reunification with Pakistani spouses virtually impossible. Those who nevertheless marry in Pakistan often move to Sweden to enjoy family reunification. In this respect, legal measures contribute to the breaking up of households and families.

After four decades in Denmark, common notions of home and belonging within transnational family networks are also being challenged. The upcoming generation to some extent see Pakistan as a strange, exotic place of the past, associated with poverty, authority, 'backwardness' and numerous relatives who will go to great lengths to get their hands on their resources. Even elders of the first generation have begun to acknowledge that, when they occasionally return for longer or shorter periods, the homeland of their dreams and memories is nowhere to be found. On the contrary, they have a difficult time fitting into and enjoying the more simple village life. In many respects, they have become strangers.

The current reorganisation of the migrant family is taking place in the environment of a Danish welfare state that has also changed radically since the late 1960s. The booms and busts of social and economic conditions have especially affected vulnerable groups such as immigrants. In the first period, immigrants from the European periphery were generally approached and conceptualised by the Danish majority as 'exotic others'. However, the critical event of September 11, 2001 – and all the effects it has generated locally and globally – changed the perception of immigrants in Danish public and political discourse. Today, they are primarily addressed as Muslims and conceptualised as 'radical others' who are supposedly threatening Danish culture, values and identity. The state of emergency that took form in the aftermath of September 11 – and today seems to have become more or less naturalised – along with a growing cultural anxiety (Grillo 2003) regarding the very constitution of Danish culture and society have had far-reaching implications for the local and transnational family lives of Pakistani migrants and for common ideas of identity and belonging.

This book is an ethnographic study of Pakistani migrant families in Denmark. It will explore and analyse how, why and at what cost notions of relatedness, identity and belonging are being renegotiated within local families and transnational kinship networks in a specific ethno-national, post-September 11 context, where Pakistani migrants are subjected to processes of non-recognition, exclusion and securitisation. In this respect, the book connects the micro-politics of immigrants' family lives with the macro-politics of the receiving nation-state and global conjunctures in general in order to discuss the current processes of family upheaval.

The family revisited

In migration studies, much emphasis has been placed on how family networks facilitate the migration process or help newly arrived immigrants to settle and find jobs after arrival. The family has often been presented as a resource and a significant push–pull factor facilitating the migration process. Recently there has been much emphasis on the transnational family (Bryceson and Vuorela 2002; Chamberlain and Leydesdorff 2004) or the global family (Sørensen 2005; Eastmond and Åkesson 2007; Olwig 2007) in order to understand how migrants are engaged in more than one place simultaneously (Levitt and Glick Schiller 2004). However, the ways family relations are being destabilised, renegotiated or invented over time in the context of migration, and how these transformations in multiple ways affect the everyday life of migrant families have so far received limited attention in the literature on South Asia (Gardner and Osella 2003: xvii).

My approach to the changing family institution among Pakistani immigrants in Denmark emphasises the migrant family as a specific arena in which notions of identity and belonging are constantly being tested, contested and negotiated. I furthermore stress the importance of the 'family history', as well as the position of the 'family in history', in order to understand the process of continuity and change in the Pakistani family institution in the context of migration.

First of all, many studies of migrant families tend to focus on either the first or the second generations. In contrast, I propose an analytical framework that focuses on the relationship between the two generations and on the ongoing interfamilial negotiations of relatedness, with a special emphasis on what it actually means and implies to be and do family. Such negotiations not only take place between the first and the second generations of Pakistanis living in Denmark, they also structure and redefine relations within wider transnational family networks. In order to address the often conflicting perspectives and experiences in and of dynamic migrant families, I analytically deconstruct the family into a number of individual positions, narratives and trajectories. Contrary to the research literature and public images that to some extent treat the Pakistani family a priori as a corporate unit with common interests (Donnan 1997a: 4),[1] here the family will be conceptualised as an arena in which personal trajectories connect different pasts, presents and possible futures. This approach does not deny the importance of the migrant family as a unit constituted by common history and descent, economy, emotions or morality, but it does insist on being sensitive to the partial perspectives (Haraway 1991) of individuals within households and families. Approaching the Pakistani migrant family as 'a site of dynamic interplay between structure, culture and agency, where creative

---

1. The image of the Muslim immigrant family that dominates the media and public discourse is often oversimplified and relies on a basic pattern of a few stereotypes. Whatever does not fit the perspective is largely ignored (Beck-Gernsheim 2006: 186). Commonly held stereotypes of the 'Asian' population in Britain, which is also salient with the wider Danish public, include that 'all families are extended, children respect their elders, religious faith is total and unquestioning, and women are veiled creatures living in the shadows' (Ali 1992: 109, in Grillo 2008: 23).

culture-building takes place in the context of external social and economic forces as well as immigrants' premigration cultural frameworks' (Foner 1997: 961) is an analytical move that brings to the fore conflicting ideas of what it means to be and to do family. Husbands and wives, parents and children, siblings, cousins, in-laws, etc., all to varying extents, and with different degrees of power and resources, engage in ongoing negotiations about the kinds of responsibilities, obligations and moralities that constitute the family on both the local and transnational levels. These negotiations, where actors mobilise various cultural understandings, meanings and symbols related to their common Pakistani background, along with resources from their years and lives in Denmark, constitute what I call the 'destructive–productive' forces of family life, as in time they will inevitably erode existing moral orders of what it means to be and to do family, as well as facilitating a process in which new possibilities, identities and lines of affiliation and belonging will emerge. In all, the family constitutes a certain modality oriented towards maintaining and recreating close relations grounded in the past, while also being preoccupied with creating alternative future scenarios. Here migrants walk a delicate tightrope, as they challenge certain aspects of traditional family systems while trying to retain others.

Secondly, in order to grasp family upheaval and change as a historical dynamic, I stress the importance of a dual perspective both of migrants' 'family history' and of situating the migrant 'family in history'. The migration project was from its inception part of family history, as young men – and later women and children – in the 1960s and 1970s were sent out in the world in order to move beyond the limited resources at home, expand their socio-economic opportunities and support their relatives. Even today, family histories continue to affect the everyday lives of Pakistanis in Denmark. Karen Fog Olwig (2007: 218) suggests that the migrant family constitutes both a *centrifugal* and a *centripetal* force, thus helping individual members move away to various destinations of social and economic opportunity, while at the same time offering a source of belonging and identity to those family members who, through social practices and displays of moral worth, confirm that they are the members of a particular family. The long-term perspective covering the history of Pakistani families in Denmark over the last four decades enables us to grasp the significance and meaning of the life-course transitions and family cycles that currently contribute to the upheavals going on within the family institution.

Life in and of migrant families is, however, also influenced by historical, social and political conditions in the receiving society.[2] I therefore move beyond the micro-perspective of family history and explore from a macro-perspective how immigrant families have been affected and formed

---

2. We should also keep in mind that the migrant's place of origin, in this case Pakistan, also changes while they are living abroad. This aspect tends to be neglected in transnational studies.

by the changing circumstances of Danish society, and especially how the securitisation of Muslim minorities following September 11 has affected the everyday family lives of Pakistani immigrants. It is, however, important to emphasise that in this process migrants are not passive individuals who are acted upon: they play an active role in reconstructing and redefining the meaning and functions of the family based on the repertoire of cultural understandings, meanings and symbols that they bring with them from the specific migration destination (Foner 1997: 962).

Basically, therefore, I approach the migrant family as an arena where common notions of relatedness, identity and belonging are being negotiated, partly between generations of family members living in Denmark and partly between different branches of the wider transnational family networks. I also emphasise that these negotiations are conditioned by specific social, historical and political conditions in the Danish context that inevitably affect family members in different ways in different periods of time. The current negative attitudes that dominate Danish public and political discourses regarding Muslim minorities have, for different reasons, had a deep impact on the family institution.

In order to explore the dynamics of Pakistani migrant families in Denmark, I approach the family from four different angles in the four parts of this book: the long-term dynamics of family mobility and community competition; the institution of marriage; the contested notion of homelands; and finally, sorcery and afflictions. The four parts constitute different entry-points into the complex micro-politics and social dramas of migrants' family lives, and support the overall argument that Pakistanis in Denmark are currently going through turbulent times, when the family institution is being subjected to transformation and upheaval.

It would, however, be misleading to see the transformations and upheavals of the migrant family as an isolated phenomenon. Currently it is generally the case across Europe – maybe even worldwide – that established forms of morality and cohabitation are changing rapidly, which again leads to a general uncertainty about the condition of the family (Grillo 2008: 15; Carsten 2004: 7). The process is more likely an aspect of modernity itself. According to Zygmunt Bauman, we are currently going through a transition from a 'solid' to a 'liquid' variation of modernity (2006, 2007), one that challenges modern subjects to adapt to ever-changing situations and creates a constant risk of failure. In this age of uncertainty, institutions like the family are no longer stable but have become fluid. Similarly, Anthony Giddens (1991: 58) suggests that spheres of intimacy are changing, as people enter so-called 'pure relationships' for their own sake. These relationships are only maintained as long as both parties gain some kind of satisfaction from them, and family relationships are just one of many alternatives to choose from. According to Arjun Appadurai (1996: 33), modernity is characterised by de-territorialisation, which enables the circulation of fantasies and desires of alternative future lives on a global scale. In this process, we are confronted with 'marriage-scapes' and 'family-scapes' that offer alternative visions of family life to be imagined and acted upon. The processes of globalisation and modernity are affecting relationships and notions of intimacy and morality in local and global families. It is no longer obvious what kinds of emotional, practical, material and symbolic exchanges are implied in being family. Still, the case of Pakistani migrant families in Denmark seems to constitute a specific variation of the more general crisis of the family institution.

In order to discuss the scope and character of family relations, I will use the concept of relatedness, but first I offer some tentative definitions of 'generation' and 'family'.

Generation and family

Generation is a powerful analytical tool for studying society, because it implies a relation in time. Susan Whyte et al. (2008) remind us of the double meaning of generation as both a passive and active verb. In the passive form we may talk of 'being generated', as is the case for offspring, progeny, descendants, etc. We are born into this world as part of a family and a culture, including values, norms and language (Whyte et al. 2008: 2). In this way, the passive form of generation refers to our specific position and 'location in history' (Mannheim 1972 [1952]: 289). In contrast, the active meaning of generation refers to the act of generating, as something akin to creativity and agency, and emphasises that members of a given generation are never reduced to their cultural and social positions, but are always able to use those positions to bring about new ideas and practices and pursue their own interests within specific historical circumstances (Whyte et al. 2008: 3).

In the context of migration, generations are not only generated in different times, but also in different places. In this respect generation not only connects the past, present and future of a given family, but is also intertwined with different experiences of living in, and being formed by, different local settings and societies around the world. As a consequence of the relatively short history of immigration to Denmark, Pakistanis today roughly consist of the first generation, who were born and raised in Pakistan in the 1940s, 1950s and 1960s, their children – the second generation of immigrants, who were born and raised in Denmark – and the emerging third generation, some of whom were born and raised in Sweden. A distinction between first and second generational cohorts is in line with a Pakistani worldview, where it is common to categorise one another as belonging to either 'the parents' generation' or 'the younger generation'.

In his monograph on Pakistanis/Mirpuris in Oldham, England, Virinder Kalra adapts the emic distinction between *babas* and *kakas*. The former is a generic term of respect for an older male, widely used in the north of the subcontinent, and is used to refer to those men who came to Britain in the early or mid-1960s. Conversely, *kakas* are the real or classificatory sons of the *babas* (Kalra 2000: 40). Using emic terminology, Kalra imitates the respectful distance between the two generations and emphasises that generation is always a relational concept, as a *kaka* can in principle be sixty if the *baba* is eighty.

I refer to the first and second generations as emic categories (as they are used in interviews conducted in Danish). The first generation refers to the pioneers: those who were born and raised in Pakistan and settled in Denmark in the 1960s and 1970s either as labour migrants or as wives joining their husbands through family reunification. The second generation refers to the succeeding generation of children, many of whom were born and raised in Denmark. The spouses of the second generation from Pakistan are in principle first-generation migrants, but are included in the historical generation of second-generation Pakistanis because they are in the same structural relationship to parents-in-law as to the 'aunts' and 'uncles' of the first generation.

In order to make it clear where specific interlocutors are located in the migration history and generational structure, I will refer to members of the first generation as Mrs or Mr followed by a surname, while members of the second generation are simply represented by their first names. In doing this, I am attempting to follow Kalra's example and imitate the respectful gesture that second-generation Pakistanis (and myself as an ethnographer) often display in relation to elders of the first generation, as well as emphasising the more egalitarian relationship I had toward my peers of the second generation.

Families consist of individuals of different generations. It is, however, difficult to come up with an exact definition of the Pakistani migrant family. First of all, the Pakistani migrant family comprises at least one household. But the family of the household is also a part of extended networks that span household units and family members scattered across the globe, not only in Denmark and Pakistan but also, for instance, in Sweden, Norway, Britain, the Middle East or North America. In this respect, Pakistani interlocutors operate with a flexible notion of the family depending on the context and the spoken language. The nuanced vocabulary of family and kin that can be employed in Urdu or Punjabi is often lost in translation when family (*familie*) issues are discussed in Danish. Depending on the context, family may refer to the immediate household (*khandan*) of parents and children, sometimes including grandchildren as well, or to the transnational family, including relatives in Pakistan or in other destinations. Family may also refer to the classificatory brotherhood of the *biraderi* from where spouses are typically recruited, or it can refer to the patrilineal clan (*zaat*). It can even in some contexts refer to the global religious fraternity of the *umma*, in which all Muslims are considered to be 'brothers and sisters'.[3]

---

3. The nuances may be 'lost in translation' from Urdu or Punjabi to Danish, but they may also be 'lost in time' between generations, as when second-generation Pakistanis do not understand or reject the notions of *zaat* or *biraderi* as significant for their everyday lives in Denmark.

Secondly, the migrant family escapes formal definition because it is more of a process than a stable unit (Gardner 2002; Harriss and Shaw 2009). The cycle of Pakistani families has different phases, growing from a nuclear family, when a recently married couple establishes a separate household, into an extended family, when the sons and sometimes daughters continue to live with their parents after marriage for a few years, although eventually separating to start the cycle again (Qadeer 2007: 196). The family is basically a dynamic form of social organisation.

When I use the concept 'family', I am referring to the unit of first-generation migrants and their second-generation (often grown-up) children, their spouses (from Denmark or Pakistan) and possibly minors of the third generation. This is what I refer to as the *vertical* family relations.[4] These families may live within the same household, as is prescribed in the ideal of the patrilocal tradition, or they may have split into separate households of the same family. At the same time, the local vertical family is also part of a transnational extended family, constituted of *horizontal* relations. When I discuss the transnational network and relations between family members – between, for example, households of siblings in different locations in the transnational social field (Pakistan, Denmark, Sweden) – I use the term 'transnational family'. But, as will be discussed, this definition is very preliminary, as the family is not only ascribed – as the definition presented above seems to imply – but also to a large extent achieved.

The concept of 'relatedness' offers an alternative to previous, more biological and functionalist understandings of family and kinship; it suggests that we should take indigenous idioms of relatedness seriously and thus study the real and symbolic practices used locally to create, maintain or contest notions of family and kinship (Carsten 2000: 4). Applied to migration studies, this approach directs us to look at the local and transnational practices through which family relations are maintained, created or contested (see Carsten 1995; Eastmond and Åkesson 2007; Olwig 2007; Pedersen 2009; Rytter and Olwig 2011).

The concept of relatedness has two distinct meanings. First, relatedness refers to the indigenous idioms of kinship and family, emphasising that even metaphors of shared blood or substance have to be acted upon locally if they are to be more than an imagined connection between people. In short, we not only *have* family (as the biological argument seems to claim), but we also *do* family (Carsten 2000, 2004). Secondly, notions of relatedness are intertwined with ideas about identity and belonging to different places such as a village, region or nation-state. In this respect, relatedness constitutes a specific relationship between people and places articulated within an idiom of ownership; it is therefore not sufficient to analyse how people imagine,

---

4. First-generation migrants in Denmark obviously also have vertical relations to their own parents, but since most of them have passed away, the vertical family relations refer to family located in the Danish context.

maintain or create sentiments of belonging to specific places. We must also analyse how the place can be said to belong to them (Edwards and Strathern 2000: 149).

Relatedness as making family

So far I have introduced a flexible definition of the migrant family that distinguishes between vertical intergenerational relations and horizontal transnational relations. Vertical family relationships are formed by the moral obligations and widespread expectations of the 'generational contract', whereby the birth, care and protection that parents provide to their offspring should ultimately be reciprocated when they in old age are unable to take care of themselves (cf. Shaw 2004; Mian 2007; Moen 2008). This generalised reciprocity forms the basis of the preference for patrilocality. However, the moral order of what it means to be a family is contested when, for instance, members of the second generation move out and start their own households, prioritise their careers, find their own spouses and in general neglect their parents.

In the horizontal perspective, Pakistani families form part of wider transnational networks of real and classificatory kin. Here, family and kinship relations can either be ascribed or achieved. Relations are ascribed within the patrilineage, when newborn children are classified as belonging to the *zaat* (clan) of their father. In Pakistan, the *zaat* used to be an occupational rank and class position that, like an ethnic identity, was used to distinguish between families (Lefebvre 1999; Shaw 2000 [1988]). In Denmark, the *zaat* of a person or family is believed to reflect an essence of identity: who they are! In this respect, *zaat* is destiny (Werbner 1990: 87).[5] Still, in the Danish context, *zaat* is a name rather than a real group: it is a category primarily used to distinguish between families, one that can be evoked strategically in different situations.

Family and kinship are, on the other hand, also achieved. According to Anjum Alvi, Punjabi Muslims express kinship primarily through exchanging gifts in the network of classificatory brothers and their families known as the *biraderi* (2007: 657). In her ethnography of a Punjabi village, Zekiye Eglar (1960: 105ff.) shows how the institutionalised exchange system of *vartan bhanji* (dealing in sweets / relationships) brings relatives together and creates lasting moral and emotional bonds between them. Pnina Werbner (1990) emphasises the importance of symbolic exchanges in the migration

---

5. Despite the ideology of blood-relation, South Asian family and kinship are a creative process. Steven Lyon suggests distinguishing between being of 'gujar' *zaat* and 'gujarism': whereas the former is simply an identity category, the latter emphasises one's active involvement in the duties and obligations of generalised reciprocity within the imagined community of Gujars that makes the notion of *zaat* relevant in people's everyday lives (Lyon 1999).

and settlement process among Pakistani families in Manchester, and Alison Shaw (2000) stresses the importance of *lena–dena* (take–give) as a formalised exchange of resources (food, money, daughters) used in the migratory context of Oxford to connect Pakistani migrant families to one another. All the cases point to the importance of reciprocity as a basic principle for creating and consolidating *biraderi* solidarity[6] between family units, and all emphasise the active and creative dimensions of making family and kinship through ongoing exchanges of gifts, ranging from small presents of sweets or flowers to the greatest gift, giving daughters in marriage. Roughly speaking, *zaat* is an ascribed identity reflecting 'who you and your family are', while *biraderi* is an achieved status created and maintained through reciprocal exchange: it is 'who you and your family become'.[7]

But again, even though there are many similarities between studies of Pakistani family and kinship in a British context (i.e., the monographs by Werbner 1990 or Shaw 2000) and in Denmark, it should be emphasised that, at least in this case, size matters. Compared to the United Kingdom, the Pakistani population in Denmark is small, and even though the principle of *biraderi* was very important in the families' settlement process and still is on certain occasions (i.e., weddings or political elections), the *biraderi* seems to have lost many of its virtues in the upcoming second generation. That second generation, on the other hand, may form *biraderi*-like relationships according to new criteria such as educational level or religious affiliation.

Taking it as our point of departure that the family is no longer just a biological unit defined by shared blood and descent, but also an entity produced and reproduced by the continued exchanges of gifts in the widest sense, then the exchanges themselves become a means by which family relations can be

---

6. *Biraderi* is a flexible concept. The *biraderi* includes mainly consanguineal (related by blood/descent) and affinal (related by marriage) kin, but at the widest level can include the entire *zaat*. In the Danish context, this flexibility may be extended further, so that the *biraderi* sometimes also includes neighbours or friends, or even those originating from the same village in Pakistan (for a discussion of the flexibility of the *biraderi*, see Donnan 1988: 74; Lefebvre 1999: 45). In relation to the work and significance of *biraderi*, an old Punjabi proverb states: 'When the fence gets old, it is your duty to put new wood in it' (Werbner 1990: 96): This not only emphasises *biraderi* as the fence protecting the group (i.e. the family) from the outer world; it also emphasises the duty to continue to work to consolidate the *biraderi* relationship. This is done through reciprocal exchange between families – and in the last instance, by the exchange of daughters within the *biraderi*.

7. To clarify the similarities and significant differences between *zaat* and *biraderi*, they can be listed opposite each other as follows. *Zaat:* 1) ascribed status as part of a patrilineal clan; 2) a primordial and (in principle) stable status; 3) exclusive endogamy: we marry here, because they are our equals! 4) 'the one you are'. Cf *Biraderi:* 1) achieved status as part of a classificatory brotherhood; 2) you are only part of the group as long as you fulfil the reciprocal obligations of giving and taking; 3) inclusive endogamy: we are equals because we marry here! 4) 'the one you become'.

contested or redefined altogether. If a Pakistani woman does *not* wish to live with her parents-in-law; if a married man living with his wife and children does *not* regularly visit his parents; if a first-generation migrant couple reduces the remittances to their siblings in Pakistan, or rejects a *rishta* (marriage proposal) from the transnational family – then the shared understandings about filial obligations can (and will) be broken, and the content and constitution of the relationship will open for redefinition. As Marcel Mauss (2001 [1924]: 26–7) emphasised almost a century ago, when a gift is not accepted or reciprocated, it is basically a rejection of the person who gave it, and a gesture that will ultimately bring the social relationship to an end.

Relatedness as belonging

Constructing a sense of belonging is a process, rather than a once-and-for-all achieved sense of being, and may therefore change during the individual life-course and be subject to negotiation between family members. In a study of dispersed Caribbean family networks, Karen Fog Olwig (2007: 19) shows that the sharing and circulation of narratives, memories and gossip is a crucial means to maintain or reshape relations and moral orders of local (vertical) and transnational (horizontal) families. To 'relate' is not only to *tell* a story, but also a way to create or contest family relations, solidarity and notions of unity (see also Chamberlain and Leydesdorff 2004). When narratives of stories, memories, dreams, hopes and fears are shared over a cup of tea, on the phone, written in letters or on the internet, or related as gossip on social visits in the migrant community or on journeys back to one's village of origin, they become important means to sustain moral orders and notions of relatedness between family members.

However, aspirations of relatedness and belonging have to be recognised by significant others in order to have an impact. We only belong to places that also belong to us (Edwards and Strathern 2000: 149). In her study of the English village of Elmdon, Marilyn Strathern (1981) found that the inhabitants were divided into two overall categories, the 'real Elmdoners' and the newcomers. To be considered a 'real Elmdoner', one had to be born in the village and furthermore to come from one of the old families. It was therefore not only place of origin, but also family history and affiliation that constituted a real Elmdoner (Strathern 1981: 6). Even though many Pakistanis, especially of the second generation, are Danish citizens born and raised in Denmark, they are often not recognised as 'real' Danes belonging to Denmark, but kept in a structural limbo as 'not-quite-real' Danes in the eyes of the wider public (see Chapters 1 and 5). Similarly, when migrant families return to Pakistan for holidays or longer stays, they often realise that members of the transnational family do not see them as belonging to the village or the family. The economic prosperity and upward social mobility of the migrants, along with decades of separation, have in many respects made the branches of the transnational families strangers to one another (see Chapters 6 and 7).

Any history of family, belonging and relatedness is also a political history (Carsten 2007: 22). It may be concerned with the micro-politics of family affairs, but it is inevitably also affected by macro-processes of changing national politics, the labour market, the economy and differing forms of racism. Established notions of relatedness and belonging may be challenged on an individual level at 'vital conjunctures' (Johnson-Hanks 2002, 2006), critical turning-points where decisions that redirect life trajectories and entire family histories are (have to be) made. A vital conjuncture could, for instance, be migration, a pregnancy, health problems or a sudden divorce that disrupts expected trajectories and opens up new horizons (see Chapter 3). Notions of relatedness and belonging can also be challenged by major 'critical events' that institute a new modality of historical action and redefine already established categories (Das 1995: 5–6). Examples of global critical events affecting the Pakistanis in Denmark in this material are September 11 (see Chapter 1) and the earthquake in Kashmir 2005 (see Chapter 8), both of which, in their different ways, have altered notions of relatedness, identity and belonging.

The following section provides basic information about the origin and constitution of Pakistanis in Denmark, and discusses the numerous emic and etic identity-categories that my interlocutors navigated between.

Methodological nationalism and symbolic violence

Denmark is a relatively small country in northern Europe, with approximately 5.5 million inhabitants and no significant colonial past or prior history of pronounced immigration.[8] In fact, the Danish population is often referred to as 'ethnically homogeneous' (Gundelach 2002: 58). However, since labour migrants and refugees started coming to Denmark in the 1950s, this picture has changed. Currently eight per cent of the total population in Denmark has a different ethnic background than Danish.

In 2008 there were 8,691 Pakistani citizens and 10,787 Danish citizens of Pakistani background in Denmark.[9] Furthermore, there are an unknown

---

8. In fact, this statement neglects certain points of Danish colonial history. The national border changed with the military loss of present southern Sweden in 1658, the independence of Norway in 1814, the loss of present northern parts of Germany in 1864 and the plebiscite deciding the southern borders in 1920, the relative independence of Iceland in 1918, the Faroe Islands in 1948 and Greenland in 1979, along with the disposal of part of the Gold Coast (now Ghana) in 1850, Tranquebar in Southern India in 1885 and the Caribbean Virgin Islands in 1917.
9. http://www.statistikbanken.dk

number of British citizens with a Pakistani background who moved from England to Denmark after the two countries joined the European Community in 1973 (Quraishy 1999: 19), or fled to Denmark from Uganda and Kenya (Bajaj and Laursen 1988: 128). Thus today there are approximately 25,000 people in Denmark who have a family history related to Pakistan and are Danish, Pakistani or British citizens.

Despite the different nationalities, I use the term 'Pakistani' throughout the book. Doing so is an act of symbolic violence (Bourdieu 1997: 188) through which I deny my interlocutors the right to be recognised as 'real' Danes, despite their Danish citizenship, and neglect the various other ways my interlocutors may have wanted to represent themselves. From the beginning my focus on 'Pakistani migrant families' has been biased by a methodological nationalism (Wimmer and Glick Schiller 2003), and the only justification for using the national category 'Pakistani' is that all my interlocutors, regardless of citizenship, used it as a self-description in relation to me (marked as a non-Pakistani), as well as to each other with reference to their common background and family history. However, my informants juggled numerous alternative identity-categories in relation to each other based on place of origin, language, religiosity, occupation or *zaat* background, all serving to distinguish between individuals and families within the migrant community.[10]

The vast majority of Pakistani families in Denmark have settled in or around Copenhagen.[11] Over the last forty years the individual trajectories and life stories have criss-crossed, and it is generally believed that Pakistanis form a village-like community where 'everyone knows everyone else' (*alle kender alle*). It is estimated that seventy-five per cent of families originate from villages in the Gujrat and Jhelum district of rural Punjab (Quraishy 1999). The rest come from larger cities such as Rawalpindi, Sialkot, Quetta, Lahore or Karachi. The most frequent native languages spoken by the elders are Punjabi or Urdu. Some also speak English. Most of the second generation prefer to speak Danish, but also, to some extent, master the language of their parents, which they have learned at home or in mother-tongue teaching after school.[12]

---

10. Even though I agree with the overall critique raised by the concept of 'methodological nationalism', this study also emphasises the importance of national context formed by unique political, economic, social and cultural conditions, in order to understand the local everyday life and dynamics of migrant families.
11. Significant exceptions are the estimated 200–300 families in Odense and 50–75 families in Frederiksværk.
12. Education in 'mother-tongue teaching' was obligatory until 2002. The obligatory teaching was abandoned as a means of 'social engineering' in order to make immigrants become more Danish by making them speak Danish in their homes and families (cf. Holmen 2002).

It is estimated that 95 per cent of Pakistanis in Denmark are Muslims. Approximately 600 individuals are Ahmadiyya-Muslims,[13] and the rest are said to be Christians (Kühle 2006: 112). The population of Pakistani Muslims is itself divided into a majority of 94 per cent Sunni Muslims and 6 per cent Shi'a Muslims (Kühle 2006: 112). Within both groups, some are highly orthodox, while others call themselves Muslims primarily because it is the religion they were born into. Another significant division is the classic Islamic opposition between neo-fundamentalists like Wahhabi, Salafi or Deobandi, and those of the South Asian Barelwi tradition, who are often *murids* (followers) of living or dead *pirs*. The contours of the religious landscape also divide the Pakistani community.

Migrants are also divided along the lines of their professions. Distinctions are made between families who count as self-employed, for instance driving a taxi or managing a corner shop, and those families who have pursued higher education as a socio-economic strategy of social mobility (see Chapter 2). Last but not least, in specific contexts and situations, many Pakistanis will differentiate between families on the basis of *zaat* affiliation. Solidarity within the patrilineage was an important means of organisation in the early phases of the migration and settlement process, and is furthermore an identity category that has regained importance as the second generation has started to marry (see Chapters 3 and 7).

This overview of some of the relevant emic categories emphasises that migrants are never 'just' Pakistanis. In her study of local politics among Pakistanis in Manchester, Pnina Werbner suggests that when it comes to identity, solidarity and political mobilisation, the community is transformed into a 'segmented Diaspora', where migrants can (must) position themselves within changing socio-political contexts as: '*british-pakistani-muslim-punjabi-asian-black-mancunian-sunni-deobandi-jhelmi-gujar*' (Werbner 2002: 64). Likewise Sissel Østberg explains that Pakistani families in Oslo, Norway, share an 'integrated plural identity' ('integreret plural identitet') that contains many different narratives of places, communities and routes, thus making it possible for the migrants either to emphasise or to downplay markers of similarity and difference depending on appropriateness and social context (Østberg 2003: 46). The multiplicity of identities among South Asian migrants in Manchester, Oslo and Copenhagen has its roots in the recent emigration out of Pakistan, as well as in the legacy of successive imperial regimes, religious movements, population displacements, the modern rise of nationalism(s) and religious hostilities, all of which have made the

---

13. Ahmadiyya are often not recognised by other Muslims as belonging to the community of Muslims. In 1974, they were excommunicated in Pakistan through a constitutional amendment, and placed on a level with other non-Muslim minority communities. During General Zia Ul-Haq's Islamisation phase, the Ahmadiyyas were also statutorily denied the right to follow Islamic rituals and symbols. Among the majority of Muslims in Denmark, too, the beliefs and practices of Ahmadiyya Muslims are considered to be controversial, and they are often referred to as non-Muslims.

subcontinent a vast border-zone of social actors bearing multiple, often contradictory identities (Werbner 2002: 58). Pakistani migrants therefore embody a range of identities. These are not necessarily contradictory, but constitute a repertoire of identity and belonging which can (or which perhaps may not) be mobilised in different social contexts. These various identities, loyalties and affiliations also challenge the emic idea of a coherent community (cf. Bauman 1996) in relation to the wider Danish society; however, people evoke and relate with pride to a common identity as being Pakistanis.

Ethnographic data from transnational social fields

According to Akhil Gupta and James Ferguson (1997: 31), ethnographic fieldwork is 'a form of dwelling that legitimises knowledge production by the familiarity that the fieldworker gains with the ways of life of a group of people'. The methodological consequence of this is that we focus on shifting locations rather than on bounded fields. Similarly, George Marcus calls for a 'multi-sited ethnography' (1995: 112) that not only includes several locations, but also implies moving between public and private spheres of activity, from official to unofficial contexts and between discourses that in some cases inevitably overlap with those of the ethnographer. Likewise, the material for this book was generated in the transnational social field stretched out between the significant people, places and spaces in Denmark, Pakistan and Sweden. A transnational social field can be defined as 'a set of multiple interlocking networks of social relationships through which ideas, practices and resources are unequally exchanged, organised and transformed' (Levitt and Glick Schiller 2004: 1009). The field consists of the complex networks of relations significant to the people involved in the study, rather than a geographical field site (cf. Hastrup and Olwig 1997: 8). Despite a geographical distance from Denmark of approximately 6,000 km, Pakistan is nevertheless only a seven-hour flight, a phone call, a click on the internet or a daydream away. Contemporary means of transportation and telecommunication have contributed to the development of time-space compression (Harvey 1989) and simultaneity (Levitt and Glick Schiller 2004) in the transnational social field. These have become manifest in the movement of people, finances (such as charity; see Chapter 8) and communication (such as gossip or suspicions of sorcery; see Chapter 9). Pakistan is always present among migrants in Denmark: even the deliberate choice of not going to Pakistan, not calling the family or sending remittances is a way of relating to people and places in the transnational social field.

Life stories and family histories

A focus on trajectories and life stories provides an opportunity to analyse the relationship between structure and agency, or more generally the development of individual trajectories, family, community, society and history (Peacock and Holland 1993; Atkinson 1998). Due to different locations in history, first- and second-generation Pakistanis not only have different narrative styles, but also often contradictory perspectives on their current and future lives. According to the Norwegian anthropologist Ingrid Rudie (2001), parents and children belong to different 'cultural generations' (*kulturelle generationer*), as they were born, raised and socialised in different times and, we may add in the context of migration, places.

Focusing on the negotiation of family relatedness can be like opening a Pandora's box of disruptive themes and conflicts. When one is confronted with interlocutors who are dissatisfied with their needy parents or narratives of indifferent children who neglect their reciprocal obligations, stories of demanding in-laws or unfaithful husbands and complaints about wives who want careers or are unable to cook decent food, one is dealing with the micro-politics of everyday family life, which must be treated with discretion – especially in a relatively small, village-like migrant community, where there is a lot of internal gossip.

According to Max Gluckman (1963: 308–9), gossip can have important positive virtues, as it maintains the unity, morals and values of social groups and is used to mark themselves off from others by talking about one another. Gossip is also a power mechanism, which those who consider themselves higher in status may use to put those whom they consider lower in their proper place. Robert Paine (1967: 279) advocates a transactional perspective on gossip, and suggests that gossip is a form of 'information-management' put forward with the intention of protecting personal interests. Thus gossip is purposive behaviour, and a way to manage competition. Both perspectives seem relevant in relation to the Pakistani community, where gossip has an integrative function in the ongoing creation of an exclusive community and in enforcing heavy social control over individuals and families. But gossip is also used to manage family status and reputation, through attempts to control what kind of intimate information circulates in the wider migrant community or in transnational networks. In this environment, an important part of gaining access to and understanding the dynamics of the migrant community is to learn its scandals; it not only became a means of access, but also a proof that I was to some extent considered an insider.

In a competitive community where people attempt to control the flows of information, strong elements of 'impression management' (Goffman 1959) often emerge when the anthropologist approaches the 'inside' of the migrant family (cf. Grillo 2008). In interviews, there are always both real audiences (the ethnographer, along with relatives, children or visitors, who are often present at interviews in private settings) and imagined ones. There can be numerous reasons for presenting slightly changed narratives so that an interlocutor can make him- or herself stand out as the one who has solved family conflicts; can present the youth organisation one is part of as progressive; can represent one's family or *biraderi* as honourable, or the Muslim community as intrinsically peaceable and tolerant. Such edited narratives not only confirm on a personal level that one's life and migration have been successful; they also reflect the dynamics of a competitive community in which families strive to accumulate symbolic capital and to gain a favourable position within the changing hierarchies (see Chapter 2). Many younger Pakistanis have warned me over the years not to trust what their elders in the first generation relate, because they are infamous for exaggerating or even lying when it comes to describing the virtues of their lives. However, rather than seeing some interviews as false statements and morally condemning the interlocutors delivering them, I see them as a premise of family histories, resulting from personal ambitions to succeed and the community dynamics of competition.

Conducting interviews

My lack of fluency in Urdu and Punjabi has created specific conditions for my research. Most of my interviews have been conducted in Danish, the language spoken most frequently by my younger interlocutors. Many older Pakistanis also speak Danish, but some have preferred to express themselves in their native language. In these cases, their grown-up children helped as translators. Many spouses who have married second-generation Pakistanis and entered Denmark through family reunification have learnt to speak Danish (or are fluent in English). Among returnee families in Pakistan, interviews were mainly conducted in Danish or English. However, in Denmark, Sweden and Pakistan, I have been excluded from following and participating in conversations whenever my interlocutors have turned to Urdu or Punjabi.

There are several obstacles beside language to be overcome when carrying out research within the discursive terrain of the Pakistani family. First of all, it has been emphasised how the terror attacks on September 11, 2001, and in London on July 7, 2005, and the global political situation in general, have had a major impact on research methodology within Muslim communities in Britain (Bolognani 2007a: 280). People have become more suspicious of the curious investigator, more reluctant to give the researcher access to private spheres. These observations on the basic conditions for fieldwork also apply to the situation in Denmark (see Chapter 1).

Secondly, much research on immigration, immigrants and Muslims conducted in Denmark is sponsored by state donors, often articulated within a political framework of problems and solutions defined a priori (Jöhncke et al. 2004). Very often the research will have a narrow focus on a specific 'problem' instead of an open and more exploratory approach. Furthermore, many studies tend to focus on the eloquent, educated and well-organised second generation and their representations of Islam and of themselves as Muslims (e.g. Johansen 2002; Schmidt 2007; Christiansen 2011). The discursive analysis tends to privilege specific perspectives of the immigrant family and of Islam, and to neglect the complex practices and experiences of everyday life. In this respect, academia actually contributes to the production of a specific kind of knowledge about Muslim immigrants in Denmark.

Finally, Pakistani interlocutors are well aware that some aspects of everyday life and immigrant experience are to be treated with discretion, which sets up important epistemological conditions for the ethnographic fieldwork. Interlocutors with higher education are not only familiar with the genre of interviews, writing dissertations or making academic careers, they also often have prior experience of participating as informants in surveys, studies or interviews. Due to the relatively small Pakistani and Muslim community in Copenhagen, associations and organisations, mosques and educational settings are frequently used (and in fact are over-run) by students and researchers from such fields as anthropology, sociology, political science, psychology, journalism, public health, education and social work, who are interested in studying and analysing the lives of immigrants within the politically defined framework of 'integration'. Even those who are seldom asked or always decline to participate in the scrutiny and exposure of their everyday lives are familiar with the genre of the interview.

Discussing a similar situation, Peter van der Veer (2001: 9) states that: 'Work on arguments about Islam in high school discussions in Western Europe describe in detail how Muslim students acquire skills to defend their religion and culture, appropriate to the discursive styles characteristic for the discursive styles in the nation-states of immigration.' Likewise Roger Ballard suggests that second-generation individuals 'have acquired the navigational skills which enable them to order their presentation of themselves in terms of majority conventions and expectations as and when they choose' (2008: 41). It is also my general impression that many interlocutors have acquired a sophisticated awareness about what to speak of and what not to speak of in public when it comes to both family affairs and topics related to the Pakistani community or Islam in general. This reservation is not the result of some kind of deliberate conspiracy, but an awareness that the social games which are significant in the transnational social field may be misunderstood and even be used against them, their family, the community of Pakistanis or Muslims in general, if they are discussed with an ethnographer, or with non-Pakistani Danes. Therefore, while interviews with second-generation Pakistanis are not necessarily false, they should be treated as explanations on a certain level and within a particular framework, defined by the external norms of the Danish majority.

These epistemological and methodological challenges have to be taken into consideration when conducting interviews. It is, however, possible to go beyond the impression-management, information-control and general precautions when talking to an outsider – a Dane who probably does not understand – if one takes the postcolonial repertoire of identity into consideration.

Figurative worlds

As already suggested, the postcolonial legacy provides Pakistanis in the diaspora with a complex repertoire of identities. The second generation especially are experts in 'code switching', whereby they navigate between different languages, norms and cultural codes (Ballard 1994: 30ff.). Emphasising the ability to switch codes is not to suggest that Pakistanis in Denmark are split personalities, nor am I suggesting that there is a post-modern, nightmarish vision in which identity-configurations are free-floating and solely dependent on individual choice. On the contrary, enactments of the historical repertoire of identities are embedded in specific local contexts and in the recognition of significant others.

In order to address the emic practice of code-switching methodologically, I suggest the heuristic concept of 'figurative worlds'. Figurative worlds basically rest on people's ability to form and be formed in collectively realised 'as if' realms (cf. Holland et al. 1998: 49). A figurative world is defined as a:

> Socially and culturally constructed realm of interpretation in which particular characters and actors are recognized, significance is assigned to certain acts and particular outcomes valued over others ... these collective 'as-if' worlds are socio-historic, contrived interpretations of imaginations that mediate behaviour and so, from the perspective of heuristic developments, inform participants' outlook. The ability to sense (see, hear, touch, taste, feel) the figured world becomes embodied over time through continual participation (Holland et al. 1998: 52–3).

The repertoire of identity-configurations available to Pakistani migrants can be seen as collective 'figurative worlds' that they can move into and out of: frames that set the conditions for social interaction in specific ways. Each identity-configuration of the 'segmented diaspora' (cf. 'British', 'Pakistani', 'Muslim', 'Deobandi', 'Gujar', etc.; Werbner 2002) has its own sanctioned rules, discourses, characters, performances and morality.

Approaching the social world as constituted by different figurative worlds that Pakistani interlocutors can move into and out of enables us to explain on a theoretical level why over the years one of my male interlocutors has frequently taken a strong position against forced marriage, although he ended up guiding his younger sister towards the marriage candidate favoured by their parents. Or why a Pakistani medicine student can be absorbed in scientific discussions about human physiology all day long, but later on the very same day is convinced that sorcery committed by family members in Pakistan is the main reason for a broken engagement. It may also give some clues as to why a highly educated, formerly active socialist claimed to be willing to stand up and defend the Raja *zaat* against unjust allegations. Or how a female law student eager to defend the rights of Muslims in Denmark suddenly, in an interview, began to talk about how important it is for young Pakistani women to protect their reputations and ultimately their virginity in order to protect the honour (*izzat*) of the family.

Logically all these shifts seem contradictory. However, if we consider them to be expressions of the postcolonial repertoire of identities put forward within different 'figurative worlds', we understand how interlocutors can accommodate these apparently conflicting positions and statements in their everyday lives. But how do figurative worlds come into being, and as outsiders, can we enter them?

Entering figurative worlds

Figured worlds are evoked by the use of artefacts. Describing the ability to enter into imagined worlds, Lev S. Vygotsky speaks of the 'pivot' as a mediating symbolic device that can be used to shift into the frame of a different world (Holland et al. 1998: 50).[14] As an example of the ability of material objects to function as a pivot, Vygotsky mentions a broomstick that in children's play can become the sword of a knight or the wand of a witch. Material objects, words, gesticulations and postures can all function as a pivot; they can not only set the frame for a specific figurative world, but also help position the ethnographer within the framework, along with his or her interlocutors.

It is my experience that ethnic Urdu and Punjabi concepts used in interviews conducted in Danish can work as pivots, and give access to specific figurative worlds. When an ethnographer is provisionally accepted as an insider and positioned as 'someone who knows', the interlocutor does not have to 'translate' defensively between different Pakistani and Danish norms and values. When, for example, in discussions of the dilemmas of arranged marriages (who, where from, when, why ...) you evoke emic concepts such as the wish and will of the *biraderi* or discuss the art of giving *rishta* (marriage connection), which opens up discussions on a different level than whether or not this kind of marriage practice should be accepted in Denmark.

Other examples could be to comment on an older interlocutor's complaints about problems within the patrilocal household using the typical emic expression that recognises their situation as 'a real headache' (*en stor hovedpine*); to suggest that experiences among the second generation are the outcome of discrimination or Islamophobia; or to ask interlocutors as a matter of course whether they ever suspected a specific family conflict to be the outcome of *kala jaddu* (sorcery). Common to all these examples is the fact that the pivot enables the interview to change from being an asymmetrical relationship in which an insider is trying to translate and contextualise the dilemmas of Pakistani migrant family life for an outsider, to instead becoming an informed conversation between two insiders.

---

14. Framing social situations is, however, often a question of power; therefore artefacts are not only mental tools, but also potentially tools of persuasion or suppression (Holland and Cole 1995: 481).

When emic concepts or gestures are used in interviews or conversations in Danish, they can function as a pivot and open different figurative worlds: at other times, this methodological strategy does not work at all. This happens when, for instance, interlocutors do not understand my questions when I suddenly refer to Urdu or Punjabi concepts, or if they simply do not accept me as an insider or credible interlocutor of the figurative world. These situations are characterised by awkward silences. However, when it does work, the pivot provides an entry into frameworks that are otherwise inaccessible to non-Pakistani outsiders. Finally, it should be emphasised that when I utilise this interview strategy, I am only doing what my interlocutors, especially those of the second generation, do every day when they switch codes and move in and out of the figurative worlds that are built up around different identity-configurations.

Ethical considerations and the politics of representation

Monica Ali's award winning novel *Brick Lane* (Ali 2003), about Nazneen and her family in a London neighbourhood dominated by Bangladeshi immigrants, created a lot of discussion. Many Bangladeshis in Britain found it difficult to accept her unflattering description of them and their everyday lives. Germaine Greer also criticised Monica Ali for writing a novel about immigrants from an English perspective. In the *Guardian* she wrote:

> Writers are treacherous; they will sneak up on you and write about you in terms that you don't recognize. They will take your reality, pull strands from it and weave them with their own impressions into a tissue that is more real than your reality because it is text. Text is made of characters. A character is, as it were, graven in stone; when you are charactered you will last for ever, or pretty nearly, but what lasts will not be you. Every individual, every community ever to be written about suffers the same shock of non-recognition, and feels the same sense of invasion and betrayal (Greer, *Guardian*, 24 July 2006).

The novel became a 'defining caricature' in the wider public, as it was the first description of the Bangladeshi families in that particular neighbourhood.[15] Regardless of what is real and what is fiction, however, the novel stands out to the wider British audience as a valid and authoritative representation. From now on, whenever anyone writes about Bangladeshis in Britain or migrants living in the neighbourhood Brick Lane, their descriptions will inevitably be compared, explicitly or implicitly, to the universe presented by Monica Ali. In this way the novel has created a certain social imaginary that will inform future approaches.

---

15. 'Forfatter-fight: Ytingsfrihed eller Fordomme', Marie Tetzlaff, *Politiken*, 6 August 2006.

Muslim immigrants in Denmark have also for years been locked into a defining caricature, presented in the book *Ære og Skam* (Honour and Shame), published in 1996 by Naser Khader, born in Syria and from 2001 to 2011 a member of the Danish parliament.[16] The book supposedly describes everyday life in Muslim families, and uses anecdotes and personal experiences from the author's own family. Regardless of numerous documented errors and shortcuts,[17] the book had sold 90,000 copies in 2004 and made the author a millionaire.[18] The book has become an authoritative manual of what Muslim immigrant family life is supposed to be like, and is read by, among others, teachers and students, social workers, pedagogues, journalists and politicians.

A defining caricature of the Pakistani community was produced when Rushy Rashid, then known as the first newscaster on Danish television with 'a different ethnic background than Danish', published her autobiography *Et løft af sløret* (Lifting the veil) in 2000. In this book she writes about her family problems and failed arranged engagements and marriages. Rashid soon became a popular lecturer, was given her own correspondence column in one of the major tabloids (*BT*) and in 2001 was awarded the annual 'Women's prize' (*kvindeprisen*) by the weekly women's magazine *Alt For Damerne*. After publishing her second book, *Bag sløret* (Behind the veil) (Rashid and Højbjerg 2003), focusing on her romance with and marriage to another television host, Rashid was criticised for making her Danish husband convert to Islam and insisting on having their son circumcised.[19] Rushy Rashid and her family were also criticised and ridiculed in the Pakistani community for exposing her family life to public scrutiny – but that is not the point here.

The books of Rashid and Khader have reached a wide Danish audience and provided an entry into the intimate sphere of the Muslim immigrant family. They have satisfied the curiosity of the Danish readership by pretending to 'go beyond the veil', and to a large extent confirm dominant orientalist fantasies in the Danish public imaginary about gender roles, power and authority in Muslim immigrant families. Any ethnography of Pakistani Muslim families

16. Due to his political work, especially on issues of integration, and his popularity in the media, Naser Khader was elected to parliament in 2001 to represent the Social Liberals (*Det Radikale Venstre*), and soon achieved star status for speaking out against Muslim fundamentalism, especially during the 'cartoon controversy' in 2005–6 and 2008. In 2007 he created his own political party, New Alliance (*Ny Alliance*) and was for a short while portrayed as the man who could solve every problem in Denmark related to immigrants and Muslims. At the end of his period in the Parliament, he represented the Conservative People's Party (*Det Konservative Folkeparti*) (see also Hervik 2011).
17. Amminah Tønnesen 2001, Ære og Skam – Fup og Fakta, 2001. See http://www.islamstudie.dk/boeger_aereogskam.1.htm
18. Torben Bagge, *BT*, 24 April 2004.
19. The third volume of her autobiographical trilogy is called *Du lovede, vi skulle hjem* (You promised we would go home). This book relates how her parents arrived and settled in Denmark, and of their prolonged dream of returning to Pakistan (Rashid 2006).

in Denmark is inevitably written (and probably read) in relation to the defining caricature. Giving voice to Pakistani migrants is not only a matter of deconstructing the ethnographic authority of the anthropologist, as in the 'representation debate' of the 1980s (cf. Clifford and Marcus 1986; Geertz 1988); it also becomes a question of adequately describing and analysing people's everyday lives in such a way as to destabilise the defining caricature. In this respect, writing ethnography becomes a political endeavour, where much more than academic evaluation of my work and text is at stake.

The problems of consent and visibility

Any ethnography of family life within the largely hidden public sphere of the Pakistani migrant community is exposure, to a certain extent. Every interview I have conducted has had the informed consent of my interlocutors, but interviews often take unforeseen turns; and when I have been 'hanging out' or met interlocutors at informal social gatherings, I have not lectured them every time about my role and position as an ethnographer and writing anthropologist. It can also be difficult for informants to know what anthropologists do with their data and how it will be presented in texts later on: we often do not know this ourselves before writing up the final draft.

In order to protect the identity and integrity of individuals and families, I have changed the names of people, their ages, the cities they live in, the number of siblings and their place of origin in Pakistan when finally writing up the data. Still, it is probably impossible to conceal fully the identity of interlocutors in a small migrant community where 'everyone knows everyone else' (*alle kender alle*).

In representing individuals and families, I am moving them into the limelight of public attention, and thereby contributing to the hyper-visibility from which Muslim immigrants suffer when moral panics cause episodes and events of their everyday life to grow out of proportion, and in turn motivate political action and intervention. The material presented in this book not only deals with sensitive moral questions of family life; it also discusses the semi-legal life of transnational married couples commuting between Sweden and Denmark (see Chapter 4). In this endeavour, some of my interlocutors are actually breaking the law and violating the conditions of their residence permits. This is an important reason to be extra cautious and thorough in making the families anonymous.

Emic description versus etic analysis

Some interlocutors may be disappointed to learn how their perspectives, instructions or life stories are presented (or not presented at all) in the final text. Others will probably find that they do not feel sufficiently represented, or maybe even in misleading ways. The problem is exactly as stated in the quote cited earlier from Germaine Greer: one of taking bits and pieces of the reality presented to me by Pakistani interlocutors over the years of fieldwork, pulling strands from it, and weaving them together in order to create an academic argument. In this endeavour, the anthropologist will inevitably be guilty of symbolic violence.

Addressing the relationship between emic and etic perspectives, Kirsten Hastrup explains that 'the native is a practical expert on local lifeways, and is constantly engaged in self-description. Yet the point of anthropology is to transcend self-description – not through a bypassing of it but by way of incorporating it into a language of a higher-order generality' (1995: 148). In the theoretical analysis, the writing anthropologist draws things, episodes and perspectives together in a way that may not be obvious to his or her interlocutors. As result of this editing and abstraction, interlocutors may find themselves represented in other ways than they would have represented themselves.

One theme of this book that many Pakistanis would probably object to is my treatment of circulating suspicions of *kala jaddu* (sorcery[20]) discussed in the final part. Several times I have been told by interlocutors not to focus on the topic. Some speak from a religious position and explain that *kala jaddu* is not part of Islamic orthodoxy and should therefore not be included in a proper analysis. Others discount the suspicions and practices related to *kala jaddu* as 'backward', associated with village life, a leftover from the cultural past that Pakistani migrant families put behind them when they settled in Denmark and improved their literacy and education. I have also been criticised for generalising about people originating from the geographical territory currently called Pakistan, and for assuming that every migrant believes in 'the evil eye', amulets and sorcery. Pakistanis in Denmark have for years been represented in the wider public as determined by notions of 'culture' and honour, arranged and forced marriages or religious extremism – now my research will turn them into superstitious believers and practitioners of *kala jaddu* and the like.

These different objections have taught me valuable lessons about identity politics and the ambivalent feelings that Pakistanis may have towards the more mystical dimensions of Islam, and of what I suggest we call the 'destructive-productive' forces of family struggles in local households or transnational networks. Even though to some extent I agree with the problems of representation raised, I have ended up using the material on *kala jaddu* anyway. First of all, I nowhere claim to speak for or about every Pakistani in Denmark. On the contrary, I fully recognise that, by approaching the inside of the family as an arena for both the production and contestation of values, morality and beliefs, the analysis will never be more than 'a partial

---

20. I prefer to use the emic term *kala jaddu* (occasionally translated into English as sorcery), because it was the most common expression used by my interlocutors. See Part IV.

truth' (Clifford 1986: 7) about Pakistani families and the migrant community. Secondly, following the advice of Kirsten Hastrup quoted above, I insist that there is – and that there should be – a fundamental difference between the emic descriptions provided by interlocutors and the etic analysis that the anthropologist ends up with.

The structure of the book

The book is organised in four parts, each constituting an empirical and analytical entry into the Pakistani families in order to shed light on different aspects of ongoing family dynamics. It is a truly multi-sited ethnography (Marcus 1995), because not only is it based on ethnographic material generated in different locations such as Denmark, Sweden and Pakistan, but also it uses four different analytical perspectives in order to address urgent aspects of both the local and transnational lives of Pakistani migrant families and their changing notions of relatedness and belonging.

Part I: Histories

The first part presents two radically different perspectives on the migration and settlement process of Pakistani families. Chapter 1 outline the macro-history of the Danish nation-state in relation to the changing attitudes towards the growing number of immigrants and refugees. It is suggested that September 11, 2001 has facilitated – and in time naturalised – a situation where Muslim immigrants and Pakistanis in particular have become *the usual suspects* for terrorism and various anti-democratic tendencies. Contrarily, Chapter 2 uses life-story material and the scattered literature on Pakistanis in Denmark to reconstruct the micro-history of the settlement process and dynamics of the migrant community. It is argued that the pronounced success and upward social mobility of second-generation Pakistanis can be explained by the fierce competition between migrant families for status and recognition, which has led them to take advantage of the free educational system of the Danish welfare state.

Part II: Marriages

The second part focuses on the institution of marriage. Chapter 3 discusses partner choice as a 'vital conjuncture', where second-generation Pakistanis have to make a decision regarding the direction of their trajectories and future lives. Presenting the case of a young couple who enter a controversial love marriage against the will of their parents, I discuss what is at stake with regard to marriage in Pakistani migrant families, and how the institution of arranged marriage is changing.

Chapter 4 presents a case study of the hundreds of newly-weds who, following Danish legislation introduced in 2002, have moved to Sweden in order to obtain family reunification with their Pakistani spouses. The chapter discusses how the legal interventions have made the expanding group of marriage migrants semi-legal in both legal and moral terms as, attempting to keep up with Pakistani ideals of patrilocality and intergenerational obligations, they commute on a regular, often daily basis between their legal residence in Sweden and their work, friends and natal families in Denmark.

In Chapter 5 the requirement of 'national attachment', as formulated in the Danish national legislation on family reunification introduced in 2002, is used as a starting-point for a more general discussion of how 'kinship images' in the dominant public discourse and imaginary tend to distinguish between 'real' and 'not-quite-real' Danes, leaving little room for Danish citizens with a Pakistani background to be recognised as belonging to the nation and to the welfare state.

Part III: Homelands

The third part discusses how the notion and status of Pakistan as a homeland are contested between generations within migrant families. Chapter 6 focuses on migrant families who, after decades in Denmark, return to Pakistan in an attempt to realise the ideal of the happy extended family, and discusses some of the numerous problems returnees face in this endeavour.

Chapter 7 presents the case of a stage play performed by members of OPSA (the Organisation of Pakistani Students and Academics), and discusses how the play's narrative, performance and reception came to represent an imagined return and a possible reconciliation with Pakistan among the well-educated second generation.

Chapter 8 focuses on the period of 'intensive transnationalism' following the earthquake in Kashmir in 2005, and analyses how the disaster affected common notions of identity and belonging within and beyond the Pakistani community in Denmark.

Overall, Part III engages with how notions of relatedness and belonging in relation to Pakistan and Denmark are being negotiated within families, and how they change over time. Pakistan simply means something different to the family members of first- and second-generation immigrants.

Part IV: Afflictions

The final part focuses on the suspicions of *kala jaddu* (sorcery) that circulate both within and between families. Chapter 9 discusses how suspicions of *kala jaddu* become a way of relating to other family members, and are a significant means of re-organising expectations and obligations within both local and transnational family networks.

Chapter 10 discusses how the better-educated 'new-born religious' second generation relates to a 'cultural' phenomenon such as *kala jaddu* which they claim not to believe in. It is furthermore discussed whether suspicions of sorcery have regained importance in personal narratives, families and the community at large due to demographic changes, and to the uncertain status of Pakistani Muslim immigrants in general.

Conclusion: family upheaval

The final chapter discusses the current situation of family upheaval among Pakistani migrants in Denmark, and it is suggested that intergenerational renegotiation and recreation of fragile family relations and moral orders makes a certain amount of upheaval an inevitable aspect of the 'diasporic condition'. However, the current dubious status of Muslims in Danish society, and the ongoing securitisation of migration and immigrants' family lives that Pakistanis experience, have speeded up, escalated and exaggerated these processes.

Part I

Histories

The first part of the book is concerned with various aspects of Pakistani settlement and family life during the last four decades, and how the processes of securitisation which followed the terrorist attacks of September 11 have affected the general status of Muslims in Denmark. It engages with what, from the position of the external observer, could be called 'the Pakistani paradox'. On the one hand, Pakistani migrants are renowned entrepreneurs who are willing to take chances and start up private businesses; the upcoming generation of young Pakistanis is doing extremely well in the educational system; families have started to leave the cramped apartments of the inner city and settle in single-family homes in the suburbs; and the relatively small community has produced a considerable number of first- and second-generation politicians who run for office in municipal and national government.[1] All in all, Pakistanis stand out as a successful and well-integrated migrant community. On the other hand, Pakistanis have gained a questionable reputation in public discourse and are suspected of forming 'a parallel society' (*parallel samfund*) consisting of extended families populated by authoritarian patriarchs and oppressed women; their community is imagined to be plagued by high rates of forced marriage, and violence motivated by a shared conception of honour (*izzat*); they are accused of egregious exploitation of welfare state benefits; and – since 2001 – they have been suspected of religious extremism, and are considered to pose serious threat to the Danish population and to Danish values and society. Accordingly, Pakistanis are perceived and approached as *the usual suspects*, a community from which only the worst can be expected.

In order to deal with the Pakistani paradox, the two chapters of Part I distinguish analytically between perspectives 'from above' and 'from below' (cf. Mahler 1998). While the first chapter addresses recent developments in the Danish welfare state, with a specific focus on the changing perceptions and positions of Muslim migrants and refugees after September 11, the second chapter discusses the settlement of Pakistani families and historical dynamics of the migrant community. Even though the two perspectives are part of the same overall history, they are very different.

---

1. One of the first members of the Danish *Folketing* (parliament) with an immigrant background was Kamal Qureshi, a medical doctor of Pakistani origin who was elected in 2001 to represent the Socialist People's Party (*Socialistisk Folkeparti*).

Chapter 1 addresses the Pakistani paradox from the macro-perspective of Danish public discourses and imaginaries, and suggests that the terrorist attacks in New York and Washington on September 11 constituted a critical event (Das 1996) that prompted Western nation-states to react with a 'security/integration-response' (Bleich 2009), comprising numerous pre-emptive policies and laws aimed at the diffuse but omnipresent threat of terror. The suicide bombings in London in 2005 further emphasised the growing insecurity regarding 'home-grown terrorism', and focused media and government attention on Muslim minorities, leading to the redefinition of this entire segment of the population as a potential enemy within. Discussing 'World Risk Society' after 2001, Ulrich Beck suggests that 'the perception of terrorist threats replaces *active trust* with *active mistrust*. It therefore undermines the trust in fellow citizens, foreigners and governments all over the world' (2002: 44; italics in original). Thus, using a concept from Ghassan Hage, the current situation and political culture can be diagnosed as 'anthrax-culture':

> Anthrax-culture prevails when a generalised culture of 'threat' permeates the whole society. The national interior becomes subverted; the citizens begin to perceive everything and everywhere as a threat, as a border; a supposed Islamic threat on the border becomes an Islamic threat everywhere. Every breath of fresh air becomes imagined as a line behind which the enemy (always ready to infiltrate the nation) lurks. Slowly but surely, the love, affection and friendship that animate the interior are replaced by the aggression, suspicion and hatred that were supposedly deployed to protect them (Hage 2003: 45–6).

In this process, the mutual trust, reciprocity and solidarity on which the welfare society rests are eroded, and the relationship between majorities and minorities redefined. Using migrants and immigration as a prism, the chapter attempts to outline recent developments in Danish history that cast light on how and why a country formerly known for its liberal lifestyle and generous welfare state has recently gained an international reputation as one of the most anti-Islamic and anti-immigrant nations in Europe.

By way of contrast, the micro-perspective provided in Chapter 2 shows what has preoccupied Pakistani families in their immediate everyday lives since the late 1960s: having a nice job and standard of living, raising and educating their children properly, arranging good *rishtas*, being on good terms with relatives back in Pakistan, and in general gaining a reputation as successful, well-functioning and respectable families. By tracing immigrant life stories back to rural Punjab and describing the different phases of settlement, I suggest that differing emic notions of improvement have emerged over time to shape and reshape the status hierarchies of the migrant community.

The Pakistani paradox is generated by the gap between the macro- and micro-histories outlined in these chapters, a gap which itself illustrates the different access to power and resources available to majorities and minorities in Danish society. Most often, the majority defines what kind of practices, relations and values constitute 'a good life' in Denmark; Muslim minorities are subjected to this dominant 'social imaginary' (Taylor 2004),[2] as it is inscribed in structures of power such as political discourses, the media, educational curricula and legislation. Still, it has to some extent been possible for Pakistani migrants to live in Danish society with a difference, and maintain some of the values, traditions and ways of life they knew from Pakistan.

---

2. Charles Taylor: 'By social imaginary, I mean something much broader and deeper than the intellectual schemes people may entertain when they think about social reality in a disengaged mode. I am thinking, rather, of the ways people imagine their social existence, how they fit together with others, how things go on between them and their fellows, the expectations that are normally met, and the deeper normative notions and images that underlie these expectations' (2004: 23).

Chapter 1

Macro-perspectives

The usual suspects

The terror attacks of September 11 promoted a new agenda for international relations and securitisation. Nation-states around the world responded to September 11 according to their own particular history, political system and general situation (Grillo 2004). In Denmark, the terrorist attack became a significant element in the new reorganisation of the welfare state and redefinition of the country's relations to the wider world.

First of all, September 11 tapped into existing discussions and discourses about the problematic nature of Muslim immigration. Right-wing populist parties such as the Progress Party (*Fremskridts Partiet*) since 1973 and the Danish People's Party (*Dansk Folkeparti*) since 1995 have with varying success argued that immigrants pose a threat to Danish identity, culture and values. From the 1960s, increased inflows of labour migrants, family reunifications and refugees from non-European countries where Islam is the dominant religion changed the demographic composition of the Danish population, which had previously been quite homogeneous. In nationalist narratives, this development was presented as the beginnings of occupation by foreign invaders let in by the naive and sloppy immigration policies of the Social Democrats, the ruling party in government to 2001 (Kvaale 2011: 232–3; Hervik 2011: 118).[1] A crucial problem is that immigrants are presumed to exploit the benefits of the welfare state. The welfare state, which has been expanding since it came into being in its modern form with the Social Reform Act of 1933, functions as a gigantic mutual insurance scheme, where, against a background of high taxes (often around fifty per cent of income), all are entitled to the benefits of free education, free university tuition, comprehensive health services, subsidised childcare institutions, theatres and libraries, paid maternity and paternity leave for one year per child, pensions

---

1. Another aspect of the nationalist narrative of diminishing control and loss of sovereignty is the expanding European Union, including the European monetary union (of which Denmark is still not a member) and the Schengen Agreement.

and so on (Jöhncke 2011: 37, 43). Immigrants, who for various reasons rank high in the unemployment statistics, are presented as taking advantage of the mutual benefits without giving or contributing. September 11 added a security dimension to these moral concerns. No longer did Muslim immigrants merely exploit the welfare state model and the Danish way of life; now they threatened state institutions and the actual lives of Danes (cf. Gad 2011).

Secondly, September 11 consolidated new directions in Danish foreign policy. Formerly a country which had taken the position of critical observer, Denmark became actively involved in the US-led 'war on terror' in Iraq and Afghanistan, and participated in NATO military operations in Libya. It became notorious for the 'cartoons controversy' of 2005–6, when *Jyllands-Posten*, the country's largest newspaper, printed twelve caricatures of the Prophet Muhammad on the front page, accompanied by an editorial instructing Muslims that they must put up with insults, mockery and ridicule as prerequisites of contemporary democracy and freedom of speech (Klausen 2009; Lindekilde et al. 2009; Hervik 2011; Stage 2011). The result was demonstrations, boycotts and burnings of the Danish flag in numerous countries around the world. Broadly speaking, Denmark's perceived role and position in the international community had changed: from being an open, liberal society with equal opportunities for all citizens and a tradition of defending the civil and human rights of minorities worldwide, the country had become insular, discriminatory and exclusionist. Furthermore, rather than a cosy little corner of the world, Denmark had become a significant player (at least in the minds of many Danes) in international politics.

This chapter discusses how the ongoing process of securitisation following September 11 has affected the everyday lives of Muslim immigrants in general, and Danish Pakistanis in particular. The chapter presents a macro-perspective on how the Danish nation-state has conceptualised and governed Muslim immigrants since the late 1960s, and how the growing political and public concern with terror has changed the relationship between majorities and minorities. In this process, Muslim diasporic spaces have changed. What used to be more or less invisible benign spaces have increasingly come to be regarded as conspiratorial (Werbner 2009: 20). Furthermore, Pakistanis have gained a particularly unfavourable position in the national discourse and imagination, because the media have in recent years contributed to creating and confirming the disturbing image of an immigrant community forming 'a parallel society'. Even though there are obvious differences in scale and scope between international terrorist attacks like September 11 or July 7, on the one hand, and Danish news stories about Pakistani taxi drivers cheating on their tax payments or young women being forced into marriage on the other, this chapter suggests that such media-borne events and images are connected. In contemporary media-scapes (cf. Appadurai 1996) the here and there, the then and now, large-scale events and small-scale incidents conflate and mutually reinforce each other. They have cast Pakistani migrants as a particular problematic and vulnerable minority group in Danish society. They have, by and large, become *the usual suspects*.

A critical event

According to Veena Das (1996), a critical event is characterised by the institution of a new modality of historical action: the reconfiguration of established categories inevitably generates new meanings, and produces spaces for social imaginaries and political action which were not previously possible, or even conceivable. The French Revolution in 1789 exemplifies a critical event which redistributed power, rights and resources in French society and challenged the hitherto indisputable position of both king and God. Another example of a critical event is the partition of India and Pakistan in 1947, which not only had long-term effects on economic, social and political conditions and security relations in the region, but also affected millions of people's notions of identity, belonging and family relations. In the same way, ten years after the event, we may conclude that the way in which President George W. Bush's administration framed and reacted to the September 11 attacks made them into a critical event which still continues to generate meaning and to have consequences on a global scale (Kapferer 2010: 211–12). Not only has September 11 affected international politics and security relations, it has also motivated numerous new national policies and laws, as well as altering notions of identity, belonging and day-to-day relations between majorities and minorities.

A common effect in many European countries has been an ongoing process of 'securitisation'; the process where 'something' (a referent object) is deemed threatened and security actions taken in its defence (Laustsen and Wæver 2000: 706). On the one hand, European nation-states have introduced far-reaching pre-emptive policies and legislation in order to protect and secure the nation-state and their institutions and citizens against religiously motivated terrorism. On the other hand, individuals and groups have taken measures to protect the religious practices, traditions, beliefs and icons which they feel are being threatened by external forces. The dynamics of mutual securitisation can mobilise people and groups into political activism and action; they may even transform legitimate religious conservatism and fundamentalism into violent acts directed at specific identified others in the name of religion (Cesari 2010: 9). In this respect securitisation is a mutual process: both sides feel threatened, and both react accordingly. The process of securitisation is thus a 'spiral of alienation' (cf. Werbner 2004), where humanist ideals and liberal values tend to become less important than the urgent need to protect beloved family members, values and institutions.

However, September 11 derived its extraordinary impact from its interpretation in the light of historical processes and trajectories which began long before the event itself (Soares and Osella 2009: 1; Bleich 2009: 354). The event mobilised the image of Islam as a dangerous and threatening religion – a concern which has been part of European history and identity since the expansion of the Ottoman Empire (cf. Said 2003 [1978]: 86ff). Peter Hervik suggests 1989 as a critical turning-point. The fall of the Berlin Wall, along with the dissolution of the Soviet Union in 1991, marked the end of the Cold War. However, 1989 was also the year when the Rushdie affair mobilised a visible Muslim public in Europe. So at about the same time as the Cold War ended, the Rushdie affair presented – or created – a new enemy to European values, identity and sovereignty. The threat of communism was succeeded by the threat of Islamism (Hervik 2011; see also Werbner 2002). After September 11, Samuel Huntington's 'clash of civilisations' (2006 [1993]) suddenly seemed a realistic scenario and an adequate analysis to some Danish commentators (e.g., Pittelkow 2002).

Even though September 11 was the most spectacular example, numerous other national and international events were important in facilitating the processes of securitisation after 2001: the terrorist attacks in Bali (2002), Madrid (2004), London (2005) and Mumbai (2008), as well as the failed suicide attacks in Glasgow (2007) and Stockholm (2010); the active involvement of Danish troops in the US-led 'war on terror' in Iraq and Afghanistan; the suicide bombing of the Danish embassy in Islamabad in 2008; several terrorist attacks supposedly planned by Danish Muslims and prevented by the secret service, PET; the so-called 'cartoon controversy', which in 2005–6 and again in 2008 provoked demonstrations and protests all over Denmark and in several Asian and Middle Eastern countries; and the attempt to kill cartoonist Kurt Westergaard in 2010 by a Somali man presumably affiliated with the terror organisation al-Shabaab. While the list is in no way complete, it exemplifies the series of post-September 11 events which have simultaneously created and substantiated the widespread impression that Denmark, its interests and values are currently under attack by Islamists.

September 11 was thus a critical event, which continues to produce numerous effects on the local and global scale. The terrorist attack not only created new ways of perceiving and imagining identities, social relations and religions; it also mobilised individuals, groups and nation-states into political action. The national concerns with immigrants' integration, which had dominated previous decades, were replaced by urgent questions of national security. In the ongoing process of securitisation, not only the external borders of the country, but also the internal 'margins of the state' (Poole and Das 2005) – represented by the Muslim immigrant family – needed to be monitored and governed.

Danish immigration and integration policies

In Denmark, September 11 was also the turning-point for the creation of a new political reality and ways of perceiving and conceptualising ethnic and religious minorities. The national election in November 2001 focused primarily on issues of immigration and integration, and parties from across the political spectrum reacted strongly in order to safeguard their voters' support (Nielsen 2004: 168). After the election the Liberals (*Venstre*) and the

Conservative People's Party (*Konservativt Folkeparti*) formed a government with support from the right-wing Danish People's Party (*Dansk Folkeparti*). Uniquely in recent Danish parliamentary history, these three parties were in power from 2001 to 2011, and enjoyed an absolute majority during the entire period.[2] The 2001 election is often referred to as 'the system change' due to the fact that the Social Democrats were ousted and a new trajectory of right-wing politics was set (Jöhncke 2011: 46). Soon after the election, the governing coalition's mandate was used to introduce far-reaching anti-terror legislation and strict legislation on family reunification, and to reduce the number of refugees. With the formation of the new Liberal-Conservative government, a Ministry of Integration was created in order to deal with the urgent political questions concerning immigrants and refugees in Danish society (Olwig and Paerregaard 2011: 11).

Since 2001, Danish integration politics have taken on a new security dimension. This becomes apparent if we look at the historical development. Roughly speaking, we can identify three different periods of integration in Denmark: the 'laissez-faire integration' of the 1960s and 1970s; the 'integration as assimilation' policy of the 1980s and 1990s; and the post-2001 'security/integration-response'. In the next section, I will outline these three historical periods and the different way immigrants have been conceptualised in Danish politics and social imaginaries.

Laissez-faire integration, 1960–1970

In the first period, the 1960s and 1970s, there was relatively little public or political focus on the everyday lives of the newly arrived immigrants: the newcomers were expected to stay and work hard for a couple of years and then return home. This was also the plan which most of the Pakistanis originally had themselves, but as male migrants began sending for their wives and children in the 1970s and the 1980s, their plans and prospects for the future changed. Despite the numerous new families settling in greater Copenhagen, remarkably little attention was paid to these immigrants. The unions warned against bringing too many foreign workers into the country, because it might affect minimum wages (cf. Østergaard 2007), but besides that there was not much discussion; on the contrary, in the emerging consumer culture of the period, the foreign 'guest workers' personified the wider unknown world of exotic cultures, languages and religions. In retrospect, one can also suggest that the labour migrants and their families from Pakistan, Yugoslavia and Turkey attracted relatively little attention because they managed to organise themselves in networks and formal associations on the basis of different notions of

2. At national elections in 2001, 2004 and 2007, the main issues in the campaigns of the Liberal-Conservative government and the Danish People's Party were foreigners, immigrants and integration.

relatedness, that is, for Pakistanis as members of a *biraderi*, as fellow villagers or countrymen. Furthermore, they started to rebuild some of the institutions they knew from back home, such as cultural associations, political organisations and mosques (Simonsen 2001: 171). These informal networks and institutions provided newcomers with practical and economic help, support and solace.

Integration as assimilation, 1980–1990

During the late 1970s and 1980s, the overall picture changed. According to Jonathan Schwartz, the migrants' decision to stay in Denmark permanently was generally perceived as a breach of faith by the wider Danish population and as a violation of the 'contract' between the Danish state and the labour migrants: that they were to work for a limited period of time and then return home (1990: 46). As the labour migrants began to settle permanently in Denmark, they suddenly posed a new challenge to politicians, and to the welfare state system in general.

As the Pakistani families expanded by natural increase, they started to draw on welfare institutions such as day-care centres (*dagsinstitutioner*), schools (*folkeskoler*), the health system (*sundhedssystemet*) and the social service departments (*socialforvaltning*). The new group of clients confronted the welfare state system with a range of unforeseen 'cultural' problems, which intensified when Denmark began to accept large groups of refugees from areas of conflict in the Middle East, Sri Lanka, Bosnia and Somalia (Fenger-Grøn and Grøndahl 2004). Norwegian anthropologist Unni Wikan has criticised the welfare state system and its public servants (teachers, social workers, etc.) in this period for neglecting problems within immigrant families related to such issues as child-rearing practices, domestic violence and arranged marriage. These problems were generally viewed as part of 'immigrant culture', and therefore something that public servants should and would not interfere with (Wikan 1995; see also 2002).

During the 1980s and 1990s, however, a more general scepticism and mistrust of immigrants took shape in the Danish population, a new perspective which was forcefully articulated by the nationalist Danish People's Party, established in 1995. While at first this party represented a position on the extreme right wing of the Danish political spectrum, today many of its ideas and positions are widely accepted and acknowledged by political opponents in the national parliament.[3]

---

3. The Danish People's Party has gained more and more voters at every election since 1995. In the national election in 2007, it won 13.9 per cent of the votes. After 2001 the party supported the Liberal-Conservative government: they were often referred to as 'the third party in government'. Since its establishment, the Danish People's Party has succeeded in moving from the margins to become a central and decisive factor in Danish national politics.

In the 1980s and 1990s, the concept of 'integration' became increasingly dominant in public and political discourse as both means to and end of migrant improvement (Olwig and Paerregaard 2011: 11). Pakistani families, along with other immigrants and refugees, were subjected to increasing demands that they should 'integrate themselves' by subjecting themselves to vaguely defined Danish norms and standards. In this respect, 'integration' actually meant 'assimilation'. Legislation and policies were introduced to alter idiosyncratic cultural ideas and practices and to correct the apparently archaic, unhealthy and un-Danish practices of the immigrant population, helping (or making) them become just like 'real' Danes instead. Policies, campaigns and legislation were directed against almost every aspect of immigrant everyday life – family organisation, accommodation, upbringing, authority, gender roles, language spoken in the home, relations with the original homeland, dress, hygiene, nutrition, marriage. All the political initiatives launched in the name of integration in this period can be seen in retrospect as part of an overall national political strategy of social engineering, intended to alter the family life, religion and traditions of immigrants in order to make them become Danish.

Security/integration-response after 2001

In recent years, the perception of immigrant integration and improvement seems to have changed once again. It has taken on a new security dimension. In his analysis of the Liberal-Conservative government's policies and legislation in the period 2001–7, political scientist Ulrik Pram Gad (2011) finds that after an initial focus on integration understood as the inclusion of immigrants in the labour market, the discourses changed dramatically after the London bombings in 2005. Since then, Muslims have mainly been presented and discussed as suspect subjects, objects of control and surveillance. In the process, the previous challenge of integration merged with urgent questions related to national and international security. Erich Bleich calls this new situation 'the security/integration-response' and characterises it in the following terms:

> Security dimensions have been layered onto pre-existing concerns about integration, melding with parallel worries about immigration, crime and the public's association between Muslims and violence ... a rolling series of events – particular domestic ones – weighing more heavily on certain policies and public responses than others (2009: 355).[4]

The list of measures included in the security/integration-response over the last decade is long, so I will give just some examples:

---

4. Thomas Faist suggests the concept of 'the migration-security nexus' (2006: 105).

- The Intelligence Service (PET) has prevented several terrorist attacks in Denmark. The trials that followed these cases revealed that the Danish authorities monitor Muslim communities and mosques and utilise undercover informers to infiltrate certain Islamist groups (Skjoldager 2009). In a case from 2008, a Danish-Moroccan man and two Tunisians living in Denmark with their families were accused of conspiring to murder cartoonist Kurt Westergaard. Both Tunisians were deported on a so-called administrative expulsion (*administrativ udvisning*), a legal instrument in the anti-terror legislation which can be used against foreigners. They were not allowed to have their cases tried in court, or even to see the evidence against them. Evidence was presented only to the minister of justice and the minister of integration, who decided to expel them.
- Various pre-emptive measures focused both on terror on Danish soil and abroad. In order to prevent terror attacks by 'home-grown terrorists', the ministry of integration and the three largest cities in Denmark have started anti-radicalisation programmes, in which the 'front-line personnel' (*frontpersonale*) of the welfare state, such as teachers and social workers, are trained to prevent and take action against processes of religious radicalisation (Kühle 2011: 91–2).
- The criteria for being granted permanent residency as a refugee were changed. The result was that the number of accepted refugees dropped from 5,211 in 2001 to 233 in 2007. In the same period, Denmark also started to select the refugees making up its UN quota on the basis of 'integration potential'. In practice, this meant that more Christian refugees were granted residency, at the expense of refugees with a Muslim background (Whyte 2011: 128).
- The legislation on family reunification was tightened. It became extremely difficult for Danes with an immigrant background to achieve family reunification with non-European spouses. This was a means to prevent transnational arranged marriages and family reunifications with foreign spouses, and to encourage immigrants to cross ethnic and religious boundaries and marry 'real' Danes instead (see Part II).
- In 2002, the government abolished the previously obligatory mother-tongue teaching which had formerly been provided to children with an immigrant background. The political argument was that children – in the name of integration – should speak Danish at home, despite international research showing that bilingual children perform better in education if they are fluent in both languages (cf. Holmen 2002).
- The subsidies to immigrant associations were significantly reduced. While association had formerly been encouraged as a means for immigrants to enhance their engagement in civil society, in the wake of September 11, the new regime regarded and treated immigrant cultural and religious associations as suspect.
- There was increased focus on remittances sent out of the country, in order to ensure that no Danish residents supported terrorist organisations

abroad. This affected not only NGOs, but also ordinary individuals sending money to family members in their first homeland.

- A new citizenship examination was introduced, requiring applicants to pass a test on Danish history, culture and society, in addition to signing a declaration in which they swear allegiance and loyalty to Denmark and Danish society, and declare their willingness to observe and respect the national laws.
- Visitation zones (*visitations zoner*) were introduced in parts of Copenhagen in order to prevent the spread of an ongoing violent conflict between the Danish branch of the biker organisation Hell's Angels and various immigrant gangs. This pre-emptive instrument was introduced and accepted as a legitimate means to regain control in, and secure different parts of, the capital.[5] However, the result is that law-abiding citizens with immigrant background have regularly been detained and searched.
- In 2009, the government established a 'burka commission' to find out how many Muslim women in Denmark wear the burka.[6] There have been numerous discussions over the last decades about whether religious dress is oppressive for Muslim women (cf. Andreassen 2011). In the view of many Danish feminists and politicians, religious dress symbolises a patriarchal authoritarian family (Khawaja 2011: 278). There has therefore been discussion of whether the hijab should be allowed in parliament or in public administration: there has, for instance, been discussion of whether a judge can be objective if she is wearing a hijab. These discussions are also linked to emerging uncertainty and fear of unidentified passengers on public trains and buses. You never know who or what is under a burka.

These are some examples of the Danish nation-state's security/integration-response since 2001. These pre-emptive measures, both 'soft' and 'hard', are both means and ends aimed at achieving a political ambition – namely, to control and regulate the everyday lives of Muslim minorities in order to protect the common good of Danish citizens, institutions and the welfare state. Taken individually, the measures may seem reasonable, relatively harmless; taken together, they constitute a pattern of political challenge, intervention and regulation of Muslim immigrants. Giorgio Agamben (2005: 3–4) has used the concept of 'state of exception' to describe the Bush administration's response to the attacks of September 11. The state

---

5. While he was minister of international development, the Liberal Party politician (and also former minister of integration) Søren Pind expressed sympathy for a manifesto published by the biker group Hell's Angels which described immigrant gangs as 'jackals'. Intentionally or not, the minister's approval confirmed and legitimised the impression that immigrants pose an external threat and menace to Danish society.

6. 'The Report on the Use of Niqab and Burqa' was published in 2009 and estimated that between 100 and 200 women in Denmark wear this type of dress (see http://www.e-pages.dk/ku/322/, p. 13).

of exception is the immediate response of state power to the most extreme situation, a response which, among other things, erases the legal status of the individual and reduces it to 'bare life', a legally unnameable and unclassifiable being. 'The state of exception is not a special kind of law (like the law of war); rather, insofar as it is a kind of suspension of the juridical order itself, it defines law's threshold or limit concept' (Agamben 2005: 4). The Danish security/integration-response that came into being after September 11 shows similarities to Agamben's scenario, and constitutes both means and ends in the changing perception and status of immigrants. While the 'war on terror' was at first an immediate reaction to an extreme situation, it later became normalised as an obvious aspect of the resort and jurisdiction of the nation-state (Andersen 2008: 56). After 2001, the old strategy of the 1980s and 1990s, that immigrants could (at least in theory) become a part of Danish society and the national imagined community, was met by suspicion and disillusionment. The reconstruction of Muslim immigrants as a potential enemy within became a more or less permanent, naturalised condition.

Ethno-nationalism and cultural anxiety

Nonetheless, it is too simplistic to conclude that Danes or Danish society in general are racist or Islamophobic. Rather, the very constitution of the national order implies a certain kind of discrimination which tends to produce and reproduce hierarchical differences between the Danish majority and ethnic minorities (see Chapter 5).

First of all, racism is not a commonly used concept in Danish discourse (Hervik 1999: 111). Racism is associated with Nazism and the Holocaust, and has not been an important topic in Danish or Scandinavian research. However, in recent years the concept of a 'new racism' has been adopted by some researchers (Hervik 2004, 2011; Hussain 2003) in order to emphasise that the current discrimination against ethnic minorities is both an old (and all too well-known) phenomenon and also at the same time something new. One new aspect is that it is no longer the 'race' but the 'culture' of the immigrants which is regarded as problematic (Hervik 1999: 116). Another common feature of the new racism is to deny racism while representing 'others' as inferior, because they are not perceived to be as developed or civilised as 'us' (Gullestad 2002a: 151). An example of this is how arranged marriages – widely accepted by Pakistani migrants (see Chapter 3 and 4) – are systematically presented in public discourse as an anachronism and as a practice Danes abandoned centuries ago. In this way, the institution of arranged marriage becomes an anomaly brought to the country by Muslim immigrants – it becomes 'matter out of place' (Douglas 1966) and a tradition which disturbs the civilised order of Danish society. In this way, culture has replaced race when it comes to defining the problems related to the immigrant other.

Verena Stolcke (1995) proposes the concept of 'cultural fundamentalism' to capture the assertion and widespread ordering principle that everyone belongs by birth to a specific territory with a distinct culture. Physical relocation such as migration disturbs such a predetermined order and will tend to result in conflicts between cultures, which are incommensurable. Cultural fundamentalism differs from new racism in the idea that, rather than there being a hierarchy of cultures, cultures belong to different places and should be kept apart. It therefore asserts that there are 'unbridgeable differences' between the Danish majority and the Muslim minorities (cf. Hervik 2004). This difference inevitably produces a hierarchy, however, as the indigenous Danes claim to be those who naturally and rightfully belong to the territory and nation and therefore have the right to define 'proper' ways of life.

In a Norwegian context, social anthropologist Marianne Gullestad has suggested that racism, new racism and cultural fundamentalism are found combined in a specific constellation she calls 'ethno-nationalism', which she defines as:

> an imaginary geography where 'foreign' appearance and family name work as markers of cultural difference and social distance. Ethno-nationalism is a close-knit set of specific understandings about geography, history, culture, religion and perceptions about skin colour and descent, a close-knit set of ideas that has only recently been re-invented (Gullestad 2006: 302).

A similar ethno-nationalism has become widely accepted in the Danish discourse on identity and belonging. It constitutes a specific social imaginary, which privileges Danes with a long family history in the country, proper name, dialect, religion and phenotype (eye, skin, hair colour). This places Danes in a superior position as the rightful owners of the nation and welfare state. At the same time, it makes it difficult, if not impossible, for Danes with an immigrant or refugee background to achieve inclusion in the imagined national community.[7]

Along with this emerging ethno-nationalism, there has also been increased 'cultural anxiety' (Grillo 2003) in Danish public and political discourse. Cultural anxiety is motivated by disturbing feelings of losing national sovereignty, territory, history, values and identity. Cultural anxiety is directed at external transgressors: these may be supranational institutions – such as the international economy, the European Union, the Human Rights Charter or the United Nations – or local potential 'enemies within' such as the immigrant population, which personifies the disturbing forces of globalisation, transformation and change. In the beginning, this kind of anxiety was articulated and promoted mainly by the Danish People's Party,

---

7. In recent years, religious affiliation has become so important in the national social imaginary that ethnic Danes who convert to Islam are seen and treated as traitors by those around them, even their own families (Jensen 2008, 2011).

but currently it seems to have become a mainstream political position and concern (Gad 2011: 61).

Ethno-nationalism and cultural anxiety, which can be seen as two sides of the same coin, have risen up both the public and political agendas over the last decades in Denmark. While ethno-nationalism and cultural anxiety are not necessarily present in every social situation or encounter between minorities and majorities, it should be emphasised that they do constitute a specific framework or 'invisible fence' (Gullestad 2002b) that can be mobilised strategically anywhere: whether at a bus stop, supermarket, sports club or university. In every instance, the indigenous Danes are positioned as superior in relation to peers with different ethnic backgrounds, for example Pakistani. Such subtle social mechanisms can be very difficult to address and discuss verbally, but they are experienced again and again by Pakistanis and other immigrants in Denmark.

The usual suspects

In a political climate of ethno-nationalism and cultural anxiety, immigrants are vulnerable. For several reasons, Pakistani migrants have been at the centre of the political discussions and legal interventions, from the start. First of all, the image of Pakistani migrants in Denmark and beyond has been affected by the central position Pakistan has gained in the war against terror.[8] The coalition's war against the Taliban in Afghanistan soon spread to western and northern regions of Pakistan. From these areas, the media frequently report military confrontations, suicide bombers and American drones killing Taliban supporters and al-Qaeda leaders (and unspecified numbers of civilians). The London bombings were planned and carried out by immigrants with Pakistani background, and the Mumbai attacks partly by Pakistani citizens, just as one of the Danish terror cases includes a young man with Pakistani parentage trained in Waziristan (Crone and Harrow 2010: 16). The Pakistani religious party, *Jamaat-i Islami*, was reported in December 2005 to have offered a reward of DKr 50,000 ($10,000) for the killing of any of the twelve cartoonists (DR, 2 December 2005), and even though this was later officially denied by *Jamaat-i Islami*, the story received wide circulation in Denmark. Media-borne stories and episodes like these contribute to

---

8. These generalised scapegoat mechanisms are not only salient in Denmark. Aminah Mohammad-Arif (2009) discusses how Pakistani migrants in the United States did well in many respects and strove to realise the 'American Dream' of success, mobility and prosperity, but after September 11 became the 'internal other' and the usual suspects for criminal activity and terror. Since 2001, approximately 2,000 Pakistanis have been deported by the American authorities, while thousands have left voluntarily (Mohammad-Arif 2009: 322). In Brooklyn, New York, it is estimated that 15,000–18,000 have left for other US states, Europe and the Middle East (ibid.: 325).

transforming Pakistani immigrants into a potentially problematic minority group. In addition, besides the ongoing international conflicts and terror-related cases, Pakistani migrants have acquired a questionable reputation in Danish public opinion due to numerous stories and episodes about the local migrant community in greater Copenhagen. The following section outlines three of these: 1) The formation of 'a parallel society'; 2) Pakistani politicians and immigrant politics; and 3) Forced marriages and notions of honour.

1. The image of a parallel society

In 2004 the minister of culture, Brian Mikkelsen, representing the Conservative People's Party, intensified the government's 'cultural war of values' (*kulturkamp*).[9] On the one hand, his attack was aimed at the elite of 'cultural radicals' (*kulturradikale*) and experts whom prime minister Anders Fogh Rasmussen had already condemned as 'judges of taste' (*smagsdommere*) in his first New Year speech in 2002; on the other hand, it represented an open confrontation with immigrant culture, religion and ways of life presented as incompatible with Danish norms and values. Brian Mikkelsen explained that Danes could not accept that 'in the midst of our country a parallel society is developing in which minorities are practising their medieval norms and undemocratic mindsets'. He suggested national armament as 'the best vaccine against undemocratic tendencies within the society' (cf. Kublitz 2010: 112). Pakistanis are one of the immigrant groups associated with the negative image of a parallel society.

Even though the Pakistani presence in Copenhagen is much smaller than the South Asian communities found in several British cities, it is commonly believed that there exists 'a Pakistani society in Denmark' (cf. the title of Quraishy's monograph, 1999). Quoting James Clifford, Werbner suggests that the Pakistani community in Manchester can be characterised as 'an alternative public sphere ... leading to forms of community consciousness and solidarity that maintain identifications outside the national time/space in order to live inside, with a difference' (Clifford 1994: 308, in Werbner 2002: 263). In this respect Pakistanis in Denmark have created an alternative public sphere during the last four decades: one which, on the basis of shared history, language and place of origin, is constituted by individuals, families, *biraderi* groups and formal associations, politicians and religious leaders, local and transnational NGOs, local media consisting of newspapers, TV

---

9. The idea of a 'cultural war of values' (*kulturkamp*) had been introduced in the book *Fra Socialstat, til Minimalstat* (Samleren 1993) by Anders Fogh Rasmussen, at that time an ordinary Liberal Party member of Parliament. As prime minister, he reintroduced the concept in a newspaper interview in January 2003 in *Weekendavisen*, and thereby launched what was soon to be known as the 'cultural war of values' (see http://www.information.dk/101590)

and radio stations, several mosques, food stores, sweet shops, hairdressers and beauty parlours, travel agencies, restaurants, *shadi* halls (wedding halls), cricket clubs, cinemas, concerts, etc. Like nodes in a network, these persons, places and institutions constitute a non-local space that is shared, embodied and lived by migrants with a family history related to Pakistan.

However, when politicians like the minister of culture quoted above use the 'parallel society' image, they paint a disturbing picture of blank spots within Danish society, blank spots sealed off from the authorities and governed by independent norms and rules. The same image also raises moral concerns that immigrants in such environments are exploiting welfare state subsidies such as health insurance (*sygedagpenge*), unemployment benefit (*kontanthjælp*) or pensions (early retirement or the *førtidspension*). Chapter 2 discusses how, in the 1980s, Pakistanis successfully established their niche of corner shops, thanks to practical help and economic support from extended family and *biraderi* networks. Over the years, however, media stories created the negative image of Pakistanis as forming a mafia-like network of shop-owners, engaged in illegal tax fraud or selling illegally imported sweets, beverages and alcohol. It was also reported that money from Denmark was being used on large migrant houses, investments, luxurious lifestyles and conspicuous consumption when migrants return more or less permanently to Pakistan (see Chapter 8). Because it both creates and confirms widespread concerns that immigrants – in this case Pakistani migrants – systematically violate the generalised reciprocity and mutual solidarity on which the welfare state is based, the image of the parallel society is extremely negative in Danish discourse.

2. Pakistani politicians and immigrant politics

In spring 2001, three young people with Pakistani parents ran for candidacy in the Social-Liberal Party (*Det Radikale Venstre*). Their intentions and loyalties were questioned in the national media, because they were also members of the Muslim Youth League (MYL) or the Women's Youth League (WYL), male and female branches of the international Pakistan-based organisation, *Idara Minhaj ul-Quran*.[10] Twenty-three-year-old Mona Sheikh, in particular, repeatedly found herself in national newspapers and television having to explain her position on sharia and the death penalty. After a hectic period, she withdrew her candidacy. The episode not only added to public suspicion of politicians with a Muslim background; it also launched a conspiracy theory, that the young Pakistanis were trying to infiltrate and destabilise

---

10. *Minhaj ul-Quran* is dominated by the South Asian Barelwi tradition (cf. Lewis 2002: 40–43). However, the organisation has been presented by Danish media and Islamo-sceptic commentators as dominated by Islamism and supporting the Taliban regime in Afghanistan. For more accurate information about *Idara Minhaj ul-Quran*, see Geaves (2006) and Schmidt (2007).

the parliamentary system in order to overthrow democracy (Hervik 2011: 113–76; see also Jørgensen 2011).

Since the 'Mona Sheikh affair', numerous politicians with Muslim backgrounds (i.e. Tanwir Ahmad, Bashy Quraishy, Tanveer Sharif, Hadi Khan, Sherin Khankan, Fatima Shah and Asmaa Abdol-Hamid) have been interrogated by Danish journalists and asked to take a stand on the sharia and the death penalty.[11] When Rushy Rashid in 2007 stood for parliamentary candidacy representing the Social Democrats, she was even questioned by a priest about her political convictions.[12] Suspicions and allegations often seem to be raised by other Muslim politicians, contributing to an ongoing division between 'good' and 'bad' Muslims in the public sphere (cf. Mamdani 2002).

This political rivalry between 'good' and 'bad' Muslim figures became visible during the 2005 election for the Copenhagen city council (*Københavns Borgerrepræsentation*), when Ikram Sarwar and Sikandar Malik Sidiqque (Social Democrats) and Mr Wallait Khan (Liberal Party) all aimed at Pakistani voters in central Copenhagen. Sikandar and Mr Khan made the headlines in national newspapers with a controversy over the involvement of Mr Khan and Sikandar's father in local politics in Pakistan, and also over family rivalry within the migrant community in general.[13] This confrontation showed how politics within the Pakistani community is to some extent organised around *zaat* affiliation and *biraderi* loyalty, and in many instances related to politics in Pakistan as well.

Cases like these have created and nurtured the widespread belief that politicians of Muslim and immigrant background 'speak with two tongues' (*taler med to tunger*). This implies not only that the politicians in question are unreliable and take different political positions depending on audience, but that their main priorities and loyalties are directed at their 'own' group or community, defined in national, ethnic or religious terms, rather than in the terms of the common good of Danish society. Rather than a responsibility and obligation for all citizens, participation in the democratic political process thus becomes a suspect activity when engaged in by Muslim minorities.

3. Forced marriages and notions of honour

Marriage practices within Pakistani families have been widely discussed in the Danish public debate. Part II discusses the escalating moral panic concerning

---

11. Back in 2000, Danish-Pakistani medical doctor Mazhar Hussain, representing the Social-Liberal Party (*Det Radikale Venstre*) in Københavns Amtsråd, reached the front pages under the headline 'Doctor death' (*Doktor død*) because he, as a practising devoted Muslim, refused to denounce sharia.
12. 'Præst afhørte muslimsk S-kandidat', *Politikken*, 10 August 2007.
13. Numerous articles in the Danish media covered the controversy; see for instance, 'Khan-sagen: Pakistanske politikere i opgør', *Morgenavisen Jyllandsposten*, 29 November 2005.

immigrants' transnational arranged marriages in the late 1990s and early 2000s. Pakistanis were the immigrant group where most problems of family pressure and enforcement in relation to marriage arrangements were recorded (cf. Schmidt and Jakobsen 2004). Crisis shelters started to receive more and more married women who had been beaten by their husbands, or desperate young women with an immigrant background requesting the authorities' intervention in order for them to escape the will and wedding plans of their parents. The violence and enforcement were often framed and explained as a way to restore family honour.

In September 2005, the brutal murder of 18-year-old Ghazala Khan by her elder brother tragically provided the worst-case scenario of such an escalating family conflict. Ghazala was born in Denmark, raised by the family in Pakistan, but frequently lived for periods in Denmark. A couple of days prior to the murder, Ghazala had married Emal, an Afghani refugee living in Denmark. After several years of a secret romance, they had eloped. The family found them in the provincial town of Slagelse, where Ghazala was killed and Emal wounded by gunshots. The murder was spectacular because it was filmed, and pictures were printed in national newspapers. The subsequent trial showed that the murder was the culmination of a family conflict, and that the order to assassinate Ghazala had been given by her own father in order to restore the family's honour and reputation. The police investigation reconstructed the movements and mobile-phone communications between the people involved in the manhunt, and this gave the impression of a coordinated crime. No fewer than nine people, including Ghazala's father, brother, aunt and three uncles, were convicted for participating in, ordering or executing the killing. They were sentenced from eight years in prison to life imprisonment (see Møller 2007).

The murder tapped into the ongoing debate and concern about immigrant marriage practices and honour-related violence. The tragic circumstances of Ghazala's death portrayed to Danish audiences a family willing to kill a disobedient daughter, sister or niece to protect its reputation. In this respect the case confirmed existing stereotypes of how patriarchal authority and archaic notions of honour supposedly dominate the everyday life of Pakistani Muslim families (cf. Grillo 2008: 23). The vast majority of immigrant families that manage to negotiate marriage preferences, intergenerational relations, household reputation and family honour were relegated to the same category of (in)humanity as the murderers who executed Ghazala Khan.

Connecting the local and the global

This chapter argues that September 11 was a critical event, which continues to impact on the relationship between majorities and minorities in Denmark. September 11 was met with a security/integration-response, which altered shared ideas of what were reasonable pre-emptive measures and interventions against Muslim minorities to protect Danish citizens, institutions and values (cf. Pedersen and Rytter 2011). The state of exception has become the ordinary condition: it is difficult to remember what it was like before 2001, or to imagine alternative trajectories or future horizons. Everyone in Denmark is affected by this new situation – not least Pakistani immigrants in their everyday lives and their notions of family relatedness, identity and belonging. They are particularly vulnerable due to the involvement of Pakistan in the US-led 'war against terror', and the fact that Pakistanis abroad have engaged again and again in planning and executing terror attacks around the world. This chapter has attempted to illuminate some of the complex links and connections between critical international events, national policies and interventions, and the dynamics of local moral panics, which have given Pakistani migrants such a prominent and unfavourable position in Danish politics, discourse and imaginaries.

This macro-perspective on recent Danish history shows that intertwined local and global events, discourses and images have served to motivate, substantiate and legitimise the security/integration-response aimed at Muslim immigrants in general since 2001. By contrast with this disturbing development, the next chapter will outline the micro-history of the Pakistani migration and settlement process, and of some of the intra-familial dynamics, which have contributed to creating an innovative and socially mobile Danish-Pakistani community. From this perspective, the most recent decades of Danish history look very different.

Chapter 2

Micro-perspectives

Notions of improvement

Transnational migration is widely regarded as a way of improving living standards and future prospects for people all over the world, but some livelihood strategies are widely held to be more successful than others. This holds true for Pakistanis who have been living in Denmark for four decades. Some families have gained the reputation of being more successful than others, something that is often referred to in emic discourses as 'a family that has done well' (*en familie der har klaret sig godt*). As will be argued in this chapter, notions of improvement are contested, and may change over time.

Since I started conducting fieldwork among Pakistani migrants in Denmark in 2001, I have noticed that my interlocutors often make a sharp distinction between those families in which young people in the second generation have pursued higher education and those where they have not. Pakistani interlocutors may gossip about the new elite of self-righteous medical doctors or arrogant engineers who think they are better than their neighbours, or make jokes about having to drive a taxi or run a corner shop (*kiosk*) in order to make a living. The question of education is usually framed in terms of an evolutionary scheme in which education implies being progressive, Western or modern; the rest of the community is thus characterised, less flatteringly, as backward, traditional, and shaped by the 'cultural' mentality that is supposedly dominant in the Punjabi villages from which these families originate. This kind of reasoning is not just based on internal Pakistani stereotypes or mutual prejudices; it also reflects an actual socio-economic division in the migrant community, initiated decades ago when Pakistani families had to decide between engaging in business ventures that would generate money quickly, and pursuing education that promised future gains in the long term.

Today, a large number of second-generation Pakistanis do extremely well in the free Danish education system. The latest survey to give the national backgrounds of students dates back to 2002 and shows that, among young people aged 18–35 of Pakistani background, 30 per cent of the males and 36 per cent of the females have completed secondary education (*gymnasial uddannelse*), whereas the figures for the descendants of immigrants in Denmark in general are 24 per cent for men and 31 per cent for women. In comparison, the average national figures for young Danes who complete secondary education are 25 per cent for men and 38 per cent for women (Hummelgaard et al. 2002).[1]

Over the years, researchers have tried to explain the educational achievements of the Pakistani community. According to Jan Hjarnø (2000), the high level of achievement can be explained by the fact that Pakistanis were already investing in real estate in the 1970s and 1980s and were moving away from the badly maintained apartments of the inner city into the suburbs of Copenhagen. Here young people attended schools in 'white areas', mingled with pupils from middle-class families, and were taught by teachers who had high expectations of their pupils regardless of ethnic or linguistic background (Hjarnø 2000). Another explanation is suggested by Bolette Moldenhawer (2005), who emphasises that the education of second-generation Pakistanis has become a strategy of social mobility for the entire transnational family, and points to the importance of the transnational *biraderi* (classificatory kin group) in this context.

Though both these contrasting explanations point to important factors, neither of them seems satisfactory. I suggest that the explanations offered by Hjarnø and Moldenhawer are actually merely the effects of a more fundamental social dynamic in the migrant community. Both local middle-class aspirations and the social mobility strategies of transnational family networks are the outcomes of decades of fierce competition between migrant families, where the prize has been symbolic capital and an improved status in the local Pakistani community. This chapter analyses how notions of improvement among Pakistani migrant families in Denmark have emerged and changed over time, and how two overall strategies – of money and of education – have been shaped by changes in the Danish welfare state.

Contested notions of improvement

In ongoing public discussions concerning immigrants and refugees in Denmark, the ultimate improvement that both categories are expected to subject themselves to is integration. It is nevertheless 'exceptionally unclear' (Ejrnæs 2002: 7) what is actually meant by 'integration'. It may refer to anything from *social integration* in certain neighbourhoods or educational institutions, to *economic integration* (understood as participation in the labour market), to *political*

---

1. Recent statistics from the Ministry of Refugee, Immigration and Integration Affairs show that in 2008 60 per cent of the descendants of immigrants and refugees aged 16–24 have entered or finished secondary education. The percentage of Danish young people finishing secondary education is only 59 per cent (*Morgenavisen Jyllandsposten*, 19 January 2008). There is no reason to believe that Pakistanis have a less favourable position in the statistics of national immigrant groups today than they did in 2002.

integration (seen as participation in national elections and local associations) and *cultural integration* (measured by the extent to which immigrants and refugees have abandoned the traditions, identity or notions of belonging connected with their first homeland). Despite the unclear definition, integration has become a common political ambition, a desirable imagined horizon.

The social diagnosis of when integration is reached, or not, is always set 'from above' by politicians, the media, scientists: ultimately, that is, by people in power. In this respect, the concept of integration is part of the vocabulary of the nation-state (Sayad 2004: 216ff.). But even though immigrants and refugees often make the headlines or are the objects of political discussions, legal interventions and academic research, they continue to live their ordinary lives in spite of all the fuss (Pedersen and Rytter 2006: 10).

In their everyday lives – 'from below' – migrants themselves constantly formulate and reformulate notions of improvement that may differ considerably from the national ambition of integration. However, the standards whereby 'families who have done well' are distinguished from those who have not are never fixed, but are the result of an ongoing evaluation between examiner and examined, me and you, our family and their family. In this process, there are always real or imagined audiences monitoring the family's actions; and notions of improvement are always situated within socio-political contexts that set up specific criteria for evaluation.

According to Pierre Bourdieu, the social cosmos of modern societies is constituted by several relatively autonomous social fields, each with their own logic and demands, which are not necessarily comparable to the rules governing other fields (Bourdieu and Wacquant 2001: 85). A field can be compared to a game (ibid.: 84). By participating in a specific social game, you confirm that you recognise it as important. This mutual recognition is the basis of struggles and conflicts in any field. Furthermore, every field is characterised by a distribution of power or capital, which gives access to the values at stake in the game. Though Bourdieu distinguishes between several different types of capital, in this chapter I will discuss only the *economic capital* of money, the *cultural capital* of education and the *symbolic capital* of prestige, status and honour. Whereas the first two forms of capital are measurable – for example, the size of a fortune or the level of education reflected in a diploma – symbolic capital distinguishes itself by being primarily cognitive and based on recognition by significant others in the field (Bourdieu 1997: 163). Symbolic capital is that particular capital that 'rescues agents from insignificance, the absence of importance and meaning' (Bourdieu 2000: 242).

For Bourdieu, notions of improvement are always situated in an exclusive social field which is governed by its own rules, morals and aesthetics and comprises a unique capital economy. In what follows, in order to grasp how notions of improvement are redefined over time, I will outline the micro-history of Pakistani families in Denmark. The aim is to explore how and why these two long-term strategies, focused on money and education, have become means of improvement within the migrant community, and how they relate to the overall national project of integration.

Immigration and settlement processes

Pakistanis in Denmark constitute an interconnected network, a little village, in which the histories and trajectories of families criss-cross. The story of one family is part of the collective history of what it means to be 'Pakistani in Denmark'. In order to understand current community dynamics and changing notions of improvement, it is necessary to trace family stories back in time and space (see Fig. 1).

Rural Punjab in the 1960s

In Punjab, from where the majority of Pakistani families in Denmark originate, labour migration has for centuries been a family strategy of economic improvement. After Punjab became part of the 'British Raj' in 1849, the Indian army recruited mainly from this region, as Punjabi men had earned a reputation for being loyal to the colonial administration, one which they confirmed in the mutiny of 1857 (Ballard 1987: 23). In the First World War,

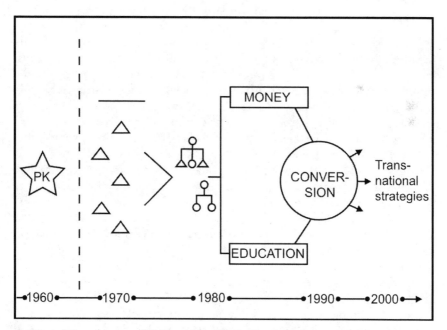

Figure 1: Micro-history of Pakistani families in Denmark

The figure illustrates the micro-history of Pakistani families in Denmark. The migrant men arrive in the 1960s and 1970s and are soon followed by women and children. In the 1980s, the community becomes split between the long-term strategies of money and education. Since the 1990s, there has been an ongoing conversion of acquired capital, and new transnational strategies have started to take shape.

350,000 Punjabis fought in the Indian army, and by the time of Partition in 1947 there were already 25,000 Punjabi migrant workers involved in constructing the railway between Kenya and Uganda (Shaw 2000 [1988]: 23). In this respect, historical conditions – imperialism – made labour migration a well-known, widely used option for families to improve their economy and prospects in some of the geographical areas that were later to become Pakistan.

Transnational migration to Europe dates back to the 1930s, when men from Mirpur in Azad Kashmir sailed between the subcontinent and Europe. During the Second World War, many started working in British industry. More and more migrants took up their privileges as 'Commonwealth citizens' to settle in the United Kingdom during the 1940s and 1950s, just when British society was in need of manual labour (Ballard 1987: 24). However, increasing unemployment changed the picture. In 1962, Britain changed its immigration rules to allow entry only to migrants with a voucher. Despite government intentions the new legislation actually intensified immigration, because it motivated migrants who were already settled in Britain to send for their relatives immediately (Lewis 2002: 17; Shaw 2000[1988]: 30ff.). In 1965, the immigration regime was tightened up once again. With restricted possibilities to enter Britain, Pakistani migrants started to look for other possibilities.

Pakistani men started migrating to Denmark as guest workers in the late 1960s. In 1973, the Danish government banned further labour-related immigration, but Pakistanis kept on arriving, first through family reunification and later through the high rate of endogamous transnational marriages in the second generation (Schmidt and Jakobsen 2004). Today approximately 25,000 people in Denmark have a family history related to Pakistan. Due to a pattern of chain migration, most Pakistani immigrants originate from villages in the Gujrat district of rural Punjab and, as this is also the case for most Pakistanis in Norway (Østberg 2003), this area is sometimes referred to as 'Little Scandinavia'.

Those who came directly from Pakistan left a developing country in a difficult period of transition following the end of the colonial era and the violent partition from India in 1947. Rural Punjab was a society consisting of villages highly divided due to the *zaat* system, a caste-like hierarchy that developed out of the historical co-existence of Islam, Hinduism and Sikhism in the region. Each village had a rigid division between the *zamindar* (who owned the land) and the *kammi* (who worked for them). These overall categories, based on descent and occupation, created a significant cleavage in the villages between the privileged and the unprivileged. As emigration was costly, the migrants who came to Denmark were primarily from landowning families belonging to various *zaat* – such as Gujar, Jat, Raja and Malik – and different types of Kashmiri background (Quraishy 1999: 91). The privileged social position of the migrants and their families is reflected in the fact that most of the migrant men had between eight and twelve years of schooling before they came to Denmark (Horst in Østergaard 2007: 353). However, even though most of the migrants came from well-off families with a relatively high ranking in the social stratification of the caste-like system, they were, from a Pakistani perspective, families with very different norms and values.

The 'Golden Age' of the late 1960s and early 1970s

Regardless of social status and economic background, the Pakistanis arrived in Denmark by the same route, travelling overland by bus via Afghanistan, Iran and Iraq, and entering Europe through Turkey. Many ended up in Germany in the late 1960s and early 1970s, where they worked on construction sites in Munich in preparation for the 1972 Olympic Games. In Germany at that time many rumours circulated about Denmark, a little country up north where it was possible to get legal work permits and where there were plenty of jobs for immigrants. The pattern of chain migration therefore continued, as immigrants who were already established in Denmark started helping friends stranded in Germany obtain the job offers that would give them permission to enter the country.

Arriving in Denmark, many Pakistanis found themselves cramped together in small and often badly maintained apartments in the centre of Copenhagen or in the suburbs. Others rented single rooms from Danish landlords. There was work available at factories needing migrant workers to do the '3-D-Jobs' of dirty, demanding and dangerous manual labour (Østergaard 2007: 351). The new lifestyle and position as immigrants made the male Pakistani migrants structurally equal. They lived, ate and slept together in small apartments, and worked side by side in the factories.[2] In Denmark, the many hierarchies and mechanisms of social stratifications from rural Punjab disappeared for a while, as everyone was 'just' an immigrant, and shared the experience of living in a strange country a long way from their loved ones back home. In the gendered masculine migration narratives, the period of the early 1970s figures as 'a golden age' when everyone was young, strong and had every opportunity in life (see Gardner 2002).

According to Pakistani life-stories, Danes had a radically different approach to immigrants during the 1960s and early 1970s than more recently. Immigrants were in most instances recognised as co-workers by their Danish colleagues, who invited them to their private homes, helped them read letters from the authorities and taught them the Danish language. This was also a time when male migrants were introduced to alcohol and dancing, and many became involved in romantic relationships with Danish women. On the one hand, the 'golden age' is looked back upon today with nostalgia; on the other hand, it was also a time when Pakistani men, who today present themselves as respectable elders, had a more exploratory approach to life in the West and transgressed several of the rules and moral boundaries they today encourage

---

2. For similar observations in United Kingdom, see Pnina Werbner (1990: 84) and Alison Shaw (2000 [1988]: 37).

their grown-up children – and maybe even grandchildren – to respect and live by. It is therefore a period in the history of Pakistani migration that is today passed over in silence, due to the many skeletons hidden in the closet.

The settlement process of the 1970s

After the Danish government banned further labour-related immigration in 1973, the most important source of continued Pakistani immigration was family reunification. In order to qualify, a male guest worker needed to have his own accommodation.

Mr Chaudry, who came to Denmark in his late teens, originates from one of the villages around Kharian in rural Punjab. His uncle sent for him and helped him settle in Denmark:

> My uncle arrived to Denmark back in 1969, so he could help me find a room … a Danish friend helped us, and let us stay in his summerhouse, so that we [could save money and] later could afford to buy an apartment. Later my cousin, my uncle and I bought an apartment in Elmegade. We bought it together and lived together. But when we got married, we agreed that only one couple should stay in the apartment and the two other couples should move out. I lived there with my wife until 1978.

After the three men were reunited with their wives in Denmark, they divided up the bachelor house and moved into separate apartments.

The general picture is that when wives and children arrived from Pakistan, the newly re-established families moved into their own apartments. In the same period, however, many workers began to lose their jobs. After the energy crises in 1973–4, Denmark faced a period of economic recession, followed by declining opportunities in the labour market. It became a period of high unemployment, during which much of Danish industry and the labour market in general were restructured (Hjarnø 2000: 101). Many factories that had benefited from the manpower of the guest workers were shut down, outsourced their activities or went through processes of rationalisation. As a result, many of the manual jobs needing low-skilled workers disappeared. Many immigrants lost their jobs and livelihoods in the process.

Generally speaking, the men lost their jobs just as the women and children started arriving; what used to be a fraternity of migrant men became a community of migrant families. This transition marked the end of the 'golden age'. Now the logic of social stratification that predominated in Pakistan was re-established, and began to frame inter-family relations. In an early article describing the dynamics of Bradford's Pakistani community, Badr Dahya suggested the existence of a two-stage process. The initial tendency towards 'fusion', when settlers associated together regardless of their background, gradually gave way to a process of 'fission' and segmentation, in which old (and new) lines of differentiation became significant within the community (Dahya 1974). The same social and historical dynamics are to be found among

Pakistani families in Denmark, but here things moved beyond the 'two-stage theory', and new lines of affiliation, identity and belonging were created. Mr Asif related that in the early years before his wife arrived, he had worked at a factory making paint and lived in a small apartment with a handful of his fellow countrymen. On my next visit I had a longer conversation with Mr Asif's son, who explained that, when his father meets some of his former co-workers today, they do not even greet each other. This example illustrates the shift from a fraternity of equal men to a community of differentiated families. In order not to be confronted with compromising stories from the past, people are highly selective about who they socialise and remain friends with (Bajaj and Laursen 1988: 140–1). This process of re-differentiation had an important impact on relations between families in the community.

A community of competition: the 1980s and 1990s

As Pakistani wives joined the men in Denmark, new families and households were established and began to recreate some of the cultural and religious institutions they knew from their country of origin. The migrant families shared life-cycle transitions, as many started having children and faced similar challenges in raising their offspring in a new social environment that in many respects was (and still is) more liberal than that of Pakistan. But even though the families helped each other with different aspects of everyday life, relations between them became more and more competitive as distinctions of status and hierarchy were asserted and renegotiated in the context of immigration.

Migrants with a middle-class background often have to accept 'a class journey' of negative social mobility when they settle in Denmark (cf. Pedersen 2009: 67ff.). Mrs Khan, who completed her education in economics in Pakistan before marrying and, in 1975, achieving family reunification, remembered from the first period after her arrival:

> My husband had his own apartment, but I was really sad, it was like a prison. I was alone all day while my husband worked in a supermarket as a chauffeur. I did not like that. In Pakistan being a chauffeur is not an occupation of high prestige, so I suggested that he started to work with something else. Then he bought a corner shop where we both could work (Mrs Khan).

Due to Mrs Khan's middle-class background and education, she was disappointed to learn that her husband was 'just' a chauffeur. This was hard to accept in an already competitive environment, but it helped when she persuaded him to become self-employed. Working in the corner shop also gave Mrs Khan the opportunity to learn to speak Danish by reading the magazines and chatting with the customers.

In this new, competitive migrant community, distinctions are made between families on the basis of their economic, educational or social merits. There are numerous arenas in which families strive to accumulate the symbolic capital of status and recognition in the Pakistani community. In these social games, participants are often divided into groups of different age and gender. Men compete at carving out careers or prosperous businesses, holding prestigious positions in the numerous Pakistani cultural, political and religious associations, or acquiring a reputation by doing volunteer work for the community or generously donating money to various causes. Women may compete to have the most beautiful dresses, the largest and best furnished homes, the most expensive jewellery, the most polite daughters-in-law, the most extensive knowledge of Islam and the best cooking (Bajaj and Laursen 1988: 130). Another female arena is the hosting of *khatmi-Quran*, where female relatives, friends and neighbours are invited to read and recite the entire Quran, followed by the serving of food. These semi-public events tend to be a means to 'show off' and to grow larger and larger (cf. Shaw 2000 [1988]: 253). In the second generation, the arenas for competition and mutual evaluation may be educational performance, demonstrations of love and respect for one's parents, knowledge of Islam, influential positions in youth organisations, volunteer work and so on. And families in general will gain in reputation by erecting three- or four-storey houses on the family's land in Pakistan (Ballard 2003: 45) or by providing 'their' village with remittances. Finally, holidays in exotic tourist destinations have also been mentioned as a way to make claims for recognition as 'a family that has done well' (Bajaj and Laursen 1988: 133; see also McLoughlin and Kalra 1999).

The demographic development of the second generation, as more and more marriages take place, has turned wedding celebrations into yet another site for community competition. Pnina Werbner calls it 'a theatre of South Asian wedding potlatches, where the basic grammar of conspicuous consumption is one of agonistic symbolic and ritual elaboration' (1990: xv).[3] Weddings are celebrated over two or three days and often include between 200 and 500 guests of the family, relatives, friends, business associates and neighbours from Denmark, Pakistan and other migrant destinations. Wedding celebrations are sites for the negotiation of inter- and intra-familial relations, and claims are made for prestige and status by conspicuous consumption and the expression of economic success.

The choice of location for a wedding celebration is an indication of the family's economic situation, and thus a claim for status in the ever-changing community hierarchy. The least expensive or prestigious option is for the family to rent an assembly hall at a school and then organise the catering, decorate the room, set up the tables and the obligatory scene in the centre of the room where the couple are to be seated. The second option is to rent

---

3. Even though in 1965 a governmental 'Commission for the Eradication of Social Evils' identified the gift-giving and extensive celebration of weddings as a major problem in Pakistani society, weddings and dowries have become increasingly extravagant ever since, and have turned into occasions for affirming the family's status and demonstrating its connections to the rich and powerful (Qadeer 2007: 1994–5).

one of the reception halls (such as *Mosaic* in Sjælør or *Thousand and One Nights* in Gladsaxe) that specialise in hosting immigrant weddings, since they have the facilities required and are connected to different restaurants. A third option that has become available within recent years is to book a regular *shadi* hall, that is, a marriage hall, like the *Taj Mahal* in Taastrup, which charges a fixed amount of money (around DKr 200–300) for each guest, providing in return a large hall with new furniture, nice food and beverages, flowers, a TV room, a lounge for the newly-weds and a playroom for the children. This is an expensive but fashionable solution, where the hosts can concentrate on receiving and entertaining their guests. The last and most exclusive option is to arrange a reception at one of the larger hotels in Copenhagen.

The agonistic potlatch-like competition between families is also expressed in the giving of extravagant presents, the wedding clothes of the bride and groom, the quality of the video-shooting team or DJ, the wedding cake, the size of the *barat* (the groom's retinue), etc. In this respect, weddings tend to become sites for creativity and invention. Families make considerable sacrifices to save up or to take out loans in order to be able to participate in the social game of community competition, and ultimately to make people talk about the wedding and gossip about the wealth of the family and expenses of the occasion. But as in any social game, participants can be more or less successful.

One example is the Javad family. Mr Javad had run a corner shop with his brother for more than twenty years, when they sold the business. His brother started driving a taxi, while Mr Javad himself remained unemployed and just waited for his pension. Mrs and Mr Javad had not been to Pakistan for years for lack of money. They had spent their savings on the *Hajj* (pilgrimage) some years before, and with two unmarried daughters it was time to start saving as much money as possible for the weddings. They preferred Pakistani husbands from families in Denmark, but had a hard time finding eligible matches. However, the biggest headache was the great expense following each marriage. As Mr Javad desperately explained, referring to a wedding we had both attended recently: 'You see, when Mr Butt hosts a big wedding for his daughter, then I have to do the same for my daughters.'

Just as wedding celebrations are a means to show off, they can also have negative consequences for the host family's reputation, and even create disagreements between the two families that are about to be connected by marriage. Family members, co-villagers or *biraderi* may not be invited in order to make a point, or invited guests may show their discontent with the hosts by not showing up. At social events like weddings, there are numerous elements that make people talk negatively about the event or the hosts: if, for instance, it is too cold or hot in the wedding hall, if there is not enough food, or if the dinner is delayed (more than expected!). At one *nikka*, we waited until just before midnight before dinner was served, and when it finally came along people literally fought over the food. This 'uncivilised behaviour' was afterwards a theme of discussion. Another issue commonly discussed among families hosting a wedding and guests attending is whether or not there should be dancing by men, women or between men and women. Dancing constitutes a disputed boundary for respectable and pious behaviour within and between families.

The above list of arenas for antagonistic symbolic competition is not exhaustive, but it illustrates the many different contexts in which families evaluate and are evaluated. Ideally each member, regardless of age or gender, contributes to the collective *izzat* (honour) and symbolic capital of the household and family. This public display of success and ongoing evaluation of 'our family' in relation to 'other families' can be a cause of happiness and pride, but also of suspicion, envy and long-lasting enmity. The competitive environment where almost anything can (and will) be measured as economic, cultural or symbolic capital was not created overnight, but is the result of changes that took place in the Pakistani community during the 1970s and 1980s.

To describe the historical emergence of this competitive community, I outline the two long-term strategies of money and education to which families resorted when the Danish labour market was restructured during the late 1970s and 1980s. These should be understood as Weberian ideal-types, not necessarily found empirically in a pure form. Nevertheless, they are constantly used by Pakistanis, both to distinguish between families and as marks of navigation within the terrain of the community.

The value of money

Jan Hjarnø, after decades of research among Pakistanis, Turks and Yugoslavs, wrote that, at the beginning of the 1980s, his conversations with Pakistanis became more and more focused on how to start up as self-employed, and which families had already done so (Hjarnø 2000: 102). These discussions reflected the emergence of a new long-term livelihood strategy in Denmark after the unskilled factory jobs disappeared. Many Pakistanis became self-employed in the late 1970s and 1980s, operating businesses such as small grocery stores or corner shops (*kiosks*), taxis or travel agencies (Hjarnø 2000: 104). The economic capital to start these businesses came from savings and loans from banks or from extended networks of family and fellow villagers, the *biraderi* that offered practical help and economic support.

In the late 1970s, the rules concerning licences for haulage contracting and taxi driving were liberalised, making it easier for Pakistanis to start their own businesses. Those who acquired licences hired fellow countrymen to keep the taxi on the street round the clock and also brought them into the business. In this way, driving a taxi became one of the largest ethnic businesses among Pakistanis in the Copenhagen area.

Small corner shops offered another opportunity for self-employment. Pakistani entrepreneurs were willing to take the economic risk of operating the traditional small-scale grocery stores (*købmænd*) that for decades have been part of Danish cities and local neighbourhoods as the main suppliers of food, dairy products, fruit and vegetables. The introduction and expansion of supermarkets had for years resulted in a declining and partly diminishing trade for these small stores. For Pakistani entrepreneurs, this was an opportunity in which networks of family and fellow villagers, who already had experience of running a corner shop or small grocery store, could help and benefit from one another.

Mr Iqbal related how several times since he arrived in 1970 he had felt badly treated by successive Danish employers. During different factory and piecework jobs, he found no continuity or economic security, because he was not a member of a trade union, or even aware of anything called a trade union. Twice he experienced peremptory dismissal. This was a precarious situation, with a wife and three small children to support. The insecurity of his job situation, along with the submissiveness and humility he had to show to his Danish employers, made him follow the advice of some of his Pakistani friends and start his own corner shop in Copenhagen in 1981. Later, in the mid-1990s, Mr Iqbal and his wife bought and managed a grocery shop in the suburbs.

Overall, therefore, Pakistanis soon became the immigrant group operating the greatest number of corner shops and small grocery stores (Rezaei 2002: 4). It has been estimated that between 600 and 800 corner shops in Copenhagen and Odense are owned by Pakistani families (Quraishy 1999: 95).

To succeed with a corner shop or a taxicab, it is not important to have many years of education, but it is necessary to economise with money and income (Hjarnø 2000: 101). Pakistanis were already doing this in order to support members of the transnational family in Pakistan as well as the household in Denmark, putting savings aside to visit the 'homeland' once in a while. However, perhaps the most important factor ensuring success as a self-employed person was a willingness to work long hours. Corner shops and taxi firms became family enterprises, pursuing a certain 'way of life' (*livsstil*), in which the husband, the wife and the grown-up children all contributed to running the business (Smith 1996).

The outcome of a successful business was 'fast money' – and more of it than people ever imagined. Mr Ahmad, in his mid-fifties, who used to drive a taxi before becoming a bus driver following a violent assault, explained:

> When you drive a taxi you start to think like you are sitting on a regular 'money-machine'. It changes your mentality. You start to work 13–14 hours in a row and nevertheless want to have more. And you start to think how to get more tips and things like that. It is not good to own or drive a taxi. I have hundreds of friends who drive cabs and they all think alike (Mr Ahmad).

Compared to their former levels of income, many Pakistani families became *nouveaux riches*. Some of the profits were invested in Denmark, and some were sent to Pakistan to support family members there who were starting up businesses or building new houses back in the migrants' village of origin. Conspicuous consumption of expensive clothes, cars and jewellery proved to the Danish migrant community and relatives back in Pakistan that here truly was 'a family that had done well'.

However, as times changed, so did the opportunities to earn fast money. Interviewees explained that it has become much more difficult to earn fast money, big money, by driving a taxi. Similarly, since the mid-1990s, corner shop business has come under pressure from chains of all-night shops like 7-Eleven (Quraishy 1999: 95), the emergence of discount supermarkets like Aldi or Netto and the long opening hours of supermarkets, which did not exist twenty years ago. Today, running a corner shop is looked down upon in the community, as it has become the business for those who cannot do anything else, especially in circles of educated families. In the corner shop business, they say, it is necessary to work long hours, just sitting in the back and waiting for customers to come. Furthermore, in order to keep these businesses alive, alcohol and possibly pornographic publications and movies are often sold, and rumours of illegal activities – selling beverages or cigarettes without paying taxes – abound.

In sum, the accumulation of money and wealth is no longer sufficient for a Pakistani family to maintain a prominent position in the changeable hierarchies of 'families that have done well'. Today the cultural capital of education is also needed.

The value of education

Despite the growing rates of unemployment in the 1970s and 1980s, some Pakistanis kept on working as wage-earners in various factories, in some cases because they did not have the skills, economic resources or luck to become self-employed. Others were successful as interpreters or teachers of Urdu in the new and expanding 'integration industry' (Preis 1998: 11), where the main task was to help less fortunate immigrants manage in Danish society. Many Pakistani women also worked as cleaners in public buildings and institutions. This meant that a large group of Pakistanis performed low-skilled manual labour, or worked as public servants in state institutions at different levels. They soon understood the importance of education if their children were to gain access to the well-paid prestigious jobs and positions in Danish society that they could not obtain for themselves. In these families, it was possible for their children to invest time and effort in their education, because they did not have to take turns behind the counter in the corner shop and were not seduced by the fast money to be made driving a cab. The tradition of living at home made it possible for unmarried young men and women to concentrate on their studies, rather than spending time earning money to pay for food and rent. Furthermore, they received a monthly stipend from the state educational fund (*Statens Uddannelsesstøtte*) to cover personal expenses.

For this segment of the Pakistani community, the educational performance of the second generation became an important new arena for competition. Through education, the second generation acquired the cultural capital that, in the long run, improved the symbolic capital of the entire family; and educational performance became a significant long-term strategy for social mobility. However, following the logic of competition, education was never just 'an education'. The first hurdle was to get the youngsters through secondary school, but higher education soon also became necessary in order to be a successful family. There is a joke among second-generation Pakistanis that parents want their children to become 'doctor, engineer and lawyer' in that order. Even though this is a joke, it also has its real aspects. Studying medicine is often regarded as the highest, most prestigious education (see Chapter 8).[4] It is a profession that both first-generation migrants and transnational families recognise as valuable and important. A medical doctor is, among many other things, a universal figure everyone can relate to – which might not be the case for a designer, a hairdresser or a social anthropologist.

Very often, education becomes a family project. Parents of the first generation explain that they have worked all their lives in order to provide the best opportunities for their children to concentrate on their studies. In return the children are expected to study hard and perform well. In this intergenerational contract, the younger generation are obliged to fulfil not only their own ambitions, but also their parents'. This kind of pressure can be very difficult to handle when young people have other plans for their future, or even lack the intellectual ability to pursue higher education at all. But when a daughter or a son actually does manage to become an engineer, a dentist or a medical doctor, it fulfils the hopes and ambitions that drove the parents to migrate to Denmark in the first place. The long absence from family members and homeland, the many years of hard work, suddenly make sense if the parents can convince real and imagined audiences that they left Pakistan years ago in order for their offspring to obtain a higher education. The emigration of the parents, which in many instances happened out of necessity and scarce resources back home, can now be presented as a deliberate strategy. The children's educational performance makes it possible to readjust the family narrative of why they left Pakistan in the first place. In this respect, educational achievements enhance not only the cultural capital of the younger generation, but the symbolic capital of the entire family.

---

4. It is not only among Pakistanis that the position of doctor is considered prestigious. In a survey from 2006, 2,155 Danes were asked to rank 99 different occupations. The position of general practitioner was ranked number three on the list, while hospital doctor was number four. Numbers one and two were pilot and lawyer respectively (Ugebrevet A4, 23/2006: 12).

Conversion of capital: the 1990s and 2000s

Today, the elevated position of families who successfully exploited the strategy of money in the 1980s and 1990s has in several respects been taken over by the families who employed the long-term strategy of education. As the educated second generation entered the labour market in high-profile positions and well-paid jobs, the hierarchies of the previous decades were turned upside down. This happened through processes of capital conversion. According to Pierre Bourdieu, capital can and will be converted from one field to another. The rate of exchange between the different kinds of valid capital is the result of an ongoing symbolic struggle between more or less powerful actors in the social field (Bourdieu 1997: 55–6). The most obvious conversion of capital in the Pakistani case occurs when the highly educated second generation begins to work, and to earn more money than their parents ever did. They use their cultural capital of higher education to improve the prestige, or symbolic capital, of the entire family.

An important arena for capital conversion is marriage. The marriage preference for Pakistani migrants in Denmark was until recently an endogamous, transnational arranged marriage. But whereas spouses used to be recruited from the *biraderi* of family, kin and fellow villagers in Pakistan, other criteria have become important today (see Chapter 3). According to the tradition of arranged marriages, couples should be matched so that they come from families that are alike (Rytter 2003a; 2006). This quest for equality and similarity is meant to give newly-weds and their families the best odds for building a future life together. In their search for a proper *rishta* (marriage match), the parents of a well-educated son or daughter will usually look for potential spouses in families of similar status and educational level. Today, families therefore often go beyond – in other words, neglect – the *biraderi* in Pakistan and look for other, more suitable options. The cultural capital of educational performance has become a point of entry into new marriage-scapes (cf. Constable 2004: 4), offering numerous new possibilities for matchmaking. It has become legitimate for families to recruit spouses for children in educated and influential families in the Pakistani community in Denmark, but also from major Pakistani cities such as Lahore, Karachi or Islamabad or from other migrant families living in Europe or North America. In this respect, marriage arrangements have become a means of consolidating social mobility and aspiring to new positions.

The discussion thus far may leave the overall impression that the families who turned, years ago, to the strategy of education live an unproblematic life today. This is not always the case. Families face huge problems, due to the fact that the generation gap widens when the second generation obtains higher education and comes to embody the ideals and lifestyles of upward social mobility. Mr Iqbal, a father of four, learned this from bitter experience. Both his sons became medical doctors. Today he lives with his younger son in a detached house south of Copenhagen. His elder son has moved to

Sweden where he works at a hospital, taking advantage of the high salary and favourable tax benefits that Danish doctors benefit from when working in other Nordic countries. Mr Iqbal describes his son as a 'workaholic' and a big spender who has lost all interest in his parents and family. He explains that he has tried several times to speak reason to his son, but that he will not listen. The son's main priority is his career and the fashionable lifestyle that follows from it. Mr Iqbal just has to accept that they no longer share the same ideas of what is important in life. However, he finds solace in the fact that he and his wife live with the other son, their daughter-in-law and grandchildren in a regular patrilocal household and extended family.

Sisyphus and the moving horizon

Chapter 1 introduced an analytical distinction between three periods in recent history, reflecting the changing attitudes of the nation-state towards the immigrant population. The three periods – laissez-faire integration in the 1960s and 1970s, integration as assimilation in the 1980s and 1990s and the security/integration-response after 2001 – illustrate the changing 'notions of improvement' that immigrants have been subjected to in Danish society. The macro-historical perspective shows how the Pakistani Muslim immigrants, who years ago were primarily seen as 'exotic others', have recently been reconfigured as 'radical others' and conceived of as a potential menace to the Danish nation, values and way of life. The current political climate of the past decade has generated a widespread 'cultural anxiety' (Grillo 2003), where the majority fears that national sovereignty and identity are under threat of extinction. This has prompted a reinvention of traditions considered typically Danish. In 2004, The Liberal-Conservative government launched the so-called *kulturkamp* (cultural war of values) campaign, stressing Danish national history and institutions and producing, among other things, new curricula and national canons. The ongoing process of reinvention has left no (or very little) room for Muslim immigrants in national history, tradition and imaginary (see Chapter 5).

These two parallel processes – the securitisation of Muslim minorities and the rearmament of national identity politics – have altered the criteria for immigrant improvement. Many migrant families have learned the hard way that, despite social mobility and their own middle-class aspirations, they face incessant demands to comply with unclear and changing criteria for what it means to be Danish. One randomly chosen example was when, in 2007, several newspaper articles drew attention to the increasing number of immigrants in higher education. Instead of interpreting the pattern in terms of the achievements of young immigrants in the educational system, or even of national integration, their educational achievements were perceived as a social problem. Thus Jacob Lange, head of student counselling (*studiechef*) at the University of Copenhagen, saw a problem in some overly ambitious immigrant parents pushing youngsters into prestigious academic education when their children did not have the intellectual capacity to complete such an education.[5] The apparent success story was turned around to become yet another example of the supposedly problematic Muslim family structure, one that does not respect freedom of choice for the young generation.

A couple of days after the Lange article appeared, I discussed it with Zubair, a highly educated young man of Pakistani parentage. To him, the twist in the story was an example of the kind of no-win situation that immigrants face in Danish public and political discourses. It confirmed his experience that, no matter how hard immigrants try to comply with the rules and norms of Danish society, they are never recognised by the wider public for these efforts. In the analytical vocabulary of Bourdieu, 'there is no worse dispossession, no worse privation, perhaps, than that of the losers in the symbolic struggle, for recognition, for access to a socially recognised social being, in a word, to humanity' (2000: 241). My disillusioned friend Zubair and other Muslim immigrants in Denmark share the fate of the Greek mythological figure Sisyphus:[6] no matter how hard they try, they will never satisfy the vague and changing criteria of integration defined by the majority, nor gain recognition as the equals of indigenous Danes. Immigrants are locked into a structural position in which their full acceptance as fellow citizens remains a horizon: they can just make out the contours of recognition, but it will never come within reach, as the horizon moves further away whenever they attempt to approach it.

The new Klondike: 2000+

Pakistanis have reacted to these social changes, and to the lack of social recognition, in various ways. Some families consider whether they should stay in Denmark or move to some other country such as the United Kingdom, Canada or Sweden, or back to Pakistan. This new aspiration is partly due to a growing feeling of insecurity among immigrants concerning their legal status and the future prospects for themselves and especially their children in Denmark. A recent study shows that 46 per cent of young immigrants between 15 and 29 years of age are considering leaving Denmark and starting a new life in another country (Shakoor and Riis 2007: 116).

The two overall family strategies of the 1980s and 1990s have created incommensurate opportunities for the second generation to leave Denmark and settle in Pakistan (see Chapter 6). Non-educated migrants have a hard time returning because, even though they may have lots of money, they do

---

5. See 'Indvandrere har æren med på skolebænken', *Morgenavisen Jyllandsposten*, 25 February 2007.
6. Sisyphus was the King of Corinth who was punished in Hades by repeatedly having to roll a huge stone up a mountain over and over again.

not necessarily have the skills to start from scratch in Pakistan. It is not possible to maintain a standard of living acceptable to a migrant family that has been living in Denmark for decades by running a little shop or driving a cab in Pakistan. The prospects are much better for the well-educated segment of the second generation, as the cultural capital of academic training is a transferable embodied resource that they bring with them wherever they decide to settle down. A dentist, medical doctor or engineer, for example, can earn a living in one of Pakistan's major cities. Those who use this opening may take their parents with them, and fulfil their long-term aspirations of return. Others have to choose a strategy of 'mobile livelihoods' (cf. Olwig and Sørensen 2002), where typically the man works for some of the year in Denmark in order to provide for his wife and children who remain in Pakistan (see Chapter 6). In this way, long-term family strategies continue to impact on the way that places and spaces in Pakistan are conceptualised by the second generation, further widening the distance between educated and non-educated families.

As the second generation utilises its high levels of education, language proficiency and transnational connections to set up businesses in Pakistan that benefit from using highly educated local employees, who work for much lower salaries than a professional in a similar position in Denmark would demand, Pakistan gains new meaning. These enterprises are often managed from offices in Denmark. They may engage in import/export, the outsourcing of manual factory work, and entrepreneurship, or may work with computer technology or telecommunication systems. As a result of these entrepreneurial activities, Pakistan is being reconfigured as 'a new Klondike' for the second generation: it is becoming a country of economic opportunity and business adventure. Just as their parents went to Denmark to improve their livelihoods, so the second generation are returning to Pakistan and setting up transnational businesses. Along with increased financial investments, risk-taking and stories of success, these transnational enterprises have become yet another site for competition between migrant families. In this respect, history is repeating itself.

Conclusion: prospects for the future

This chapter has shown how Pakistani family strategies of improvement have been shaped by historical circumstances. Of course, any account that starts out in rural Pakistan and covers the nearly fifty years from the early 1960s to the late 2000s will inevitably neglect nuances from everyday life and numerous idiosyncratic experiences, both within and between migrant families. Thus patterns of employment and educational achievements in most families are much more complex than the neat picture I have given of two family strategies. Despite these reservations, it is quite informative to take a step back and look at the broader picture of community dynamics in order to enrich our understanding of such urgent questions as the upward social mobility of Pakistanis in Denmark.

When discussing the long-term strategies of money or education, I use 'the family' as the basic unit of analysis, regardless of the many discrepancies and conflicts there are in any family. Taking the family as my context, I have argued that the social mobility of Pakistanis should neither be explained primarily as the result of economic opportunities in the Danish welfare state system nor as an orientation towards the transnational extended family. These two explanations are merely the effects of a more fundamental dynamic within the Pakistani community, whereby families have for years competed for high-ranking positions in the changeable hierarchies that are seen as important within the migrant community. The suggested micro-historical perspective on long-term family strategies contributes to contemporary migration research by insisting on the importance of combining the specific migration history, individual trajectories and family cycles as they unfold under specific circumstances in the particular national context.

I have also suggested that notions of improvement are the outcome of ongoing negotiations in different contexts, characterised by asymmetrical relations of power. The historical perspective emphasises how these dynamics work at different levels of society and how they change over time. Not only have the criteria for earning a reputation as 'a family that has done well' changed within the Pakistani community; socio-economic and political processes have also redefined the structural relationship between minorities and majorities in Denmark. In recent decades, it has become more and more difficult for Pakistani Muslim immigrants to meet the unclear, mutable standards of improvement set 'from above' and to become fully recognised as Danish citizens; instead, they have become the usual suspects. The Pakistani case illustrates that, even when migrants successfully engage in the social games that are recognised as important by the Danish population and nation-state, such as education, they cannot succeed. Regardless of efforts and of actual achievements, they are seldom seen or recognised in public and political discourses. The lack of recognition is often interpreted as an act of discrimination or racism by Pakistanis themselves, a demeaning and painful experience that substantiates the spiral of alienation and in years to come risks widening the gap between immigrant minorities and the majority population of Danish society.

The next part of the book is dedicated to the institution of marriage, which is currently being redefined as a consequence both of ongoing negotiations between first- and second-generation Pakistanis and of securitisation and interventions by the Danish nation-state.

Part II
Marriages

In South Asian traditions, and within a religious Islamic framework as part of the Sunna of Prophet Muhammad, marriage is a sacred, respected and extremely important institution. Partner choice and marriage are, ideally, once-in-a-lifetime decisions. To second-generation Pakistanis it is therefore not so much a question of whether they are going to be married or not, but rather a question of when, where and to whom. In this respect, marriage constitutes an inevitable, irrevocable decision about one's life trajectory and future horizons.

It is part of Pakistani tradition that marriages are arranged between families. It is a parental duty and obligation to find eligible partners for offspring. To arrange the marriages of one's children completes one's parenthood. Several studies have been concerned with how transnational marriage among Pakistani groups in the diaspora becomes a means to create and strengthen the bonds of affiliation, to continue labour migration, and to maintain values and identity within the close family and extended kinship networks of *biraderi* (Ballard 1990; Werbner 1990; Shaw 2001; Charsley 2005, 2006, 2007; Beck-Gernsheim 2007). Recent studies have also emphasised the importance of more emotional aspects of kinship in order to explain the preference for transnational marriages within the extended family (Shaw and Charsley 2006). To give a daughter away in marriage is the ultimate gift that migrants can make in order to reinvest in their relationships and relatedness to significant people and places in Pakistan.

All these aspects are also salient among Pakistanis in Denmark. Nevertheless, the institution of marriage is, for different reasons, currently being redefined with regard to function, meaning and content. The transformation is observable in the numbers of transnational marriages. In 1989, a national survey showed that more than eighty per cent of all marriages within the group of Danish Pakistanis aged 18–25 were contracted with spouses from Pakistan. However, fifteen years later, in 2004, a new survey showed that in the group of Danish Pakistanis aged 17–27, 'only' fifty-nine per cent were engaged or married to a spouse from Pakistan (Schmidt and Jakobsen 2004: 111). The figures are probably even lower today, as the study concluded that there was a general tendency for increasing numbers of immigrants to marry spouses from Denmark (ibid.: 112). The figures thus reflect the ongoing transformation of Pakistani marriage preferences, characterised by more and more marriages being contracted with spouses found in Denmark. The development has been facilitated by two mutual historical processes: *internally*, where new marriage ideals are being negotiated between the generations within migrant families and the community; and *externally*, through abrupt intervention by the Danish nation-state, when its new, strict policy on family reunification was introduced in the summer of 2002.

- *Internal dynamics*: The institution of arranged marriage rests on the understanding that the younger generation should comply with the wishes and decisions of their family elders. However, the upcoming educated and independent generation of young Pakistanis do not necessarily share their parents' interest in having a transnational marriage within the *biraderi*, but often want a partner with the same background as their own: in other words, a spouse with higher education, brought up in Denmark or another Western country. More importantly, the emerging trend of local marriage(s) reflects a new ideal of marrying out of love. In recent years, there has been a growing number of *love marriages* contracted between families within the migrant community. They are the result of young people meeting, falling in love and marrying, with or without the consent of their parents. When it comes to marriage, the differences in upbringing, level of education, job prospects and worldview between the first and second generation often create tensions and conflicts within the families which should not be underestimated. However, many parents have also learned from previously married children in the family that arranged marriages contracted with partners from Pakistan can be dysfunctional and may leave their children unhappy. Provided that first-generation migrants have married their oldest son or daughter within the *biraderi*, they are to some extent relieved from the pressure of family expectations and obligations, and can instead start to look in new directions in their search for spouses for their younger children. As mentioned in the previous chapter, Pakistani families in Denmark have to a large extent started to reorient themselves towards new marriage-scapes in Pakistan, or in the diaspora in general.
- *External intervention*: The decrease in transnational marriage is also an observable effect of the new Danish legislation on family reunification. Marriage migration has in many respects become the last legal entry into 'Fortress Europe', and many European countries have adjusted their rules on family reunification in order to protect their national interests against the uncontrolled inflow of foreign spouses. Denmark took a leading position in this endeavour when, in 2002, the *Folketing* (parliament) adopted new legislation on family reunification which soon acquired a reputation as the strictest in the world (Schmidt 2011: 259). On the one hand, the new immigration regime was presented within a *discourse of humanism* as a necessary means to save young, second-generation immigrants from being forced into transnational marriages by their parents and families. On the

other hand, the new legislation was part of the general securitisation and mobilisation of national sentiments and values following September 11, and as such was presented within a *discourse of nationalism* as an effective means of protecting national borders and interests (Hervik and Rytter 2004). Due to the introduction of the five requirements – minimum age, accommodation, personal finances, collateral and 'national attachment', as discussed in Chapter 5 – it has become difficult not only for foreigners but also for Danish citizens as well, and in particular those with immigrant backgrounds, to achieve family reunification with non-European spouses. While a total of 6,399 foreign spouses came to Denmark through family reunification in 2000, by 2009 the number was reduced to 3,662. While 261 spouses came from Pakistan in 2000, in 2009 there were 132.

The *internal dynamics* and *external interventions* are part of an overall transformation of the institution of marriage among Pakistanis in Denmark. Chapter 3 discusses the irrevocable decision to select a marriage partner as a 'vital conjuncture' (Johnson-Hanks 2002, 2006), in which second-generation Pakistanis are split between the preferences of the family and those of the nation-state, and suggest that the choice of a love marriage constitutes an act of 'symbolic mobility', whereby young couples redirect their common trajectory towards a future in Denmark.

Chapter 4 focuses on the everyday lives of the hundreds of newly-wed couples who, because they have chosen to comply with family tradition and marry a spouse from Pakistan, are living in Sweden: in order to achieve family reunification, these couples have to settle in another country of the European Union. These couples often commute on a regular or even daily basis between their legal residence in Sweden and their place of work or study, or to visit friends and family in Denmark. However, this move makes them 'semi-legal' in both legal and moral terms. I discuss what kind of mobile everyday lives these couples are subject to, and discuss how their semi-legality influences family relations, notions of belonging and perspectives of the future.

Finally, Chapter 5 elaborates on the developing cleavage between national majorities and minorities as I analyse the specific notions of identity, relatedness and belonging embedded in the requirement of 'national attachment' that Danish citizens have had to comply with since 2002 in order to be granted the right to family reunification with foreign spouses. The requirement of national attachment is based on a specific 'kinship image' that discriminates between Danish citizens on the basis of their family background.

All in all, the three chapters in Part II deal with the transformation of the institution of marriage among Pakistani migrants, and how this affects both vertical and horizontal family relations, as well as notions of identity and belonging.

Chapter 3

Between preferences

Love marriage as symbolic mobility

At first, Yasmeen and Imran, fellow Roskilde University students and occasional classmates, did not really notice each other and spoke only sporadically. Gradually, however, they became more and more interested in each other. They started communicating by email, talked after class, and on one occasion they even risked getting caught and went to the movies together. Yasmeen and Imran were both well aware that by doing so they were going well beyond the rules of *purdah*, the common code of acceptable behaviour for young unmarried men and women enforced by their families and the gossiping Pakistani migrant community in greater Copenhagen. Despite the interests of their respective parents, who wanted them to engage in arranged marriages with spouses from the extended family in Pakistan, they nevertheless decided to take their relationship to the next level and enter into a controversial *love marriage*. This chapter discusses the current trend of love marriages, whereby couples like Yasmeen and Imran reject the transnational marriages arranged by their parents and extended family, and engage in local marriages based on romantic feelings. Such love marriages are embedded in discourses of identity, mobility and modernity, and the growing popularity of local marriages obviously affects connections and notions of relatedness in transnational family networks.

The chapter discusses how young Pakistanis are split between the diametrically opposite marriage preferences put forward by their parents and extended family and by the nation-state, which has determined marriage preferences for all Danish citizens by means of a complex of policies and legislation on family reunification (see Chapter 5). In order to grasp and analyse the critical period in which differing aspirations for and ideas about the future meet and in which individual life-trajectories must be decided, I apply Jennifer Johnson-Hanks' notion of 'vital conjunctures' (2006: 22–3). Within this context, young Pakistanis' choice of a marriage partner on the basis of love and personal interests not only constitutes a public statement of 'who they are', but also a projection of 'who they want to be'. Love marriages are distinct from the traditional endogamous marriages which young people often associate with their parents' 'village mentality'; they are embedded in notions of individuality and modern lifestyles. In this respect, one might say that 'love has become something of a metaphor for social mobility' (Hunter 2009: 147). The irrevocable decision to marry against the preferences and interests of parents and the transnational family becomes an act of 'symbolic mobility', in which immigrant youth sets a course towards a future in Denmark for both themselves and their families. The extended case of Imran and Yasmeen will be used below to elaborate on the dilemmas and conflicts of family life when it comes to marriage in Pakistani migrant families.

Arrangement, enforcement or love …

The tradition of arranged marriage has since the 1990s been a hot topic in Danish public and political discourses. It is often conflated with that of forced marriage. However, in local discourses, young Pakistanis use three overlapping categories of marriage: arranged marriage, forced marriage and love marriage (see Fig. 2). The arranged marriage is the norm, based on negotiations between, on the one hand, the parents and child (and probably the extended family), and, on the other, the two families involved. Forced marriage is characterised by the lack of negotiation or consent of one or both of the young people involved, and can be defined as an exception to the norm of arranged marriage (Gullestad 2002a: 32). In a forced marriage, it is the parents (and maybe the extended family) who select a partner for a young

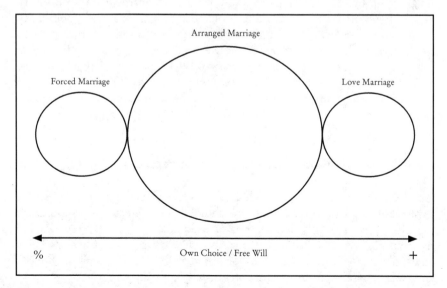

Figure 2: The continuum of choice and the three categories of marriage

person, without her or his consent. Finally there is a growing interest in the kinds of marriage that in local discourse are categorised as love marriages, and imply that the young couple have met, fallen in love and married with or without the consent of their respective parents. These three categories of marriage constitute a continuum with regard both to the amount of individual autonomy and free will involved in making the decision and to the interference of parents and family in general.

The three marriage categories can be manipulated for several reasons in differing contexts during life-courses. What was initially an arranged marriage, maybe even contracted under pressure, may eventually end up as a happy marriage as spouses grow fond of each other in time. On the other hand, there have been reports of young people representing their voluntary arranged marriage as a forced marriage to the welfare state system, whether to get back at their parents for some reason or to get special benefits from their social worker, such as a new apartment (Sareen 2003; Schmidt and Jakobsen 2004: 138–9).

Young Pakistanis often emphasise that marriage should be based on mutual romantic feelings. In this respect, the kind of love marriage that second-generation Pakistanis talk about, dream of and strive for is a marriage of companionship, where emotional closeness is understood as both the foundation for and the goal of the marriage – an ideal which worldwide seems to have become a key trope as a claim for modern identity (Collier 1997; Constable 2004; Hirsch and Wardlow 2006; Cole and Thomas 2009). But even though discussions and gossip about romantic relations have a prominent position in the minds and interactions of second-generation Pakistanis, this kind of marriage – in which the young couple go against their parents and families and may have had an illicit, perhaps even sexual relationship before marriage – is still considered controversial. In order to protect themselves and their families from becoming the target of community gossip, second-generation Pakistanis may make strenuous efforts to obtain their parents' blessing and help so that the initial secret romantic relationship can be presented to the public as a (more or less) properly arranged marriage between two migrant families. The boundaries between the three marriage categories is constantly up for negotiation and manipulation, as the extended case of Yasmeen and Imran will also illustrate.

Diametrically opposed preferences

Children represent the future, which makes it crucial for significant others to direct or even control their life-choices and trajectories in order to reproduce the existing order. Marriage affects not only the intergenerational transmission of property and values, but also class positions, knowledge and skills, as well as significant notions of identity and belonging within the family. Likewise, modern welfare states have a significant interest in governing partner choice and the family formation of their citizens. This regulation is exercised through national policies and bureaucracy, in combination with the educational system and the labour market (Sørhaug 1996: 130–1). In the following discussion, I explore how both the family and the Danish nation-state have significant interests in attempting to control and regulate the partner choice and life-trajectories of Danish Pakistani youth.

The marriage preferences of the family

The institution of arranged marriage is not only the union of two individuals; it is also a relation between two families, and there are therefore inevitably different perspectives and interests at play in most marriage arrangements. The socio-cultural and religiously justified norms of gender segregation, or *purdah* (cf. Papanek 1973), mean that unmarried Pakistani women and men have limited opportunities to meet and get to know each other before the actual marriage. It is furthermore considered a sign of respect, and a proof of a decent upbringing, for young people to allow their parents to take an active part in the decision about where (in what family, in what country) the marriage is to take place. On the other hand, it is also a parental duty and obligation to find eligible partners for their offspring. To arrange the marriages of one's children completes parenthood. But young people also need their parents' collaboration and approval, so that the parents can formally give their *rishta*, that is, suggest a marriage connection between two families. A formal proposal is seldom made by young people themselves.

Pakistanis traditionally express a preference for marriages within the extended family, and the ideal match is often considered to be between first cousins (Ballard 1990; Werbner 1990; Shaw 2000, 2001). Such marriages are believed to confirm and strengthen already existing ties and notions of relatedness within the family. Another important argument in favour of this kind of marriage is that cousins can be assumed to know each other in advance. However, close relations between two cousins can also cause problems, for example, if they have known each other since early childhood and relate to each other as siblings rather than as potential marriage partners (Charsley 2007: 1125). Marriage between first cousins is also believed to ease the bride's transition in the patrilocal system from being her parents' daughter to becoming her husband's wife and the daughter-in-law in the house of his parents. In a consanguineous marriage, the bride's mother-in-law is already her aunt, which is believed to imply that she will not be as critical or demanding as she might be with a girl from an unknown family (Charsley 2005: 89). But again, this is a generalisation. In real life, there may be numerous pragmatic reasons for not arranging marriages between children within the immediate family, and for seeking partners among more distant relatives, friends, neighbours or business partners instead. Last but not least, marriage within the family can be a strategy to protect second-generation Pakistanis from being exploited in 'bogus marriages' (Charsley 2006: 1170) or becoming 'visa brides', that is, solely a means for a man to enter Europe (Wikan 2002: 262).

A study of marriage preferences and practices among young men and their parents shows that the latter often prefer to recruit spouses from the extended family in Pakistan (Rytter 2003a). This marriage preference reflects the assumption that marriages between equals and families that are 'alike' provide the best basis for a long-lasting marriage and family relationship in the years to come.[1] However, any notion of equality naturally depends on defining criteria: the equality between families can be measured in relation to such parameters as educational level, occupation, economic resources, political orientation, religiosity, place of origin in Pakistan or the family's *zaat* background.

When parents start looking for a daughter-in-law in Denmark for one reason or another, they consider it important to find a girl from a Pakistani family they are already acquainted with and respect, typically a family from their native village or at least from the same *zaat*. The absolute minimum criterion for Pakistani parents is that their daughter-in-law should be a Muslim, while the worst-case scenario is an ethnic Danish, non-Muslim daughter-in-law (Rytter 2003a: 58ff.). In this way, the parents and the extended family distinguish between potential partners and rank them along a continuum of good and bad choices, with several gradations in between (see Fig. 3).

Choosing a daughter-in-law from the extended family network is a way to confirm and renew connections and bonds with significant people and places that the immigrant family left behind decades ago. The widespread reluctance, at least in the beginning, of the first generation to marry in Denmark has to do with the risk and uncertainty of marrying into 'strange' and unknown families (Charsley 2007: 1120). The same is the case when it comes to marrying Muslim girls in Denmark with a different background than Pakistani. Despite a common religious background and the general acknowledgement that Muslims are brothers and sisters of the *umma*, there is often deep scepticism regarding whether differences in national background, language and traditions can be overcome in everyday life in the domestic sphere. Ethnic Danish non-Muslim girls are often rejected as serious potential spouse material by both young men and their parents: one may have close relationships, even sexual affairs with them, but when it comes to marriage, ethnic Danish women are not an option. They are often described as being too independent for Pakistani family life, too promiscuous, and marriages to them are all too likely to end in divorce.

---

1. Norwegian anthropologist Thomas Walle suggests that Pakistanis in Norway, like those in Denmark, express an explicit preference for *isogamous* marriages, that is, marriage alliances contracted between families that are structurally equal and alike (Walle 2004: 120). In a British context, other scholars have suggested the term *homogamy*, which refers to the selection of a partner from a similar social background, shaped, for example, by race, class, ethnicity, religion, age and education (Samad and Eade 1996: 29).

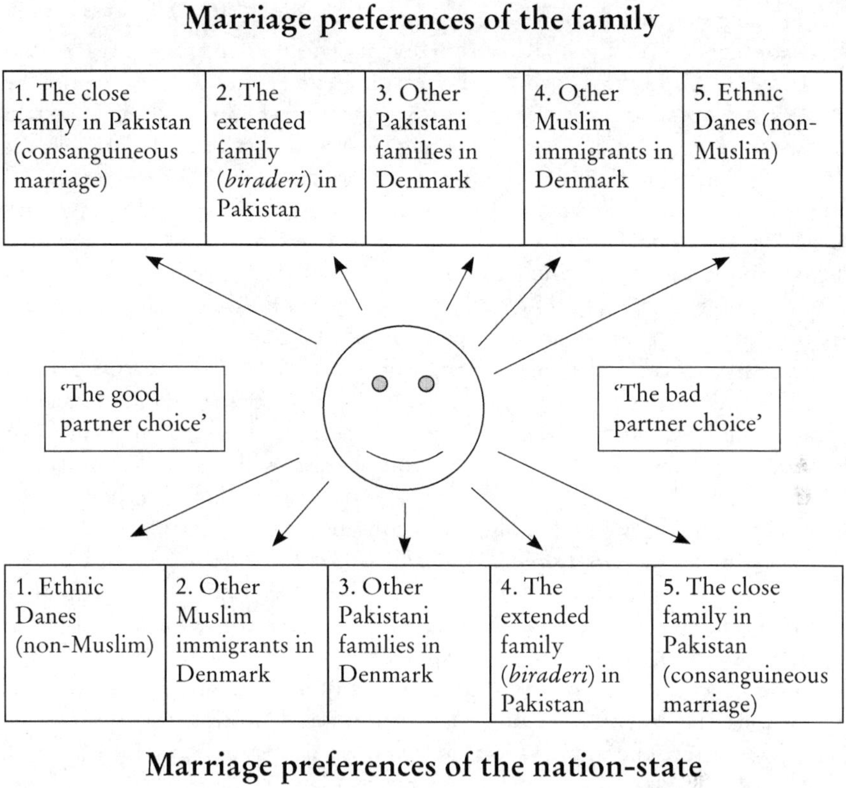

Marriage preferences of the family

1. The close family in Pakistan (consanguineous marriage)	2. The extended family (*biraderi*) in Pakistan	3. Other Pakistani families in Denmark	4. Other Muslim immigrants in Denmark	5. Ethnic Danes (non-Muslim)

'The good partner choice'   'The bad partner choice'

1. Ethnic Danes (non-Muslim)	2. Other Muslim immigrants in Denmark	3. Other Pakistani families in Denmark	4. The extended family (*biraderi*) in Pakistan	5. The close family in Pakistan (consanguineous marriage)

Marriage preferences of the nation-state

Figure 3: Marriage preferences of the family and Danish nation-state compared

The marriage preferences of the nation-state

From a historical perspective, the strict immigration legislation and policy on family reunification introduced in 2002 is the culmination of a growing public and political interest in the marriage of different immigrant groups which emerged in the 1990s in Denmark (e.g., Madsen 2002; Rytter 2003a, 2006; Sareen 2003; Schmidt and Jakobsen 2004; Schmidt et al. 2009) and in the rest of Scandinavia (e.g., Berg 1994; Bredal 1999, 2006; Wikan 2002; Schlytter 2004). This interest was motivated by a number of cases in which young people (mostly women) with a background as immigrants and Muslims stood forth in the media or in autobiographies and recounted how they were forced into marriage by their families (Heide-Jørgensen 1996; Khader 1996; Abdel 2000; Larsen 2000; Osmani 2000; Rashid 2000; Kickbusch 2001; Svane 2002; Deveci 2004). These horrible cases stimulated the creation of a sense of moral panic, and motivated politicians to take action in order to find a responsible solution to the apparently massive problems within the Muslim community. One goal has been to help young immigrants 'gain time', so that they can avoid being married at too young an age.[2] It is generally believed that higher education postpones the final decision to marry until young people reach their mid-twenties, and that this delay empowers them to take a stand against the wishes and possible pressures of their parents, their family and the Pakistani community in general (The Government's Action Plan 2003). The current strict legislation on family reunification is a political signal that transnational marriages are not wanted in Denmark. Second-generation immigrants are urged to find their partners inside the country. In this respect, the national legislation designates which partners the Danish nation-state considers 'good partner choices', while at the same time indicating clear preferences as to what constitute 'bad partner choices'. Choosing spouses from the extended transnational family is often presented in public discourse as an 'un-Danish' (*udansk*) practice, contrasting with the marriage preferences of 'real' Danes (Schmidt 2011, see Chapter 5). Transnational marriages are also seen as an indicator of a failed integration process, which in this context has connotations of a morbid state of existence. Another aspect is the heightened risk of producing disabled children in consanguineous marriages (cf. Shaw 2001), which *The Government's Action Plan for 2003–2005 on Forced, Quasi-forced and Arranged Marriages* emphasises is twice as great as in other kinds of marriages (2003: 4). This warning indicates that, from the official point of view, the only morally responsible course of action is to abolish the preference for transnational marriages within the family network. Even though marriages between cousins are legal under Danish legislation, cousin marriages within the immigrant population are presented as morally suspect and as liable to result in genetic degeneration.

In short, the Danish nation-state has set up an alternative marriage preference for the Muslim immigrant population. In contrast to the preferences of the parents, the nation-state urges second-generation immigrants to marry within Denmark and preferably to enter into an inter-ethnic and inter-religious relationship with a Danish spouse. Above all, Danish Pakistanis are encouraged to defy the tradition of transnational marriages, and especially not to marry within the extended family network, as these types of connections are presented as both irresponsible and morally reprehensible.

As illustrated in Fig. 3, the marriage preferences of the family and the Danish nation-state are diametrically opposed. In the first scenario, the family offers all the privileges, rights and obligations associated with the transnational kinship network, as well as the possibility of renewing practical and emotional connections and bonds with relatives and significant places and spaces in Pakistan. In the second scenario, the nation-state offers a future of being fully recognised and accepted as a Danish citizen, which also includes access to the privileges of the welfare system.

---

2. This is also the main political justification for introducing the minimum age of 24 for both spouses ('24-års regel') in order to be eligible for family reunification to Denmark.

The vital conjuncture of partner choices

The choice of marriage partner constitutes a critical period in the life of young Danish Pakistanis where different aspirations and ideas meet. No matter what decision they finally end up taking, it will have consequences not only for themselves, but also for numerous people in their local and transnational families. It is this kind of intense life situation that Jennifer Johnson-Hanks suggests we call 'vital conjunctures' (2002, 2006). She introduces the concept to address periods of potential transformation (such as death, divorce, pregnancy or childbirth) where the direction of individual life-trajectories changes (2006: 22–3), and suggests that structural transitions are much more open and contested temporal periods of uncertainty, innovation and ambivalence than acknowledged by traditional ethnographic categories (2002: 865). The concept of vital conjunctures can therefore be used to grasp and analyse the vital events of human life, which cause previously steady trajectories to shift direction and which lead to the formation of new horizons.

The current immigration policy and legislation on family reunification has created a vital conjuncture for young Danish Pakistanis.[3] Any decision they make will inevitably include the rejection of others. But neither the family nor the nation-state accepts the rejection of their particular preference without sanctions. If second-generation Pakistanis refuse to adopt the preference of the nation-state, they have to leave the country in order to achieve family reunification with their new spouses (see Chapter 4). If, on the other hand, the family's preference is rejected, the parents – perhaps especially the transnational family – will interpret this as a neglect of the emotional and social bonds within the family and of the norm of marriages within the *biraderi*. When migrants do not fulfil their obligations, this is often interpreted as an unmistakable sign that they feel that they have become too 'good' for their families and relatives in Pakistan and no longer want to invest in intimate family relationships. This neglect can end up creating family conflicts, and ultimately lead to the reorganisation of the transnational network. For this reason, Pakistani parents in Denmark sometimes react very strongly when their offspring do not comply with their wishes, or even reject an already planned *rishta* within the transnational family network. Young Danish Pakistanis who insist on marrying a husband or wife against the will of their parents (and transnational family) risk the sanction of longer or shorter periods of 'social death', where they are ignored and not considered part of the family (Charsley 2007: 1122). On rare occasions, young people who do not comply with the plans of the

---

3. Marriage always constitutes a vital conjuncture, where differing aspirations and interests regarding the couple's current and future lives are presented and discussed. However, since the introduction of the new national immigration policy, the Danish nation-state has interfered in this process and presented an alternative marriage preference to local spouses.

family have been punished with death, victims of so-called 'honour killings' (Møller 2007; see also Wikan 2003).

The remainder of this chapter presents the extended case of Yasmeen and Imran in order to investigate the micro-politics, dilemmas and conflicts within and between migrant families when young people no longer wish to comply with the tradition of formal transnational arranged marriages, but instead outline alternative futures for themselves and their families.

Imran and Yasmeen

Imran is 27 and a student at Roskilde University. He is the oldest of four siblings and has always lived with his parents in a suburb south of Copenhagen. Like the majority of Pakistani migrants in Denmark, his father and mother both originate from smaller villages in the Gujrat district. Imran has a relatively large family in Denmark, since one of his paternal uncles and a paternal aunt live here, with their spouses and children. Imran's grandmother also lives in Denmark.

Yasmeen is 26 and also a student at the university. Her father died years ago, so she lives alone with her mother and three siblings. Her mother comes from the city of Faisalabad in the heart of Punjab, a major city compared to the villages that Imran's family comes from. Yasmeen is the second oldest of the children in her family. Her older brother is engaged to a young woman from the family network in Pakistan. The plan is that in time they will marry and she will then come to Denmark through family reunification. Yasmeen has no other family in Denmark, but she has paternal aunts in Belgium, Holland and France. All remaining family members on the mother's side live in Pakistan.

As mentioned at the beginning of the chapter, Yasmeen and Imran met each other at university and later initiated a romantic relationship. However, they both emphasised during our conversations that their relationship back then was purely platonic, and that they did not transgress any religious boundaries regarding acceptable behaviour for unmarried women and men. When I asked whether they had made their decision to marry on the basis of love, Imran explained:

> Yes … and no. We were in love. But at the same time … it was also because we matched each other on many fronts and shared many interests. We had the same ideas about our family and married life. So it was also to some extent a pragmatic decision. We had been looking at each other for a long time. We did not just rush into it.

When Imran and Yasmeen learned that they shared common interests and dreams for the future they decided to take their relationship to the next level: they decided to get married.

Imran's troubles

In order to be married, Yasmeen and Imran needed in the first place their families' acceptance (and ideally their blessing); in the second place, they needed to get their parents to arrange the *rishta* formally between the two families. To 'do it right', the boy's parents officially ask the girl's parents for the hand of their daughter; so Imran had to confront his parents and tell them that he had met a girl that he wanted to marry. He was very nervous about the outcome of this confrontation, for three reasons.

First of all, Imran knew for a fact that his parents would prefer him to marry within the extended family in Pakistan. A year before his relationship with Yasmeen started becoming serious, he had been in Pakistan with his father and younger brother, and here his father had explained that at his age (then 25) it was time to start thinking about marriage, and now that they were already in Pakistan it would be obvious for them 'to look around' (*se os omkring*). However, the idea of a future with Yasmeen had already begun to take shape in Imran's mind, so he refrained from making any decision in that regard, though without making it clear to his father that he might not be interested in a wife from Pakistan at all, but preferred a partner from Denmark instead.

Secondly, a marriage connection between Yasmeen and Imran was complicated by the fact that the families had no prior relationship and, even worse, had different backgrounds. Not only did Imran's family come from a village while Yasmeen's came from a large city, the two families also had different *zaat* backgrounds. Imran's family were Jat and Chaudry, an overall category for families with land. There are many families in Denmark which call themselves Chaudry. However, Yasmeen's family was of the lineage of Rajputs, which converted from Hinduism to Islam generations ago. According to Imran, both *zaat* rank high in the overall hierarchy, which in the end made the *rishta* acceptable to his parents: as Imran's father confided to him later, 'Yes, after all it was good that it was not a family from a lower-ranking *zaat* that you were married to.'

But there was a third and more fundamental obstacle to their future wedding plans: Yasmeen was already engaged to a man in Pakistan. Due to the delicacy of the situation, in which Imran wanted to marry a woman outside the *biraderi*, from another *zaat* and a different part of Pakistan, and who furthermore was already engaged, it took him almost three weeks to find the courage to confront his parents and tell them about Yasmeen. By then he had no other choice, because gossip about their relationship had started to circulate in the migrant community. About this nerve-wracking period, Imran explained:

> I had told my friends that I knew a Pakistani girl, but it was a long process where we started to develop these feelings for each other. In the beginning we did not think so much about it, but when the gossip started I got really nervous. I was not concerned for myself or about what people may think of me. But there is this

with my mum and dad, they are part of this Pakistani spider's web where rumours about me would give them a hard time – and so they eventually did. It was not Imran, but Chaudry's son who had started having lady friends.

When he finally told them, his parents were very upset and disappointed that their son wanted a partner from Denmark despite their explicit preference for a daughter-in-law from Pakistan, and that he had being pursuing a secret relationship with Yasmeen and had thereby jeopardised the honour and respect of the entire family. But because Imran's romance was about to turn into an 'open secret', they had no other option but to try to arrange the marriage.

Yasmeen's engagement

When Yasmeen met Imran, she was already engaged to her maternal aunt's son. They had become engaged when she had gone on a summer holiday in Pakistan with her mother, at the age of nineteen. Back then, her mother had actively tried to influence her decision by constantly talking positively about her cousin, complimenting him on his looks, and letting her know how happy it would make her if Yasmeen were to marry him. As a widow without family in Denmark, Yasmeen's mother was uncertain about her future and old age; by having her daughter engaged to her sister's son, she could re-establish a link to her family in Pakistan. The marriage would furthermore be economically advantageous to the family, because it would give the young man the opportunity to come to Denmark, earn money and support the family back home. So to make her mother happy, Yasmeen agreed to the engagement.

Despite all these convenient reasons, Yasmeen felt a growing unease with her fiancé. For her, one potential future problem was that she herself was heading towards higher education, while her fiancé had no education at all. She asked him to acquire an education in Pakistan numerous times, so that he would be prepared to get a job when he came to Denmark later. But despite her requests nothing happened in this respect.

If Yasmeen and Imran were to be married, she would have to break off the engagement with her cousin. This, however, would put her mother in bad standing with her sister, and probably also with the rest of the family in Pakistan (see Fig. 4).

Previous episodes in the family history meant that a broken engagement would have serious consequences for Yasmeen's mother.[4] (1) Years ago, Yasmeen's maternal aunt and her husband had arranged for the engagement of two of their sons to the uncle's sister's two daughters. After a while, both engagements were annulled, because the young women and their parents wanted to find more educated and eligible partners. (2) Enraged that she and her sons had been rejected in such a humiliating way, Yasmeen's aunt

---

4. The numbers in this section refer to Fig. 4.

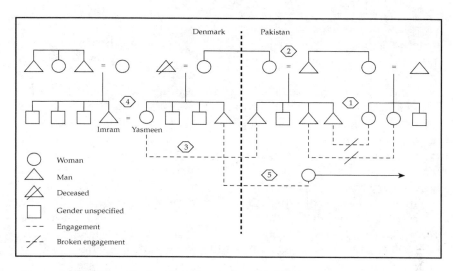

Figure 4: Family conflict between Denmark and Pakistan

demanded of her husband that he break off all contact with his sister, which he did in order to restore the family's public face and reputation. (3) When Yasmeen, years later, became engaged to a third son, her cousin in Pakistan, she inadvertently became part of this family conflict (4), because if she were to break off the engagement with her fiancé and marry Imran instead, this family history would repeat itself. In that event, her uncle would be entitled to reciprocate the ultimatum he had been given, and demand that his wife break off all contact with her sister (Yasmeen's mother) in Denmark, a demand that would restore some of the prestige and dignity lost after having a son rejected after years of engagement.

By falling in love and deciding to get married, Yasmeen and Imran had become the centre of a family drama in which the worst-case scenario was that Yasmeen's mother would be cut off from her family and network in Pakistan. Yasmeen was aware of this, so she could not tell her mother directly about her relationship with Imran. Instead, she just told her that a boy from the university and his parents would like to come for a visit. Immediately her mother understood what was going on. First she was furious, and then she started crying. In a desperate attempt to make her daughter change her mind, she declared that Yasmeen was no longer her daughter, and forbade the rest of her children to talk or listen to their sister.

When Imran's father later visited Yasmeen's mother for the first time, to meet Yasmeen and discuss the possibility of connecting the two families in marriage, the mother's concern about losing contact with her family in Pakistan was the major topic of conversation. At the time, Yasmeen's mother was also worried about her son (5). He had recently been married in Pakistan, and was waiting for his wife to be granted family reunification to Denmark. He now risked being punished by the family in retaliation if Yasmeen broke off her engagement.[5] Yasmeen's mother would therefore under no circumstances allow Yasmeen to be married before her new daughter-in-law had arrived in Denmark.

Yasmeen's mother had a hard time relating the bad news to the transnational family. In fact, she waited until after the wedding before calling her sister in Pakistan and informing her that the engagement was called off because Yasmeen had married a man from Denmark of her own accord. When Yasmeen visits her mother today, she is no longer supposed to answer the phone, because Yasmeen's mother has officially cut her connection with her disobedient, independent daughter in deference to the extended family.

Fundamentally, neither Imran's nor Yasmeen's parents approved of the marriage in the beginning, but they went along with the decision of the young couple in the end. Parents walk a tightrope between suggesting eligible candidates and attempting to orient the trajectories of their children in certain directions, all the while risking that the young people will go ahead and make decisions about their marital futures without their consent. Often parents and adult children meet somewhere in between. This was also the case for Imran and Yasmeen. About a year after Imran first told his parents about Yasmeen, they were married at a discreet wedding with 'only' a hundred guests. Yasmeen explained why they did not have the traditional big wedding: 'It would have been like inviting people to come and see all the trouble.'

Marriage and mobility

Yasmeen and Imran ended up getting married despite all the problems they initially faced in their local and transnational families. But just because young people succeed in convincing their parents to go along with and arrange a love marriage, the couples do not necessarily 'live happily ever after'. After the wedding comes the time when the strength of the newly-weds' mutual feelings and aspirations are tested against members of the two families, who might have preferred to see them married to someone else. Yasmeen's mother did not start speaking to her again until six months after the wedding, and even then never with the same level of intimacy as before. When I interviewed Yasmeen, her mother was still hurt and disappointed. When Imran visited, she gave him few openings to start building a relationship with her and fulfilling his practical and emotional duties and obligations as son-in-law. The only comfort was that Yasmeen's older brother had fully accepted Imran.

---

5. Yasmeen's mother feared that the family in Pakistan would not let her daughter-in-law come to Denmark if Yasmeen broke off the engagement with her maternal cousin. Pnina Werbner (1999) presents a case where a divorce in the *biraderi* was reciprocated by numerous other divorces in the transnational network in order to even up the balance.

Right after the wedding, Yasmeen and Imran moved into his parents' apartment, in order for them to get to know each other. In this respect, they complied with the patrilocal ideal, but after a while they realised that this housing situation gave them very little privacy to prioritise each other and their studies. Yasmeen explained:

> Imran would like to live at home, but I do not. His family is really nice. But I think that if we live too close it will increase the tensions. We lived there for a while after our wedding … Imran's father does not really speak to him anymore because we moved out. They [the first generation] see it another way [than we do]. They may think that we are leaving because we do not like them. But I would like to have some privacy.

So after six months they moved into an apartment just five minutes away. Imran's father, however, was not satisfied with this arrangement. Once again he had to listen to the community gossip about his unruly, independent son and daughter-in-law. Once again his paternal authority and ability to raise his children were called into question.

The case of Yasmeen and Imran shows that migration is never a once-and-for-all move, but rather a continuous process in which historical background still influences and guides migrants' interests, aspirations and decisions. It therefore seems useful to supplement our understanding of physical migration with a concept that can address the kind of 'symbolic mobility' that is part of any vital conjuncture. Whereas physical mobility concerns the move from Pakistan to Denmark, symbolic mobility refers to the various social practices – that is, gestures, speech acts, gifts or such life-phase transitions as marriage – through which migrants confirm, contest or recreate their sense of relatedness and belonging to specific places or significant imagined communities (cf. Carsten 2000). Though second-generation Pakistanis are often born and raised in Denmark, they are nevertheless absorbed in social games at home, among Pakistani friends or in the migrant community, through which they relate to the country their parents left behind, and to the ways in which everyday life was organised in that socio-cultural environment. While physical mobility is irrevocable relocation from A to B, symbolic mobility refers to the ways in which we constantly adjust our life-trajectories towards more or less distant horizons. Yasmeen and Imran's marriage can be interpreted as a kind of symbolic mobility: through their choice, their love for their parents, which is ultimately confirmed by accepting an arranged marriage, was redirected and transformed into their romantic love for a member of another family. In this process young Danish Pakistanis to some extent distance themselves from their parents and extended family as they head towards a common future in Denmark.

Marriage patterns and notions of relatedness

The case of Yasmeen and Imran highlights several dilemmas created by the trend of love marriages within and between migrant families. The following section will discuss how these new marriage preferences affect the Pakistani migrant community and relations of transnational family networks in general.

Currently, first-generation Pakistani parents have started to view the marriage of their offspring as a means to social mobility, whereby the middle-class status achieved in Denmark can be converted into favourable *rishtas*. In this process, the *strong ties* consolidated by transnational marriages within the family are being replaced by the creation of *weak ties* by which Pakistani migrants reach out and connect to new networks of migrant families, in Denmark or in the rest of Europe, the Middle East or North America or even upper middle-class families in Pakistan's major cities such as Karachi, Lahore or Islamabad (cf. Werbner 1999: 27–8). In this respect, the strict Danish immigration regime of 2002 has pushed the families in the direction of new marriage-scapes (Constable 2004: 4); it has made it acceptable to go beyond the transnational – but still narrow – family network, and to recruit spouses from new and wider circles.

Not everyone, however, ends up in a love marriage like Imran and Yasmeen. Members of both older and younger generations explain that it is actually difficult to find eligible matches in Denmark: first of all, there are relatively few Danish Pakistanis of the opposite sex in the same age group who are not already married or engaged. Furthermore, there is the problem of meeting candidates without jeopardising your reputation or the honour of the family – here educational settings, associations and the internet seem to be favoured options. Another crucial aspect is the increasing importance of education in matching families that are alike. On one occasion during a taxi ride in Copenhagen, my Danish Pakistani driver related how his *rishta* had been refused three times by different families because he was 'only driving a taxi'. Due to his lack of education, no Danish Pakistani woman or family would marry him. Instead his parents were now arranging a marriage for him in Pakistan. Turning this example around, it is also a growing problem that young women with an immigrant background are more successful than their male counterparts in the educational system (cf. Mikkelsen et al. 2010: 134). Getting an education is an accepted way to postpone the family's marriage plans, and many seem to use this as a deliberate strategy to get an education and start a career. Unfortunately, however, the increasing population of educated women with immigrant backgrounds (including young Pakistani· women) is not matched by men with similar backgrounds and educational qualifications to marry. One strategy in this situation is for the family to start looking for matches in other countries, or for the young woman to fall in love with a man from another ethnic background.

Numbers and categories of eligible partners are not the only causes of problems: it can also be difficult to create and cultivate lasting relationships of mutual trust and affection between two families which have previously considered each other 'strangers' due to differences in place of origin, *zaat*, religious orientation, etc. It has been suggested that endogamous marriage within the extended family is a means by which Pakistani migrants can reduce the risk and avoid the uncertainty of marrying unknown families (Charsley 2006, 2007). Conversely, the problem can also be that two families know each other too well. Many male Pakistani migrants lived and worked together in the golden age of the late 1960s and early 1970s before their wives and children arrived: back then many of the respectable elders of today had a more exploratory approach to life, which might have included consuming alcohol, illegal activities and sexual relations or extramarital affairs with Danish women (see Chapter 2). In this respect, both 'unknown' and 'all-too-well-known' families may have skeletons in the closet that disqualify them as reliable marriage potential.

Along with the strict Danish legislation on family reunification and the growing interest in local marriages, the institution of the matchmaker has gained prominence. When I interviewed Mrs Ghafoor, a middle-aged married woman and mother of three children about her informal matchmaking service, she explained that Danish Pakistani men and their families often have unrealistic expectations about what *rishta* they can expect. Mrs Ghafoor had two booklets where she listed her 'customers', including their age, height, weight, family and *zaat* background, education and current job, interests and their approach to religion. One example she gave was of a man with a university degree who worked for a large Danish company who was from what Mrs Ghafoor referred to as a 'good family'. Still, she had no potential spouses for him; not only had he been married once before, he was also below average height and had started to lose his hair. The highly educated women listed in her other booklet would never be content with this *rishta*.

Finally, many interlocutors stress their religious identities, and use the choice of life-partner as a means to emphasise that, contrary to their parents, they consider themselves to be 'Muslim' before they are 'Pakistani', which often means that they find and marry spouses who are Muslim but from another immigrant group. Such religiously motivated marriages mark a distance from the gossiping Pakistani migrant community and the various cultural traditions considered un-Islamic, such as the parents' emphasis on *zaat* endogamy. However, the choice of a Muslim but non-Pakistani spouse often results in numerous challenges after the wedding, when the couple must learn to navigate between two different nationalities, languages, traditions and family backgrounds.

All the above examples are intended to illustrate how the emerging marriage-scapes and changing notions of relatedness and intimacy not only offer possibilities, but also create numerous new challenges for Danish Pakistani youth and their families in their quest for eligible partners.

Conclusion: transformation and continuity

Anthony Giddens has suggested that an integrated aspect of late modernity is the emergence of so-called 'pure relationships', where romantic feelings and relationships are supposedly separated from wider social or familial obligation (1992: 58). Even though Danish Pakistani love marriages might constitute such a radical break from the previous traditions of arranged marriages, many young couples still try to 'do it the right way', which implies that they attempt to make their evolving romantic liaisons and love marriages follow the script of formally arranged marriages. Young couples like Yasmeen and Imran might follow their own aspirations and desires by entering more or less controversial love marriages, but they also relate to the values and traditions of *rishta*, *zaat*, patrilocality and *biraderi*, which continue to be important in the migrant community. The current trend of love marriages is clearly a symptom of an ongoing 'transformation of intimacy', as suggested by Giddens (1992). However, it does not indicate a fundamental rejection or break with previous marriage traditions in Pakistani families; rather, it constitutes a subtle redefinition of existing practices. The simultaneous processes of transformation and continuity in Pakistani marriage patterns and preferences exemplify how migrants may adapt to their new circumstances in European countries without assimilating to the whole package of individualistic values.

The case of Imran and Yasmeen also suggests that Pakistani youth often find themselves in a vital conjuncture, caught between the preferences of their family and the Danish nation-state. Much is at stake for migrants when it comes to marriage. Not only do vertical relationships with parents in Denmark risk being seriously damaged when young people 'suddenly' want to choose their partners themselves, the horizontal connections to significant people and places related to the Pakistani branch of the transnational family are also at stake. Just as marriage is the ultimate way to create or maintain transnational relations, it can also be an event that may cause conflict and reorganise the moral orders of emotions, duties and obligations within transnational family networks. Thus I have suggested that, when young Pakistanis choose to engage in a love marriage with a spouse from Denmark, the decision is often explained and justified within discourses on identity and modernity; in this respect, a love marriage constitutes an act of symbolic mobility, whereby young people map out the direction of their future life-trajectories.

Despite their popularity, love marriages are still controversial within the relatively small migrant community. Their scandalous character will most likely disappear, however, as more and more young couples meet, fall in love and get married with, or without, the blessing of their parents and families. So even though the rejection of a *rishta* from the extended family may weaken or even break up connections to significant people and places in Pakistan, love marriages are becoming the foundation on which new close relationships can be cultivated between migrant families in the diaspora. In this way, a love marriage between two families may be the first step in the creation of new *biraderi*-like relationships (Shaw 2000: 186).

Today, it is years ago since Yasmeen and Imran were married. Still, if back then Yasmeen had not broken off her engagement and married her cousin, or if Imran had complied with his parents' wishes and married a woman from the *biraderi* in Pakistan, they would probably, as result of the strict Danish rules on family reunification, have had to move to Sweden in order to achieve this. The next chapter discusses this paradoxical situation: that second-generation Pakistanis who comply with their families' marriage preferences and marry a spouse from Pakistan have to move to Sweden. As they decide to invest themselves in and become fully a part of the local and transnational family, they must also accept being separated from their parents and relatives in Denmark, and start a new life in Sweden.

Chapter 4

Welfare state nomads in the borderlands of Sweden and Denmark

'You see, I live the life of a nomad!' Zagib burst out in the cafeteria at the Panum Institute, where he was a medical student. We were having coffee at a table in a quiet corner, and Zagib had just related that he married Sara, his paternal cousin, in Pakistan in 2004. He had known from early childhood that his father and paternal uncle (father's brother) would like Sara and him to get married, so it was never really a question for him whether they should be married or not, but rather a question of when and where the big occasion should take place. None of them ever imagined that Danish legislation on family reunification would force them to leave Denmark and settle in Sweden – but so it turned out. After their wedding in Pakistan, Zagib bought an apartment in the Swedish city of Malmö and officially moved to Sweden to assure his entitlement to family reunification with Sara. To pay for their apartment and general expenses in Malmö, he worked evening and night shifts at different hospitals in and around the Danish capital, Copenhagen. He also felt emotionally obliged, as the oldest son in his family, to visit his parents in Denmark regularly, preferably every day, before returning to Sweden. Zagib's everyday life involved constant travelling back and forth between Sweden and Denmark to meet his obligations towards his studies, his work, his parents and Sara, without violating either Swedish or Danish law. In this respect, Zagib did actually live the life of a nomad. This chapter discusses the effects of Danish immigration law on the marriage patterns and everyday family life of Pakistani youth who engage in transnational marriage with a spouse from Pakistan.

In 2002 the Danish *Folketing* adopted new legislation on family reunification, with three main objectives. First, the new legislation was meant to hinder the practice of arranged and forced marriages among certain immigrant groups such as Turks and Pakistanis. Secondly, the new legislation provided a means of restricting immigration from non-European 'Third World' countries and, as such, was an aspect of the general securitisation of migration and Muslim immigrants following September 11. Finally, the authorities believed that achieving the first two objectives would provide fertile ground for a new and improved strategy of national integration for the immigrants and refugees who were already resident in Denmark.

To comply with these three political objectives, five requirements were introduced (or refined) in order to obtain family reunification:

1. Both partners must be over the age of twenty-four (*24års-reglen*).
2. The partner residing in Denmark must have 'adequate accommodation of reasonable size' at his or her disposal (*boligkravet*).
3. The partner residing in Denmark must be able to provide for his or her partner and must not have received public financial assistance for a year prior to submitting the application (*forsørgelseskravet*).
4. The partner living in Denmark must post a specified sum of money (from 30 June 2011, DKr 100,000, which is approximately $19,000) in collateral in the form of a bank guarantee to cover any possible public assistance paid by the municipality after the foreign spouse has moved to Denmark (*sikkerhedsstillelsen*).
5. The combined 'national attachment' of the married couple should be at least as great to Denmark as to any other country (*tilknytningskravet*).

These five requirements had an immediate effect on marriage-related immigration. As already mentioned, 6,499 spouses came to Denmark through family reunification in 2001, but by 2009 the number was down to 3,662. The most frequent reason for a newly married couple to be denied reunification is that their combined national attachment to Denmark is considered insufficient. Instead, an estimated 2,000 to 3,000 Danish citizens have done the same as Zagib and adopted a strategy known in Danish public discourse as the 'Swedish model' – in other words, the member of the couple with Danish citizenship moves to Sweden. He or she is then entitled to family reunification as a citizen of the European Union, which Denmark and Sweden joined in 1973 and 1995 respectively. Paradoxically, Danish citizens currently have more rights, and find it easier to obtain family reunification, in Sweden than in Denmark.

However, the current immigration regime not only hinders newly-wed transnational couples who want to live in Denmark, but it has also initiated a process whereby the practices of marriage and family organisation among Pakistanis (and other Muslim immigrant groups) have become suspect. These groups have become *semi-legal* in both legal and moral senses.

I use the concept of 'semi-legality' to refer specifically to those transnational couples who commute on a regular basis between their legal residence in Sweden and their studies or workplace, friends and family in Denmark. Whereas 'legality' refers to a legal status characterising the specific relationship constituted by mutual rights and obligations between a subject and the nation-state, 'illegality' refers to subjects who lack a legally sanctioned relationship with a nation-state (Genova 2002: 422). In principle, 'legality' and 'illegality' are one-dimensional concepts – one can (has to) be either one or the other. However, recent studies emphasise a more process-oriented approach, and document how migrants may move between the statuses of legal and illegal (Erdemir and Vasta 2007; Koser 2010; Ruhs and Anderson 2010). The concept of semi-legality refers to a specific lifestyle and mutable condition of transnational couples created by the cleavage between the Swedish and Danish legislation. On the one hand, to qualify for family reunification in the first place, the Danish partner of the married couple has to live permanently in Sweden and not leave the country for too long. On the other hand, newly arrived spouses from Pakistan must live in Sweden and may stay in Denmark only for a limited period. Newly married couples living in Sweden can go to Denmark and stay there, but only for a while before they become illegal. In this respect, one can compare semi-legality with a battery that needs recharging occasionally to function properly: after a period of time in Denmark, the couples must return to Sweden to regain their status as legal citizens.

The concept of semi-legality bears some resemblance to the concept of 'semi-compliance', recently introduced to describe and discuss the employment of migrants who are legal residents but who violate the employment restrictions attached to their immigrant status, and so move between different legal statuses (Ruhs and Anderson 2010). The concept of semi-legality can also be seen as a variant of 'overstaying', for migrants become illegal if they stay in Denmark too long (see Koser 2010: 183; Schuster and Solomos 2004: 279). In this specific case, transnational couples also risk violating the terms of their family reunification and residence permit if they 'understay' in Sweden.

Besides the legal dimensions of semi-legality, the condition also has significant moral aspects. Not only do public and political discourses frequently challenge and condemn Muslim immigrants' transnationally arranged marriages; the five requirements of the family reunification legislation inherently affirm that immigrant marriages are suspect and contradict the usual motivations of 'real' Danes in contracting marriages (see Chapter 5).

In this chapter, I first present the 'Swedish Model' and show how marriage migrants organise everyday life in the borderlands between Sweden and Denmark. Secondly, I discuss the legal and moral aspects of semi-legality. Finally, I show how external political intervention and the redirection of individual trajectories facilitate a state of uncertainty among married couples regarding their legal status and future prospects. In sum, therefore, this chapter discusses the effects of the Danish immigration regime on Pakistani marriage patterns and on everyday family life, and more generally on current and future relations between majorities and minorities in Denmark.

The 'Swedish Model'

Geographically, the Öresund region consists of part of the Danish island of Zealand and part of Scania in southern Sweden. Since 2000, the Öresund Bridge has linked Denmark to Sweden, and this has reinforced mutual political ambitions to integrate the region further (Linde-Laursen 2003: 187). Today, because of the lower cost of living and lower prices for accommodation, cars

and food, almost 6,000 Danes live in the Swedish city of Malmö, an increase
of 60 per cent since 2001 (Rapport 1, 2006: 7). Meanwhile, favourable job
opportunities in the Copenhagen area have motivated thousands of Swedes
to work in Denmark. In 2005 no fewer than 3,500 Danes moved to Sweden,
while 1,800 Swedes moved the other way and settled in Denmark. In this
respect, the many transnational couples resettling in Sweden are only part of
a larger mobile segment of the population in the Öresund region.

There are no accurate figures for how many Danes have moved to Sweden
to obtain family reunification. However, in 2005 the Swedish immigration
authorities received almost 600 applications from Danish citizens residing
in Scania. Of these, 64 per cent were men, 36 per cent women, and in half
of the marriages, one or both partners were under the age of twenty-four
(Rapport 1, 2006: 7). Based on these figures, an estimated 2,000–3,000 Danes
have moved to Sweden since 2002 to obtain family reunification. Before
2002 there were only a couple of hundred people of Pakistani origin living in
Scania, mainly in Malmö, but since then the numbers have increased. In 2004
the Swedish authorities authorised approximately 110 family reunifications
with spouses from Pakistan, and in 2007 no less than 12 per cent of Danish
Pakistanis had emigrated to Sweden by the age of twenty-five (Schmidt et al.
2009: 99). The couples typically settle in Swedish cities such as Malmö, Lund,
Landskrona, Trelleborg or Helsingborg.

In the typical case of the 'Swedish model', a Danish citizen moves to
Sweden to rent or buy an apartment or house with the sole purpose of
obtaining family reunification with his or her foreign spouse. To make the
resettlement in Sweden official, the Dane has to register at the *Folkbokföringen*
(the national registration office). Due to his or her status as a citizen of the
European Union, a Dane living in Sweden is entitled to family reunification
if he or she can support the spouse economically. In real life, this often means
that he or she must continue to work in Denmark while living in Sweden and
must commute on a daily basis between the two countries.

The siblings Sanam and Tariq, who today live in the city of Landskrona
with their spouses from Pakistan, are typical examples of the 'Swedish
Model'. In 2002, when Sanam was twenty-three, she was married to a well-
educated man from Pakistan. Their parents formally arranged the marriage,
but Sanam and her husband already knew each other and both approved of
the *rishta*. When Sanam returned to Denmark after her summer wedding
in Pakistan, she submitted an application to the Danish immigration
authority (*Udlændingeservice*) to apply for family reunification in Denmark
with her husband. They rejected her request because, according to the age
requirement, Sanam was considered too young to obtain family reunification:
she was below the age of twenty-four. She therefore had to wait before
becoming eligible for reunification. The rejection was a hard blow to the
newly-wed couple's plans, especially after their honeymoon and long intense
time together in Pakistan. In the following year, Sanam therefore made three
longer journeys to Pakistan in order to be with her new husband. The year

after, when she turned twenty-four, they applied for family reunification again. Even though they now both met the age requirement and Sanam had the required financial guarantees, a steady income and her own apartment, the immigration authorities again turned down their request for reunification. This time the reason they gave was that Sanam and her husband were no more attached to Denmark than they were to Pakistan. The Danish authorities also stressed the fact that Sanam had spent a lot of time in Pakistan in recent years. The decision made Sanam and her family very angry and frustrated, but then they heard rumours about other Pakistanis who had moved to Sweden to live with their newly arrived Pakistani spouses. The family decided that Tariq, Sanam's older brother, who already had a career in an international company, would also get married in Pakistan. Subsequently, they would both move to Landskrona and apply for family reunification with their respective spouses. Learning from his sister's experiences, Tariq did not even bother to apply in Denmark, but just left the country. After eleven weeks, the Swedish immigration authorities (*Migrationsverket*) granted Sanam and Tariq family reunification with their Pakistani spouses. Thus, Sanam's husband arrived in September 2004 and Tariq's wife followed at the beginning of 2005.

Sanam, Tariq and the other marriage migrants constitute approximately 20 per cent of all Danes who have moved to Scania since 2002 (Rapport 1, 2006: 7). But unlike the increasing number of Danes who move to Scania for economic reasons or to pursue career opportunities, Sanam, Tariq and the other transnational couples I interviewed moved only because they had no other option.

The family as an institution of integration

The new legal circumstances force transnational Pakistani marriage partners who settle in Sweden to redirect their trajectories and future prospects. The problems and frustrations related to their new lives in Sweden often dominate the period after the wedding when they are separated from family and friends, who would normally ease the structural transition from 'child' to married 'adult' and the physical transition of brides from their parents' houses to the households and families of their husbands. In transnational marriages, the family often also eases the move from Pakistan to Europe.

One can see the current pattern of transnational marriages into Europe as a continuation of the institution of arranged marriages discussed in the previous chapter. In the patrilocal tradition, newly-wed women leave their natal homes and families to become the wives and join the families of their husbands. The current transnational dimensions of marriage migration are new, however, and they often distort established structural relations and gender roles (cf. Charsley 2005). Due to the Danish immigration regime, both partners must now leave their homes and families in Denmark and Pakistan and settle in Sweden. In this new situation, it is difficult for family members to provide the help and services that a newly arrived transnational bride or groom normally needs in order to adjust to a new family and social environment. This means they often have to forgo basic supports such as economic security, the comfort of a secure haven, and help with learning the language or finding a job. Established migrant families often have networks of relatives, friends or colleagues who can help newcomers feel at home in the foreign country and the new social and bureaucratic environment. This important work of the family is difficult to continue when young, second-generation Pakistanis move to Sweden to live with their Pakistani husbands or wives. Even in cases where transnational spouses have known each other for several years and discussed the circumstances of their future lives before the wedding, they still have to face a new life in an unknown Swedish environment, where they are responsible for shopping, cooking, cleaning and paying the bills. Through marriage, they enter adulthood and confront a new moral landscape of obligations and expectations, including a physical relationship with their new spouse. To ease the structural and geographical transitions, a member of the Danish part of the family (for example, the mother or a sister) will often move to Sweden and live with the newly-weds for a period, or at first the couple will simply stay with the patrilocal household in Denmark.

On the other hand, many see advantages in living in Sweden. The Danish legislation forces young couples to find their own apartments, which is useful when the structural position of being a son- or daughter-in-law in an extended patriarchal and patrilocal family starts to be an irritant. The newly-wed couple Humaira and Waqas both mentioned Sweden as somewhere to make a fresh start and live on their own without the interference of Waqas' family. Born and raised in one of the suburbs south of Copenhagen, Waqas felt sympathetic to the Danish government's desire to reduce the number of immigrants and refugees entering the country. Humaira found it problematic that her husband, despite his Danish citizenship, was not allowed to live in Denmark, but she did not regret the fact that they now had their own apartment in Sweden.

Aspects of the semi-legal condition

The Danish immigration regime of 2002 resembles 'social engineering', as it is a deliberate political attempt to regulate those aspects of family life among Muslim immigrants that are seen as problematic. If we measure its success in reduced numbers of transnational marriages and family reunifications in Denmark, the immigration policy has been highly effective; but the official strategy has also had numerous unexpected consequences. Creating policies inevitably creates the potential for actions that contravene these policies (Bledsoe 2004: 97); and while some of these are legal, others are not. The rest of this chapter will discuss the legal and moral aspects of semi-legality separately, showing not only how the condition affects contemporary everyday life and future prospects, but also how transnational couples who have settled in Sweden react to the external intervention, and come up with different creative solutions in order to restore a 'normal' family life.

Semi-legality: the legal aspects

In the current world order, it has become self-evident that everyone belongs to a nation-state and has national citizenship. People who cross national borders without the proper documents become illegal. To be illegal is in no respect a favourable status, but an all-embracing concept that sticks to the body and defines who you are. Undocumented migrants have only limited (if any) access to the rights and privileges that the particular nation-state gives its legal citizens.

The condition I suggest we call semi-legal is slightly different. Semi-legality is the outcome of the differences between Danish and Swedish legislation, and refers to a condition where married couples move between a legal and an illegal state of being. Transnational couples settled in Sweden are semi-legal because they constantly run the risk of becoming illegal, which will happen if they spend too little time in Sweden or too much time in Denmark and thereby transgress certain legally defined periods. However, by commuting between the two countries, they can regain their status as legal subjects. The following example illustrates this point.

Zagib, introduced at the beginning of this chapter, was perfectly aware that Sara, his fiancée, would not be permitted family reunification because they were both below the age of twenty-four and therefore too young to meet the age requirement (and probably the national attachment requirement as well), so he decided to move to Sweden. To obtain permission for family reunification from the Swedish authorities, Zagib had to prove that he could provide for both of them and to confirm that he actually lived in Sweden. To live in Sweden officially, a Danish citizen has to spend at least half of his or her time in the country.

When Sara arrived from Pakistan, she was granted a Swedish residence permit from the *Migrationsverket* (Immigration Office), which allowed her to stay up to three months in another country of the European Union, for example Denmark. However, if Sara were to stay longer than the fixed time limit, she would not only become an illegal subject in Denmark, but also violate the conditions of her Swedish residence permit.

If either Sara or Zagib contravene the specific rules by 'overstaying' in Denmark or 'understaying' in Sweden, they risk the ultimate sanction of the Swedish authorities: to be sent back to Pakistan and Denmark respectively. When the couple stays in the patrilocal household of Zagib's family in Denmark, therefore, they must make sure that they regularly go back to Sweden. Like flat batteries, they need recharging. This continual movement between Sweden and Denmark can be seen as a 'technology of the self' (cf. Foucault 1988), whereby transnational couples, by careful organisation of the time they spend in different places, can legally visit friends and family in Denmark regularly and for longer periods. They must accept, however, that the structural conditions of their semi-legal status mean that they are always in the process of becoming illegal.

Married couples who violate the rules by spending too much time in Denmark take precautions in order not to attract too much attention to themselves from the Danish and Swedish authorities. One way to do this is to make the apartment in Sweden look inhabited, by making regular visits to use electricity and water, to make transactions through their Swedish bank accounts and always to reply in time to official letters from, for example, the owner of the flat or the Swedish authorities. Another strategy is to use (or have someone else use) their 'bro-bizz', a monthly season ticket to the Öresund Bridge. In this way, when requested, transnational couples can 'prove' that they return to Sweden every evening after going to work in Denmark.

Another strategy is to start renovating the Swedish apartment. Asad and his newly arrived wife lived in his parents' house in Denmark. To justify why they were not in Malmö, Asad explained that their apartment was being rebuilt and modernised. This gave them a legitimate reason for not staying in the apartment if the Swedish or Danish authorities – or a curious ethnographer – confronted them.

Finally, there are those who deliberately violate the rules. Back in 2000 Sanjeev got engaged to one of his cousins in Pakistan during a summer holiday. In 2002 they held a *nikkah* (wedding ceremony). When the Danish authorities turned down his application for family reunification in Denmark, he rented a room at a friend's apartment in Malmö and registered at the *Folkboksföringen*. Now he officially lived in Sweden and, since Sanjeev could easily come up with payslips for the previous three months to prove to the Swedish authorities that he was capable of supporting his wife, they soon granted her permission to enter Sweden. Officially, the couple lived in the rented room, but in reality they stayed in the basement of his parents' villa in Denmark. Sanjeev's wife started taking private lessons in Danish so that at some time in the future she could enter a Danish educational institution and utilise her professional training from Pakistan. Two years ago, the couple had a son, who was born at a Swedish hospital. Whenever the child had to see a doctor, Sanjeev would pay for private consultations because his son officially lived in Sweden and therefore had no access to the free Danish medical system.

On one occasion, *Migrationsverket* contacted the owner of the apartment where Sanjeev and his wife rented a small room and asked him to confirm that his tenants actually lived there. The owner was more than willing to help Sanjeev and his wife as part of the cover-up, so he confirmed that his tenants were indeed living in the apartment. After this incident, Sanjeev started to look for an apartment in Sweden because if they had their own place, they would attract less attention.

The Swedish authorities have become aware that some of the recently settled Danes and their non-European spouses seem to be spending less time in Sweden than they are supposed to. In 2004, the Swedish tax authorities (*Skatteverket*) presented a report stating that Danes sometimes move pro forma (*på papiret*) to Sweden to buy cheap cars or obtain family reunification (Rapport 2, 2004). Since then the authorities have started carrying out random checks on whether transnational couples are actually living in Sweden. They typically target couples who report that they are living in a small rented room with friends, or where the Danish partner works far away from the place of residence in Sweden. One incident that attracted attention was when the Danish partner of a married couple was supposed to be living in Malmö but worked in Esbjerg in western Denmark, approximately four hours away (*Berlingske Tidende*, 31 August 2004).

One effect of the various official actions targeting transnational couples violating the conditions of their residence permit is a creeping paranoia, so that the couples often use (and misuse) mailing lists and SMSs to circulate information and rumours through Pakistani networks in the Öresund region. For instance, the couples in question commonly assume that the Swedish and Danish authorities monitor their family lives and transnational movements. Another rumour asserts that the Swedish authorities check up on newly married couples by sending in officials disguised as workers supposedly reading the electricity or water meters in the apartment. A third rumour claims that Swedish politicians will soon follow the lead of their Danish colleagues and tighten up the legislation on family reunification. The atmosphere of paranoia is a general condition of the semi-legal lives of transnational married couples in the borderlands between Sweden and Denmark.

Besides the legal aspect, there are also some significant moral aspects connected to the status of semi-legality, to which I now turn.

Semi-legality: the moral aspects

Legislation sets up standards for proper behaviour and draws the line between right and wrong, legal and illegal. In this respect, legislation becomes a certain way of imagining society. By introducing the five requirements (on age, housing, income, collateral and national attachment) mentioned at the beginning of this chapter, the Danish immigration regime set up a normative guide on how to contract marriages and organise a proper family life. My interest is not in whether or not these requirements are reasonable, but in how policy-makers employ a certain, basically European family model to which Danish citizens, especially those of immigrant background, are expected to conform (Grillo 2008: 16; see also Kofman 2004). According to the normative framework derived from the five requirements mentioned above, people in Denmark should not get married until they are in their mid-twenties, have their own house or apartment, have a nice job with a decent salary and have money in their saving accounts. Furthermore, the Danish government published a policy on 'forced, quasi-forced and arranged marriages' for the period 2003–5 (The Government's Action Plan 2003; see Chapter 3). It clearly disapproves of arranged marriages, for it states that 'in Denmark it is customary for young people to choose their own marriage partner and enter a marriage based on a loving relationship. ... The practice of arranged marriages is a violation of the right of the individual to freely find and choose a spouse' (The Government's Action Plan 2003: 5). The five requirements and the plan of action set out a national standard for people who wish to start a family in Denmark. If Danish citizens from immigrant backgrounds ignore these standards, it tends to indicate that they are not 'real' Danes after all.

In 2003 the Danish *Folketing* intensified the moral aspects of semi-legalisation by introducing the so-called 'rule of supposition' (*formodningsreglen*) as a guiding principle for how the Danish authorities should administer the ambiguous requirement of 'national attachment'. The rule of supposition stipulates two circumstances in which a transnational marriage will inevitably result in the rejection of an application for family reunification. First, the authorities will automatically treat a marriage between 'close relatives' (e.g., first cousins) as forced, even though marriages between first cousins are legal under Danish law. Second, if a family has previously undergone a transnational marriage (e.g., of an older sibling), the authorities will see it as a family pattern and an indication that the marriage is not based on a voluntary decision by the young couple in question (Liisberg 2004: 26). In this respect, the specific intention of the rule of supposition is to hamper the practice found among immigrant groups from Pakistan, Turkey and the Middle East. That the authorities administrating the law are instructed to assume that the marriage has been forced on the young couple, which is against the law in Denmark, where one is not allowed to force anyone into marriage against their will, has now indirectly criminalised this category of marriages; certain marriage preferences and partner choices are criminalised on the sole grounds of supposition and suspicion.

Ontological insecurity and blurred horizons

As we have seen, Danes from a Pakistani background end up in Sweden with their Pakistani partners because of their decision to follow the family's preference over that of the Danish nation-state. Many informants relate that their involuntary emigration to Sweden has left them in a temporary position of waiting until they can return to Denmark and live in the patrilocal household, or at least close to their family. The period in Sweden constitutes a limbo, with a diffuse extension in time, and is characterised by the lack of a normal everyday family life. In this respect, the structural conditions of semi-legal couples resembles the situation of asylum-seekers who wait to have their cases and destinies decided by the respective authorities (see Schwartz 1998: 9ff.; Whyte 2011). Anthony Giddens (1991) introduces the concept of 'ontological security' as a description of agents who navigate and cope with a recognisable social system. In this respect, ontological security is an embodied knowledge that gives the routines of everyday life a sense of certainty. Ontological security is a basis on which agents act and understand their immediate environment, thus giving the social world a sense of continuity, so that the social world presents itself as organised and recognisable. Conversely, one can use the concept of 'ontological insecurity' analytically to describe the events and social situations in which the agents have the carpet pulled from underneath them. The social world is no longer immediately recognisable, and they therefore cannot draw on their embodied repertoire of skills and knowledge in order to predict what kind of consequences specific acts will provoke. Ontological insecurity is a condition that cancels the existing social order, which in the end can be socially paralysing and psychologically problematic. Likewise, Khalid Koser points out that irregular migration not only poses a threat to state security, but may also undermine the 'human security' of migrants themselves (Koser 2010: 190).

The ontological insecurity of everyday life results in blurred horizons. When, for instance, I confronted transnational couples with questions about where they might live in future and perhaps having children, many hesitated. Their current situation urges them to take each day at a time. Furthermore, the changing 'legal landscape' contributes to the experience of ontological insecurity, because couples utilising the 'Swedish model' can never be sure that their dreams, hopes and plans for the future can actually be carried out. Let me give three examples of this.

First, many interlocutors were surprised that the Danish legislation would actually impact on their specific marriage and family reunification. This is probably because many of the couples I interviewed were among the pioneers who had moved to Sweden. Currently, most Pakistanis have become aware of the problems and pitfalls, so they know where to get help and counselling to cope with moving to Sweden. Zagib, for one, claimed to be totally unprepared for all the problems he and Sara had to go through. He and Sara completed the ceremony of *nikkah* back in 2001, but the actual celebrations and the structural transition from being 'children' to becoming 'husband and wife' did not take place until 2004. I asked why, if they were actually already married, they had not applied for family reunification before the summer of 2002, when the new immigration regime came into force, but for Zagib this was not so obvious:

> I was not ready for marriage at the time ... and I did not believe that it [the new immigration regime] would affect me ... An angel like me, with no criminal record, a student of medicine and all – I just couldn't believe that it would affect me ... but it did.

Secondly, many interlocutors related stories that showed that they found it difficult to understand the complicated rules and changing criteria the Danish authorities used to grant or reject applications. As in the case of Sanam, presented earlier in this chapter, many had a history of one or more rejections before they eventually decided to move to Sweden. Asmaa and her husband did not meet the age requirement at their first application because her husband had not yet turned twenty-four. When they applied a second time, their application was rejected because they failed to meet the requirement of national attachment. Now, living in Malmö with her husband and infant daughter, Asmaa was convinced that no matter what they did to meet the requirements of the Danish state, it would never be enough.

Thirdly, the continual introduction of new legislation and the numerous subtle bureaucratic adjustments to how, for example, administrators interpret and administer the requirement of national attachment, are constantly changing the legal landscape – in fact, the rules sometimes change from one day to the next. For instance, in September 2005 the Danish minister of integration, Rikke Hvilshøj, declared that under certain circumstances the *Udlændingeservice* could depart from the otherwise rigid requirement that both partners needed to be aged at least twenty-four. She proposed exempting from the age requirement students who were studying for a profession such as engineering or medicine, because Denmark needed them to safeguard the future of the welfare state. Although the right-wing Danish People's Party, on whose votes the Liberal-Conservative government depended for its survival, vetoed the minister's statement the very next day, rumours of the new possible opening were already rife in the Pakistani community. Hamid, who at that time was waiting to get his Pakistani wife, Aisha, into Sweden, had seen his mother weep with joy at the prospect of her son and new daughter-in-law after all being able to live with her and her husband to form a patrilocal household in Denmark. The next day, however, Hamid had to comfort his mother when it became apparent that her dream would not come true.

In the next section, I present an extended description of the case of Hamid and Aisha to illustrate how the 'rule of supposition' undermines the legitimacy of Pakistani preferences for marriages within the family.

Territorial borders and moral boundaries

When we first met in the spring of 2005, Hamid was a student at the Technical University of Denmark (DTU). He had just become engaged to his first cousin, Aisha, the daughter of his mother's sister from Pakistan. Well aware that the choice of a transnational marriage would mean that they would have to settle down in Sweden, he bought an apartment in Malmö and did not even bother to apply for reunification in Denmark. The couple planned eventually to return to Denmark to live with Hamid's parents.

That summer Aisha and Hamid married in Pakistan, and in early January 2006 she arrived in Sweden, ready to start a new life with her husband. In December 2006, after living in Malmö for almost a year, Hamid applied for permission to return to Denmark with his wife. Newly qualified as an engineer, he was now included on the so-called 'positive list' (*positiv-listen*) of professionals (doctors, nurses, engineers, IT workers) exempted from the five requirements (Thomsen 2006). Hamid hoped that his new position would make a difference, but he had still not heard from the Danish authorities by March 2007. Meanwhile, he started working for a large Danish company and commuting each day between their apartment in Malmö and his workplace in a suburb north of Copenhagen. During the daytime, Aisha remained in Sweden. She did not attend language school, because the municipality had told her that there were no vacancies for the next seven months. It seemed a waste of time to learn Swedish and then later switch to Danish, so Hamid taught Aisha some Danish words and sentences at home in the evenings. Because of Hamid's inconvenient daytime journeys between their home and his work, and Aisha's growing homesickness and loneliness in Sweden, the couple started to spend nights at the house of Hamid's parents in Copenhagen.

On one occasion, Hamid called his case-officer. When he finally succeeded in reaching her, she implied that, since he had not yet received a positive response, there might be a problem with his application. It turned out that the rule of supposition applied to their application, which meant that the authorities had officially reclassified their union as a forced marriage.

When the *Udlændingeservice* finally rejected their application in the spring of 2007, it emphasised the kin tie between Hamid and Aisha as the decisive factor. Hamid immediately appealed against the decision and submitted more than seventy photographs of the couple together to prove that it was not a forced marriage: some photos were from their wedding in Pakistan, some from their apartment in Sweden, and he even sent photographs from a family holiday they had been on together in northern Pakistan long before their engagement. Hamid hoped that these photographs would prove to the Danish authorities that he and Aisha had known each other long before the engagement and that they had married on a voluntary basis.

By August 2007, Hamid had still not heard from the authorities regarding the appeal. He felt humiliated, discriminated against and badly treated. He bitterly regretted his honesty: 'Many of my friends do not say that they are marrying within the family, so they do not have any problems, but I do.' The worst headache, however, was the long period of uncertainty. They had already waited for nearly nine months for the rejection of their application for family reunification in the spring of 2007; now they had to wait even longer for a decision on their appeal. According to Hamid, imposing long periods of uncertainty was part of the official strategy to cause stress and thus weaken the applicants' resolve. Nevertheless, Aisha and Hamid decided that, if they lost the appeal, they would simply stay in Sweden and continue commuting between the two countries. They would not waste any more resources or valuable time trying to obtain permission to move to Denmark.

The case of Aisha and Hamid raises several of the problems related to semi-legality discussed so far. Hamid and Aisha actually lived in Sweden most of the time, but the couple had weighty practical and emotional reasons for wanting to live in Denmark. In the house of her parents-in-law, Aisha was not alone, and Hamid could be there for his father, who suffered from diabetes. For a while, they discussed the possibility of bringing Hamid's parents with them to Sweden, but abandoned the idea because his parents preferred to stay in Denmark near their friends and grandchildren (the children of Hamid's older brother and sisters).

During our conversations, on several occasions Hamid expressed his anguish that, despite his Danish citizenship, the authorities denied him permission to live with his wife in Denmark just because she was his first cousin from Pakistan. This became even more incomprehensible when the government started allowing Danish companies to bring labour migrants, for example, tradesmen from Poland and Germany or trained medical staff from Eastern Europe or India, into the country. Hamid interpreted these conflicting political attitudes as proof that he, Aisha and their family were simply the victims of racism and discrimination.

From an analytical perspective, the case illustrates how the current Danish immigration regime is turning the *territorial border* of the nation-state (the bureaucratic administration of who can and cannot enter the country) into a *moral boundary* that stipulates how to contract marriages and organise family life. This new moral judgement about immigrant marriages not only negatively affects young people who get married today, but it can also work retrospectively to affect couples who contracted arranged transnational marriages years previously.

First, Danish Pakistanis and their Pakistani partners who move to Sweden fall under suspicion the moment they enter Denmark, because their choice of marriage partner is now illegitimate. One consequence of the rule of supposition is that it automatically categorises the marriages of first cousins like Aisha and Hamid, or Sara and Zagib, as forced marriages. This redefinition invalidates such marriages according to both Islamic orthodoxies and Danish law, since in both cases forced marriages are void. Furthermore, the rule of supposition also throws suspicion on the parents of the married couple, since they arranged the marriage in the first place. If the marriage is in fact forced, then the parents are guilty of a felony.

Secondly, the rule of supposition also works retrospectively, as it makes previous transnational marriages and marriages between relatives suspect. Immigrants who have been living together in Denmark as man and wife for decades have to accept that, under contemporary legal and moral redefinitions, their marriages are now regarded as involuntary and forced.

Conclusion: prospects for the future

Sweden and Denmark, despite both belonging to the European Union, have very different immigration policies. The geographical proximity of the two countries has created a unique situation in which Danish Pakistanis can move to Sweden and obtain family reunification with a spouse from Pakistan, while continuing to spend much of their time with family members in Denmark. The popularity of the 'Swedish Model' obviously threatens the agenda of the Danish immigration regime. On several occasions, the Danish government has urged its Swedish colleagues to stop semi-legal couples exploiting the loopholes. In response, the (now former) Swedish minister of justice, Thomas Bodström, called the Danish legislation 'silly and discriminatory'. Likewise, the (also former) minister of integration, Mona Sahlin, stated that 'it's Denmark's problem that so many Danish-foreign married couples settle in Malmö'. The confrontation is symptomatic of the differences between the official multicultural politics of Sweden and the rearmament of national sentiments and identity in Denmark (Hedetoft 2006: 391).

Transnational couples settling in Sweden have different strategies for the future, and we can roughly class them into two groups. Those in the first group claim that they have emigrated for the last time and have started to build a new life in Sweden. Couples with social and economic resources, in the form of a good education or a well-paid job, are most likely to choose this strategy. They present Sweden as a good place in which to live, with lower living expenses and a political system that endorses multiculturalism; they feel more accepted and appreciated there than they ever did in Denmark. Tariq, whom I introduced earlier in this article, stated that he would never return. 'If Denmark does not want us, we do not want Denmark either!' He elaborated on the statement by comparing his situation with his parents' situation when they arrived in Denmark in the 1970s. According to Tariq, his parents had spent all their adult lives in Denmark working hard, while dreaming in their spare time of returning to Pakistan. Tariq would not make the same mistake. He would not live in Sweden and use all his time and resources imagining his future return to Denmark. Out of a combination of anger, defiance and realism, he planned to settle permanently in Sweden. Another significant reason for staying in Sweden is that the pioneers of the 'Swedish Model' have started having children who attend local day-care centres and kindergartens and have started to speak Swedish. Many couples accept that they have to stay in Sweden for the sake of their children, and often encourage friends and family members to follow them. The second group of transnational couples sees life in Sweden as a demarcated period they have to endure before they can return to Denmark. The complicated and changing legal landscape and conflicting immigration regimes create different legal loopholes that they can exploit in pursuit of these aims. Statistics indicate that many may have started applying for student visas or work permits for their spouses instead of applying for family reunification. In 2001, fewer than 100 Pakistanis applied for a student visa for Denmark. However, by 2008 the figure had increased to 324. As it has become more and more difficult to obtain family reunification, the number of students has increased drastically.

Hamid and Aisha actually ended up moving permanently to Denmark when, early in 2008, Hamid was granted Swedish citizenship. It normally takes 'just' two years of legal residence for a Dane to become a Swede. Changing his citizenship from Danish to Swedish thus allowed Hamid to bring his Pakistani wife with him to Denmark and settle with his parents. In late 2008, the couple had a daughter, who became a Swedish citizen just like her father. Another option, of which I know some examples, is for the Pakistani spouse to become a Swedish citizen. This also makes it possible for the married couple to return to Denmark.

Other couples like Sara and Zagib will continue their semi-legal nomadic lifestyle, and commute between Denmark and Sweden to 'recharge their batteries' and avoid breaking the law. They are part of a large group in the borderlands between Denmark and Sweden caught between having to accept a common future in Sweden or finding a legal way of returning permanently to Denmark.

Overall, this chapter highlights some of the problematic effects of the restrictive legislation the Danish parliament passed on family reunification in 2002 and 2003. The Danish immigration regime successfully converges with transnational marriage patterns and family practices among certain immigrant groups, but the cases presented here also illustrate how, despite the obstructions and interventions, Pakistani transnational couples manage to restructure their everyday lives and aspirations for the future. Nevertheless, the legislation has created a semi-legal condition that affects Danish citizens with a Pakistani background and their families residing in Denmark: a condition which not only generates new insecurities in family life, but also widens the gap between the indigenous Danish majority and the immigrant minorities.

Chapter 5

'The Danish family' and 'the aliens'

The previous chapter discussed how transnational couples become semi-legal when they commute between their legal residence in Sweden and family, friends and work in Denmark. This chapter analyses how ideas of national identity, relatedness and belonging are embedded in the Danish legislation on family reunification of 2002, and more specifically in the requirement of 'national attachment'. As several of the cases presented in the previous chapter illustrate, the requirement of national attachment is very difficult to comply with. Actually it is currently the most frequent reason for newly-weds to be denied family reunification in Denmark.

Applying insights from anthropological studies of kinship, I will argue in this chapter that the requirement for national attachment is both a model of and a model for a more basic, systematic exclusion of Danish citizens with immigrant backgrounds from the national discourse and imaginaries: it not only distinguishes between Danes and foreigners, but also, within the pool of Danish citizens, between the majority of 'real' Danes and the minority of 'not-quite-real' Danes. The latter group comprises the large group of Pakistani immigrants who have obtained Danish citizenship in the past four decades. The persistent distinction between 'real' and 'not-quite-real' Danes is not only made possible, but also perceived as legitimate, because of the widespread use of what we could call 'kinship images'. The former minister of integration, Bertel Haarder, representing the Liberal Party, used this kinship image when in 2003 he wrote about Danes in one of the major Danish newspapers:

> We [the Danes] have a job, because we care about what our family and neighbours think about us, and because we want to set a good example for our children. But foreigners do not feel these inhibitions in the same way. They live in a subculture outside the Danish tribe. That is why they so quickly learn about the possibilities for getting money [out of the welfare system] without making an effort (*Berlingske Tidende*, 20 September 2003).

Here, the minister not only offered a generalised, derogatory description of foreigners in Denmark, he also introduced an explanation for the differences between Danes and foreigners: the latter live 'outside the Danish tribe', and the ways 'they' live and think are radically different from the ways 'we' (the Danes) do so. Kinship images constitute an indigenous theory of how Danes are related to each other (Carsten 2000), and are a specific way of talking and thinking about the nation that continuously marks out who belongs to the national community and who does not. Even though they may not necessarily be intended to harm or exclude anyone, kinship images nevertheless produce and reproduce 'invisible fences' (Gullestad 2002b) between different segments of the Danish population.

This chapter discusses the basic conditions for integration in the current historical situation, where both national legislation and popular kinship images tend to distinguish between different types of citizens, and in the same process to question the legitimate rights and attachments that some groups have in relation to the nation and the welfare state. First, I explore how ideas of national relatedness are embedded in the requirement of national attachment; secondly, I analyse the notions of integration implied in the current immigration regime, and discuss how people categorised as 'not-quite-real' can aspire to become 'real' Danes.

Notions of national attachment

When the requirement of national attachment was first introduced in 2000, it was only applied to foreigners living in Denmark who were requesting family reunification. At that time, the total national attachment of the married couple was to be *at least as great* to Denmark as to any other country. When the new legislation was introduced in 2002, the requirement was changed in two ways. First, it was now applied additionally to Danish citizens marrying foreigners, and secondly, the total national attachment of the married couple now had to *be greater* to Denmark than to any other country (Jacobsen 2004: 104). These apparently minor changes had a major impact.

When the Danish Immigration Service (*Udlændingeservice*) has to decide the total national attachment of a newly-wed transnational couple applying for family reunification, it does so on the basis of various predefined parameters. These parameters have been adjusted several times since 2002, and constitute a flexible political tool when it comes to regulating which foreigners are to be allowed family reunification. In 2008, the parameters for deciding the total national attachment of a married couple were as follows:

- How long you and your spouse/partner have lived in Denmark.
- Whether one or both of you have family or other acquaintances in Denmark.
- Whether one or both of you have custody of or visiting rights to a child under the age of 18 living in Denmark.
- Whether one or both of you have completed an educational programme in Denmark, or have a solid connection to the Danish labour market.
- How well you and your spouse/partner speak Danish.
- The extent of both of your ties to any other country, including whether any or both of you have made extended visits to that country.

- Whether you have children or other family members in any other country.

The evaluation procedure amounts to a calculation which is intended to decide whether or not a married couple fulfils the requirement of national attachment and should be given permission to live together in Denmark. The following example of Nadia (from Pakistan) and Sohail (from Denmark) is a real case, taken from a report published by the Danish Institute for Human Rights (Olsen et al. 2004), where it was used to exemplify how the Immigration Service evaluates the total national attachment of a newly-wed couple:

> Sohail is twenty-five years of age, born and raised in Denmark by parents originating from Pakistan. He is a Danish citizen and his parents and siblings all live in Denmark. At the time of handing in the application, Sohail has worked continuously as a salesperson for almost six years and is furthermore representing Denmark on the national team in an unnamed sport. Nadia is a Pakistani citizen. She is twenty-four years of age and has never visited Denmark before. Nadia has a sister who is already living in Denmark, but this is not considered to be a circumstance that enhances the attachment of Nadia to Denmark. The married couple met during Sohail's holiday in Pakistan, and were soon after married. The couple communicates in Urdu. It cannot be seen in the decision whether or not Sohail has been on a longer holiday in Pakistan or if he has been there frequently. In their final decision the Immigration Service denied them family reunification because Nadia's and Sohail's total national attachment to Denmark was not seen as greater than their total national attachment to Pakistan. In the decision the Immigration Service emphasized that Nadia had no independent attachment to Denmark. (Case reproduced from Liisberg 2004: 32)

The case of Sohail and Nadia shows that Danish citizens with parents originating in another country have a hard time fulfilling the requirement of national attachment, because they lack a long family history and genealogy related to Denmark. In this case it was not enough that Sohail was a Danish citizen and had his entire family in the country, that he had worked steadily since he was nineteen and that he represented Denmark at international sports events. Despite these circumstances, Nadia's and Sohail's total national attachment to Denmark was not considered great enough.

In an ideal 'national order', there is an absolute correlation between the territorial boundaries of the nation-state and the nationality of its citizens living there. In the real world, the picture is often more blurred. Groups of immigrants, refugees, spouses and relatives who have entered the country from non-western countries and in time obtained citizenship embody the disparity between the Danish nation and Danish citizens. Despite their achieved legal status, they are still not regarded as 'real' Danes. The requirement of national attachment elevates the ongoing division within the pool of Danish citizens to a legal principle – which again legitimises the idea that some citizens have more rights to and ownership of the benefits of the welfare state than others, due to their 'natural' relatedness to the nation.

Kinship image: the family of Denmark

The power of kinship images is their ability to construct and characterise the national community through metaphors. In *Metaphors We Live By*, George Lakoff and Mark Johnson (1980) emphasise that metaphors are embedded in language, and therefore in the very ways in which we comprehend the world. A metaphor is not a single arbitrary, more or less poetic, construction, but an element in a broader structure of concepts and meanings. As an example, the nation itself is a concept we can *love, build up, nurse* or *defend* in meaningful speech-acts.

Metaphors are also grounded in bodily experiences of the physical and cultural environment. When we cope with abstract phenomena, such as the nation, we use a *Gestalt* from one domain of experience to structure another domain (Lakoff and Johnson 1980: 230). In this respect, the nation has been described metaphorically as a biological organism, for instance a body (Eriksen 1997), or as grounded in local idioms of solidarity within family and kin groups (Herzfeld 1997: 75; Gullestad 2006). The nation is also represented as complementary parental figures. On the one hand, the nation is the caring mother who protects and nurtures the children of the nation (mother's milk, mother tongue). On the other hand, the nation is described as the vigilant father, the fatherland, ready to defend the territory and the children of the nation against external aggression (Hage 2003: 31ff; Carsten 2004: 158). These examples show how we use tangible experiences from the primary sphere of the family to grasp the abstract imagined community of the nation.

In the Danish socio-political context, the notion of 'the family of Denmark' (*Familien Danmark*) is one such significant and productive kinship image. As the social anthropologist Anne Knudsen observes, there is a certain poetry to this: 'the family of Denmark has a beautiful ring to it' (*'Familien Danmark har en smuk klang'*) (Knudsen 1996: 64). This beauty is embedded in the condensed figure signalling coherence, solidarity and security, but it is also associated with peacefulness, cosiness and happiness – all values found in the ideal family. Evoking the notion of 'the family of Denmark' in public discourses is a way to speak of average people such as Jensen, Hansen or Olsen without differentiating between them or privileging one over the others. In that respect, the 'family of Denmark' also sometimes signals mediocrity, and may be used with a touch of sarcasm. It also represents the envious side of Scandinavian egalitarianism, where no one is supposed to stand out from fellow kinsmen, friends, colleagues or neighbours. The notion of the 'family of Denmark' combines real experiences (or idealised fantasies) of family life with the more abstract national community.

The 'family of Denmark' has been discussed in ethnographic studies in and of Denmark. Knudsen provides a polemical discussion of the Danish welfare state and illustrates, through numerous examples, how the family is the general model for social organisation at different levels. Relations between case-workers and clients, teachers and pupils and between medical staff and patients (and, one might add, between Danes and foreigners and between majorities and minorities) are all modelled on the structures of authority and intimacy found in the family (Knudsen 1996: 56–7). In particular, the relationship between mother and child is to be found everywhere in the Danish welfare system (Knudsen 1996: 73). Similarly, American-born anthropologist Jonathan Schwartz, who has lived and worked for decades in Denmark, notes how immigrants and refugees are often reduced to symbolic children when they are represented by the majority:

> One of the obvious differences between our [immigrants'] situation in Denmark and that of France and Britain is that voices of the settlers in the two large countries are audible. They may not be *listened to*, but at least they can be *heard* … Danish journalists, politicians, social workers and social scientists talk about us sometimes as if we were not even present – something like the way children are talked about when they misbehave or are 'so cute' (Schwartz 1990: 43, italics in original).

A number of studies conducted in Denmark are preoccupied with the same power-mechanism, and point out how dominant ideas of national 'selves' and 'others' are structured as relations between 'hosts' and 'guests' (Schwartz 1985; Hervik 1999, 2004; Rytter 2003b). The logic is straightforward: The indigenous Danes invited guestworkers from the European periphery in the 1960s and 1970s, and more or less voluntarily accepted groups of refugees and spouses who entered through family reunification. To reciprocate this gesture, the newcomers should submit to the explicit and implicit rules of the country.

There are several examples of how the Danes and the Danish nation are constructed as an imagined kinship, and how basic ideas of what it means to be a family structure the relations between majorities and minorities. Kinship images are often taken for granted, which only serves to conceal their impact. It is even difficult for the people exercising the power of 'familism' to see and understand what they are doing. They have no evil intentions, but act as they do for the common good, as they see it (Knudsen 1996: 61).

I will now go on to test the range and validity of these kinship images against some of the findings in recent anthropological studies of kinship.

Euro-American kinship

In *American Kinship*, David Schneider (1980 [1968]) explores dominant understandings of family and kinship in North America. According to Schneider, a core element of American and European kinship is the idea that 'blood is thicker than water'. Schneider finds two distinct types of family relations defined within *the order of nature* and *the order of law*, respectively.

Family and kinship relations of *the order of nature* are divided into two categories of family and kin, which are both considered variations of natural connections. First there are relations based on substance, referring to the idea that each parent provides one-half of the child's biogenetic constitution. In this respect, people are said to contain a part of their mother and of their father and therefore also parts of their grandparents, and so on. The second type of natural bond is that understood as a relation of blood. Common blood relates ego to his or her siblings, aunts, uncles, cousins, etc. Even though these are two different ideas of relatedness, they are both considered to be part of what Schneider calls *the order of nature*, and contain categories of relatives that cannot be terminated or changed, because it is never possible to have an ex-mother, ex-child or ex-brother (Schneider 1980 [1968]: 23ff.).

By contrast, family and kin belonging to *the order of law* are created through marriage, for example spouses, in-laws, the children of a spouse's previous marriages, and so on. These relations are not seen as natural but rather as purely juridical, and constituted by laws on marriage, divorce, divisions of property, inheritance and so on. These family and kinship relations can in both theory and practice be changed and replaced with similar ones (Schneider 1980 [1968]: 25ff.).

Generally, Schneider claims that family and kinship are integrated and work over time due to a 'diffuse, enduring solidarity' (Schneider 1980 [1968]: 97): 'diffuse' because the relations are not necessarily directed at any specific goal; 'enduring' because they last and are often irrevocable; 'solidarity' because they are based on mutual trust and imply – indeed, often demand – help, support and cooperation (Smedal 2001: 13).

In the history of anthropology, David Schneider's analytical approach to family and kinship was groundbreaking; it marked the transition from studying kin and family as biological and functional units, to conceptualising them as cultural and symbolic domains. In an article published in 1977, nine years after the first edition of *American Kinship*, Schneider suggests that his findings on family and kinship could also be applied to other domains such as religion or nationalism (Schneider 1977). I will try to follow this suggestion and apply his analytical vocabulary to the Danish national community and the logic behind the legislation on family reunification. The Danish people, the 'real' Danes, are part of a coherent national community based on a common history and cultural heritage. The national community too can be characterised as a diffuse, enduring solidarity. We are Danes, and we belong to the land as our parents, grandparents and ancestors did before us. Our presence within the national territory and our national citizenship (*indfødsret*) are of *the order of nature*, and comply with the global 'national order' of people and nation-states.

It is a totally different situation when we talk about the immigrants and refugees who have entered and settled in Denmark since the 1950s. They are in the country because they have been granted permission, through work permits, residence permits, asylum, etc. People from this group have, over the years, obtained Danish citizenship, but only by abandoning their original citizenship. Also the so-called second-generation immigrants, who were born and raised in Denmark and may never have had any other citizenship than Danish, are regarded as abnormal in relation to *the order of nature*, because even though they live in Denmark, they are supposed to live in another country in another part of the world. The presence of this expanding group of people is the result of *the order of law*. The people in this group are only in Denmark due to labour migration, family reunification, wars, or oppressive regimes elsewhere. Since they cannot refer to a specific national birthplace, a local place of origin, a family business or a family farm that substantiates their natural and legitimate belonging and attachment to Denmark, they are structurally excluded from being part of 'the family of Denmark'. Just as the domain of family and kinship contains different kinds of relatives, so, too, is the national community constituted by different kinds of citizens (Schneider 1977: 68). In this respect, Schneider's analysis not only explains how and why it has been legitimate to distinguish between 'real' and 'not-quite-real' Danes in the legislation on family reunification; it also captures current tendencies in Danish public and political discourses towards a more hierarchical and exclusive 'ethnic nationalism', in contrast to the previously egalitarian and inclusive 'civic nationalism' (Ignatieff 1993) that used to characterise the national community and welfare state system.

The distinction between the two categories of national citizens was further stressed in 2003, when the *Folketing* introduced law no. 1204 in order to remove some of the unintended consequences of the new immigration regime. In the summer of 2002, it became clear that the rules on family reunification affected not only arranged and forced marriages, but every transnational marriage. Expatriates who for years had served Danish interests in the diplomatic corps, as employees of NGOs or international companies all over the world were no longer allowed to bring their foreign spouses back home. Their situation was reported in the media, and soon put on the political agenda. As a result, the requirement of national attachment was supplemented by the so-called '28-year rule' (*28 års-regel*) that exempted everyone who had held Danish citizenship for at least twenty-eight years from the requirement of national attachment. As a result of this adjustment, Danes by *the order of nature* were relieved of the requirement of national attachment when they turned twenty-eight. By contrast, Danes by *the order of law*, who had often obtained Danish citizenship later in life, had to wait twenty-eight years before the requirement of national attachment was removed.

The *Folketing* introduced law no. 1204 as a necessary adjustment so that the strict rules on family reunification would not affect the 'wrong' groups of citizens (Jacobsen 2004: 115–18). However, in making this legal adjustment, national legislation was once again used to emphasise and expand the distinction between 'real' and 'not-quite-real' Danes.

Changing identities

So far Schneider has provided an analytical perspective that explains why the division of the national community, emblematised by the requirement of national attachment, is widely considered legitimate. On the other hand, his model does not allow much room for contestation or local creativity in response to the mechanisms of differentiation and submission. In this respect, a recent study conducted by Signe Howell (2001, 2003) on childless Norwegians and their ideas and practices concerning the adoption of children from Asia, Latin America and Eastern Europe is much more instructive. Howell shows how newly arrived children are soon given a position within the family that adopts them and within Norwegian society as a whole, despite the fact that the adopted children and their new parents do not share any biological substance. These adopted children are included in their adoptive families by Norwegian law, but the families also adopt symbolic gestures themselves, such as narratives and social practices, to transform the children into 'real' family members. Howell calls this process of social and cultural becoming 'kinning' (2001: 207).

In a critical discussion of the concept of integration, Abdelmalek Sayad makes a very similar observation, when he suggests that the discourse on integration is about identity. When politicians and policy-makers speak of integration, they imagine a movement 'from the most radical alterity to the most *total* identity' (Sayad 2004: 216; italics in original). This new total identity is bound to be a national identity, as the concept of integration is part of the 'identitarian' vocabulary of the nation-state (ibid.) that distinguishes between 'the children of the nation' and the aliens.

Uniting the insights of Howell and Sayad, there are resemblances between the changes a subject will have to go through when it comes to the process of *kinning* and *integration*. Both imply an ontological change in the subjects involved. They constitute specific, locally recognised ways of including aliens in the community of the family or the nation, and, by the same process, of granting them obligations, responsibilities and ownership of the common good.

In the Danish case, there are at least two processes of kinning in which citizens categorised as 'not-quite-real' Danes engage in attempts to become 'real' Danes. The first is the long-term strategy of intermarriage. The second strategy relies on various technologies, which transnational couples settled in Sweden can be subjected to.

Intermarriage as a strategy of kinning

As discussed in Chapters 3 and 4, the explicit political agenda of the new immigration regime was to reduce the inflow of newcomers by preventing transnational marriages. Immigrants with a tradition of transnational arranged marriages are urged to redirect their marriage preferences in favour of inter-ethnic and inter-religious marriages with spouses found in Denmark (see Fig. 4). The ambition of national politicians to govern the marriage market and to alter existing transnational marriage patterns in many respects resembles a state-defined preference for endogamy within Danish territory, the Danish nation and – following Bertel Haarder, the former minister of integration, quoted at beginning of this chapter – the Danish tribe.

The current legislation on family reunification assumes that the intermarriage of immigrants already residing in Denmark with ethnic Danes, together with their subsequent biological reproduction within the national territory, will inevitably make them and their offspring more Danish. It is generally assumed that during the process of kinning, immigrants will abandon their cultural idiosyncrasies within a generation or two, and start to become 'real' Danes.

In a study of transnational belonging among Somalis in Denmark, sociologist Nauja Kleist (2006) presents a case that illustrates how marriage and biological reproduction are intended gradually to relate people to 'the family of Denmark'. Saphia, a Somali woman, fled Somalia in the 1990s and went through a long transit period in an institution for asylum-seekers before she managed to establish a meaningful life in Denmark. She has, among other things, married a 'real' Danish man and given birth to their daughter. Nevertheless, the reactions their daughter meets depend on whether she is accompanied by her father or her mother. When she is with Saphia, the girl is often treated as an unwanted immigrant, whereas, in the company of her father, she is seen and treated as a lovely little girl with beautiful hair and a radiant skin (Kleist 2006: 124). Following my line of argument, one could say that in the company of Saphia the daughter is regarded as an alien. In the company of her father, however, she is perceived as a person undergoing transformation, moving away from the embodied radical alterity. She is a girl who, through the practice of kinning, is gradually being recognised as a 'real' Dane by her surroundings.

The case of Saphia illustrates how it is widely accepted in the Danish social imaginary that biological reproduction within the territory and nation initiates the process of kinning, and gives citizens who are categorised as 'not-quite-real' Danes partial rights over national places and spaces. Danish history has several examples of how aliens have been absorbed into both the local as well as the national community. The many French, Dutch and German surnames in the population bear witness to the fact that, if one goes back a sufficient number of generations in family genealogies, many forefathers of 'real' Danes are actually immigrants.

Kinning as a technology of the self

In the work of Signe Howell, kinning is an ontological change that adoptive parents can initiate in favour of their newly arrived children, but Howell does not discuss how the newly arrived children themselves can contribute to this transformation. This is actually possible in the Danish case. As the Immigration Service (*Udlændingeservice*) applies relatively few parameters in deciding the national attachment of newly-weds, it becomes possible for transnational couples to initiate and stimulate the process of kinning themselves. In this way, a couple who were first denied family reunification because their attachment to Denmark was considered insufficient can in time actually improve their record of national belonging and make the evaluation tip over in favour of Denmark. Paradoxically, this happens while they live their semi-legal family life in Sweden (see Chapter 4). In order to explain how this process takes place, I return to the case of Nadia and Sohail, who were denied family reunification because their combined national attachment was considered to be greater to Pakistan than to Denmark. I use the real case of Nadia and Sohail to set up a further, hypothetical scenario of how national attachment and belonging can be acquired.

> After his application for family reunification to Denmark is denied, Sohail decides to move to Malmö in Sweden in order to utilise his status as a European citizen to bring Nadia to Europe. He buys an apartment and leaves home. Four months later Nadia is granted permission to go to Sweden, and they start living together as husband and wife in Malmö. Sohail continues to work in Denmark, commuting across the Öresund Bridge. After a while Nadia begins to attend the local language school in order to learn Swedish. Every evening she voluntarily studies the social conditions and history of Denmark, partly by talking with Sohail and partly from books, TV and the internet. They spend almost every weekend in Denmark, where they typically spend the night in the house of Sohail's parents. Nadia soon establishes a network of female friends centred around her sister, who is already living in Denmark, and around her sisters-in-law and their friends. In time Nadia learns to speak both Swedish and Danish, and she takes a job at a shopping mall in Malmö. However, she quits her job when she becomes pregnant. After living together for two years, Nadia and Sohail are blessed with a daughter, who they decide should become a Danish citizen, just like her father.

If the Immigration Service were asked to re-evaluate the total national attachment of Nadia and Sohail after their stay in Sweden, they *might* end up deciding that they now have become much more attached to Denmark than they were two years earlier. This change has happened because they spend every weekend in Denmark, Sohail commutes to work in Denmark every day, Nadia has learned to speak Danish, and they now have a daughter with Danish citizenship. The parameters for deciding national attachment give priority to certain practices, such as command of language, level of education, work, transnational mobility and reproduction, through which transnational couples in Sweden can increase national attachment and belonging. These practices constitute a number of 'technologies of self' (cf. Foucault 1988) that married couples must subject themselves to in order to continue the process of kinning and to increase their degree of relatedness to Denmark.

As mentioned, the case of Nadia and Sohail is fictitious. In real life, it is not so easy to have a decision on national attachment re-evaluated. The Danish authorities will only deal with applicants living in Denmark, so before a re-evaluation can take place, the Danish spouse, in this case Sohail, must move back to Denmark. This also means that the foreign spouse must go back to his or her country of origin, which in this case means that Nadia must return to Pakistan. From there they can apply for family reunification in Denmark – but there are no guarantees. Few, if any, married couples dare jeopardise their possibilities of building a future together in this way.

Conclusion: integration of new Danes

Analysing the Danish legislation on family reunification, this chapter has suggested that kinship images not only delimit and characterise the national community, but also at the same time disqualify a large number of people on the basis of their family history.

I have given examples of how Danes categorised as 'not-quite-real' can work in order to change their position and status. In doing so, I present a relatively unproblematic scenario, which neglects the fact that the cultural system itself changes over time. What today constitutes a 'real' Dane will change as more and more people with an immigrant background obtain Danish citizenship, get married, and start making claims for recognition as 'real' Danes and for ownership of the nation and welfare state. Even though these groups will, in time, become part of what Schneider called *the order of nature*, they will continue to have black hair, coloured skin, names associated with other parts of the world, and not least other religious practices and affiliations than Evangelical-Lutheran Protestantism – all features that are incompatible with the title and status of being a 'real' Dane. Contemporary Danish politics has in many respects turned into a battle of identity politics, in which the criteria used to define which citizens should be recognised as 'real' Danes are contested and redefined.

However, the kinship images themselves are also changing. The notion of 'the family of Denmark' is powerful because it is capable of presenting the abstract national community as one big happy family, but due to current divorce rates the nuclear family is just one among numerous ways to organise family life. Single parents, couples 'sharing' children, the experience of having 'weekend siblings', alternative collective families, long-distance relationships of transnational families, the legal possibility of gay marriages and the right for lesbians to have artificial insemination: all are urging indigenous Danes to rethink the concept of family fundamentally. This will probably also have effects on the kinship images of the future. Upcoming generations of Danish society might not have the same kind of experiences and sentimental feelings attached to the family as those dominant today, and they will therefore probably develop new images and ideas of the abstract national community. Only time will tell whether this redefinition will make the national community more open or more restricted than it is today when it comes to distributing recognition, ownership and identity – meanwhile, hundreds of Danes with a Pakistani immigrant background continue to move to Sweden in order to achieve family reunification with their foreign spouses. In this respect the immigration regime is not only having immediate effects on Pakistani marriage preferences and practices; it is also contributing to and substantiating the developing cleavage in the Danish population between 'real' and 'not-quite-real' Danes, and ultimately between the indigenous Danish majority and the immigrant Muslim minority.

The third part of this book discusses how notions of 'homelands' are being narrated, staged and contested in and between Pakistani families in Denmark. It is clear that these inter- and intra-familial discussions have been influenced by the current situation in which many second-generation Pakistanis are moving to Sweden, and where the legitimacy, rights and belonging of Danes with an immigrant background are being questioned and undermined.

Part III

Homelands

Pakistani migrant families are situated in a transnational social field stretched out between Pakistan and Denmark (and Sweden). For migrants in the diaspora, Pakistan constitutes a 'homeland' distant in time and space, ascribed with multiple meanings. The notion of the homeland is never fixed, but inevitably subject to change over time: in personal biographies, during family cycles, or when transmitted between the first- and second-generation cohorts of migrants.

The homeland has always been a rallying point among Pakistani migrants in Denmark. Pakistan is significant in every family history and is present among first-generation elders in the narratives, experiences and (often nostalgic) memories of the people and places that formed their childhood and youth before emigration. Second-generation Pakistanis, on the other hand, often have few if any first-hand experiences of Pakistan, as they were born and raised in Denmark. To them, the homeland is mainly constituted by family narratives, community gossip, more or less pleasant experiences of holidays or longer stays with relatives, and second-hand experiences they obtain from the media. Finally, Pakistan also becomes salient among first-, second- and even third-generation immigrants in Denmark, when again and again they are confronted with the inevitable question, 'Where do you come from?', referring to the phenotypic markers of skin colour, brown eyes and dark hair that often distinguish citizens of immigrant origin from the indigenous majority of 'real' Danes. Even though many migrants may consider Denmark to be their homeland after four decades abroad, their aspirations to belong in Denmark are often not recognised in the wider society.

Since their settlement in Denmark in the 1960s and 1970s, Pakistani migrants have been involved in transnational activities in order to maintain intimate relationships with people and places back home. In the early years, this happened through letters, long-distance telephone calls and occasional return visits to the family back home. More recently, contemporary means of telecommunication and cheap tickets for the numerous air routes connecting Europe and South Asia have improved these options. Migrants have sent remittances in order to support relatives in Pakistan, erected multi-storey houses on family land and invested in the infrastructure, sanitation and general modernisation of their villages or local mosques. And, as discussed in Chapters 3 and 4, arranged marriages within the transnational *biraderi* have over the years been an important way to confirm or create bonds between families, despite decades of separation. Lately, due to the demographic development of the migrant community, an increasing number of dead bodies are being transported to Pakistan and buried in their villages of origin (Rytter 2005). These various transnational activities have been a means to create or maintain emotional and material connections with significant people and places in Pakistan. In this respect the homeland has always been there.

Local media stories and moral panics of recent years, however, have contributed to giving Pakistan a bad image with the Danish public. Likewise, several international events – such as Pakistan's increased military confrontations with Taliban and al-Qaeda, US special forces' assassination of Osama Bin Laden, fierce demonstrations against Denmark during the cartoon controversy, or the suicide attack on the Danish embassy in Islamabad in 2008 – have given Pakistan a prominent, but unflattering, position in the media (see Chapter 1). The negative exposure also affects Pakistani families in Denmark and their notions of home and homelands. On the one hand, migrants are proud of their national background and origin, but on the other, many also acknowledge problematic aspects of Pakistani society, such as poverty, violence, corruption, fundamentalism, including various social and cultural practices they thought they had put behind them in the process of migration. Part III of the book discusses how the meanings of Pakistan as a homeland are contested and negotiated between the first and second generations within migrant families in Denmark.

Chapter 6 discusses how families over the years have attempted to return to Pakistan. For several reasons, the project has often failed; many have. moved back to Denmark, disappointed and shocked at being unable to live in Pakistan and be reintegrated in their families or villages of origin. However, currently the idea of return has resurfaced, as the highly educated second generation turn to Pakistan because they want to give their children a proper upbringing in a Muslim country, or start up different transnational companies and businesses. Still, individual members of migrant families often have differing aspirations and ideas as to whether or not to return, and Chapter 6 discusses how parents and children, husbands and wives are struggling to define whether the homeland of the family is Pakistan or Denmark.

In Chapter 7 the perspective is again the Danish context, as I discuss an 'imagined return' in the guise of a stage play written and performed by members of the OPSA (the Organisation of Pakistani Students and Academics). The narrative of the play, concerning a family who return to Pakistan on their summer holiday after decades in Denmark, evoked strong sentiments of patriotism and national pride in the actors and the audience, sentiments that were not necessarily articulated among OPSA members in other situations or contexts. The stage play became a means for the second generation to negotiate sensitive issues related to contested notions of homelands, identity and belonging with their parents.

Finally, Chapter 8 focuses on the period of 'intensive transnationalism' in the Pakistani community in Denmark following the earthquake in Kashmir in October 2005. By analysing the waxing and waning of the ad hoc association, Medical Doctors in Assistance of the Earthquake Victims in Pakistan, I discuss how the catastrophe in Pakistan became a vehicle to confirm, contest or redefine notions of identity and belonging within the rising elite of medical doctors and the migrant community in Denmark more generally. In its own tragic way, the disaster made Pakistan stand out as an undisputed 'momentary homeland' in the migrant community – but only for a while.

Generally speaking, all three chapters provide empirical findings that substantiate my overall argument that notions of homelands are open to negotiation and contestation within and between Pakistani migrant families. This is why I refer to 'homelands' in the plural.

Chapter 6

Pakistan – Denmark

Back and forth

'Old people love Pakistan, their children hate it!' Mr Shah snapped impatiently, in response to my series of questions about returnee families and the potential intergenerational problems such returns may involve, when I visited him for the first time in the office of his tile factory outside Kharian. Back in 1990 he sold his business in Copenhagen and returned to Pakistan with his wife and two sons, and settled in an impressive three-storey house just outside his native village. But Mrs Shah, who had been born and raised in the United Kingdom, found it very difficult to adapt and accept the new living conditions in the rural village, so she soon moved out and settled in Britain with their two sons, leaving Mr Shah alone in Pakistan with the responsibility for their big house, his newly opened factory and the dream of returning to Pakistan. Today, both sons are adults. They do not share their father's vision of reuniting in Pakistan and taking over the factory and family business. Mr Shah's conclusion – that 'children hate Pakistan' – was probably based on experiences with his own sons.

This chapter is about return migration, or more precisely about the recurring dreams and attempts at return that are salient in the life stories and family histories of Pakistani migrants. When a family returns after years or even decades in Denmark, it is not necessarily all members of the family involved that support the decision. People have differing opinions, aspirations and interests in preferring to live in one or the other country (or a third country, for that matter). Russell King (2000: 13–18) lists four reasons for labour migrants to return: (1) economic: either economic development in the homeland, or general economic downturns in the country of immigration; (2) social: such as homesickness, nostalgia, experience of racism, the desire for enhanced status at home; (3) family/life-cycle, including kinship ties to and retirement in the country of origin; and (4) political: changing policies, whether in the country of immigration or of origin, or both. This chapter suggests a fifth reason. Return migration among Pakistani migrants settled in Denmark is often an attempt to pursue and realise an idealised vision of the family that is an integral part in shared images of Pakistan. In contrast to the often disappointing situation in Denmark, where treasured family values and relations seem to become corrupted, break down or disappear, Pakistan comes to represent a place of moral superiority, where there is the time, will, economy and plenty of room in the multi-storey migrant house to recreate a well-functioning, caring and happy extended family.

Many first-generation migrants dream of returning to Pakistan so they can spend the last years of their life in the place they grew up, surrounded by siblings, cousins, children and grandchildren. When relating their life stories and family histories, elders often explain how, once or several times, they have tried to realise the dream of returning to Pakistan, but ended up moving back to Denmark because it was too difficult for them to accept the bureaucracy and corruption, because they needed some sort of medical treatment, or because the possibilities of providing their children with a good education were much better in Denmark (cf. Bajaj and Laursen 1988: 53). Returnees also explain that they experienced being treated as strangers and foreigners in their native village, sometimes even by their own relatives, and that they soon began to miss family members and friends who had remained in Denmark. A survey conducted in Rødovre municipality shows that older migrants from Turkey and Pakistan may wish to return, but only on the condition that their children and grandchildren join them; otherwise they prefer to stay in Denmark (Mølgaard and Lindblad 1995: 129). In such cases, emotional connections with close family members are more important than the longing to return.

Among the upcoming generation, I found a general scepticism towards moving permanently to Pakistan. People prefer to stay in Denmark, where they were born, raised and where they have their friends and social networks. However, this general picture seems to be changing. Many express a smouldering frustration that they, as children of immigrants and as a religious minority, are, almost on a daily basis, portrayed in the national media as a social problem or security issue, subjected to demeaning taunting on the streets and hateful stares at the supermarket, or rejected, due to their foreign names, when applying for apartments or jobs. According to most of my interlocutors, such incidents have intensified since September 11 (cf. Koefoed and Simonsen 2010; Mikkelsen et al. 2010; Jakobsen 2011; Khawaja 2011). Experiences like these substantiate the frequently held belief that Muslim immigrants are not politically or socially recognised as the equals of 'real' Danes, which again motivates discussions within the second generation of whether or not to move their families to Pakistan or some other country in order to escape the stigma and experience of being second-rate citizens. In this respect, Marta Bolognani suggests that current return migration has become much more idealistic, as Pakistan is being presented as a place where it is possible to escape European racism and Islamophobia (2007b: 65–6).

This chapter discusses the experiences, obstacles and disappointments confronting Pakistani families when they attempt to return to the 'homeland' and re-establish the shared family ideals of an ideal family.

Preparing to return

In the 1970s and 1980s, most Pakistani migrants expected to return. It was not a question of whether or not to move back, but when the inevitable return would take place. In this respect, the first generation of migrants shared a 'myth of return' (Anwar 1979), where, in a combination of economic reasoning and growing homesickness, they prepared to go back to Pakistan. However, the return was postponed again and again, because there was always a little more money to be made, another child to be born, etc. As Anders Stefansson puts it: 'Many exiles evoke "next year in Jerusalem", "next year in Havana", etc., but with the passing of time the likelihood that the dream of return will be carried out seems to diminish' (2003: 116).

One example of how a family's plans to return were taken up for reconsideration is illustrated by the narrative of Mr Rasool, who was only seventeen when he left his family back in Sialkot. From 1968 to 1970 he worked illegally in Germany, but when some of his old classmates in Denmark invited him to join them and obtain legal residence there, he did so. In Denmark he lived in a small apartment on Vesterbro; first alone, later together with his new wife and their children. While in the early years Mrs Rasool mainly took care of the children, Mr Rasool worked as a manual labourer in different factories. In 1977 he bought his first taxi and started what later turned out to be a very successful taxi business. I provide a relatively long quotation from one of our recorded conversations in order to let Mr Rasool explain his changing attitude towards Pakistan:

> It is every foreigner's dream one day to return. I had that dream too. I had planned that in December 1982 I would return. That would be my last day abroad. I wanted to return because I cared so much for my father and wanted to be with him. Therefore, I enrolled Ali [his son] in a boarding school in Pakistan. In Denmark children are six when they start at school but in Pakistan they are four, and there are high demands. If you later on want to enter the military or the state bureaucracy, age is very important. You have to be well educated at a young age, otherwise you do not stand a chance. So in order not to ruin the future prospects of my son I sent him to Pakistan … [pause]. When I went there [to Pakistan] in late 1982 I was ready to move back. It was the first time I came to Pakistan to stay permanently. I had visited my father several times for two, three or four months at a time. However, back in Pakistan I soon realised that I had grown away from Pakistan. My mind and patterns of reactions had become too European. I had always been very outspoken. If I saw something which I considered to be a wrongdoing, if for example I saw a person being exploited by someone in power, I would interfere and say: 'What are you doing? Who do you think you are?' But that is not something you do in Pakistan. So I ended up at the local police station. And if I had stayed in Pakistan I probably would have been arrested every week. So I had to decide either to change myself and become more egoistic or to simply stay in Denmark. Still I hoped that … well, it took me a couple of years to accept that it [Pakistan] was no longer a place for me. When I finally reached that conclusion, I immediately took my son out of the boarding school and brought him to Denmark. When I could not live in Pakistan, there was no reason for him to stay there either.

Today, Ali, Mr Rasool's son, is making his career in an international company. I have known him for several years and have always been intrigued by the way he mixes Danish, English and Urdu in conversation. One afternoon, while the three of us were having tea, Ali explained, on his own initiative, that his mixed language was the result of his father's decision to send him to Pakistan. His father's decision back then deprived him of having a single language today. Judging from Mr Rasool's intense stare into his teacup, I assume he agreed.

While several parents in the 1970s and 1980s sent their children to boarding schools or placed them with relatives in Pakistan to prepare them for the inevitable return, others enrolled their children in one of the two Pakistani private schools (*friskoler*) in Copenhagen: the Jinnah International School or the Iqbal International School, which opened in 1984 and 1986 respectively. A study of one of these schools finds that parents enrol their children so that lessons in Urdu and teachings in the Quran can become an integral part of their school education. Another important reason is the prolonged uncertainty over whether the family will, in time, actually return (Shakoor 2004: 14); by sending the children to a Pakistani private school, parents feel that the option of return is still open.

Imagined homelands

Pakistanis who have lived abroad for decades are divided between two significant places in the transnational social field, *desh* and *pardesh*. Referring to his material on Punjabi migrants in Britain, Roger Ballard discusses the meaning attributed to *desh* and *pardesh*. Using her material on Bangladeshi migrants in Britain, Katy Gardner discusses the meanings attributed to *desh* and *bidesh*. In my readings of the work, the difference is mainly between Urdu and Bangla, not so much in the conversations of 'home' and 'abroad'. *Desh* is the place of inalienable family land associated with fertility, spirituality and religiosity (Gardner 1993: 5ff.). In contrast, *pardesh* can be translated as 'a home abroad' (Ballard 1994: 5) and is associated with economic and political power that is not accessible in *desh*. But, even though *pardesh* potentially means prosperity and social mobility, it is not an unconditionally desirable place to live. Modern life in the West is often regarded as amoral and heathen, and people in these parts of the world are believed to be struggling with less favourable symptoms of decay (anomie) such as promiscuity, alcoholism or a high number of divorces.

Katy Gardner's ethnography (2002), based on life stories narrated by first-generation Bengalis at a centre for the elderly in Tower Hamlets in East London, discusses how notions of *desh* and *pardesh* are contested. The life stories of the older generation reflect their structural position as aging immigrants in a diaspora context they find it difficult to understand and navigate in. A common disturbing experience is that the family institution is changing at a rapid rate, as manifest in the fact that families break up and their elders are left to fend for themselves. Especially the second generation are blamed for this moral decay, as they tend to neglect the generalised reciprocity that is crucial to the continuation of vertical family relations. In contrast to this disappointment, the past in Bangladesh is remembered and narrated as a superior moral order, where family members fulfilled their duties and obligations and took care of one another, especially in relation to respecting and taking care of the elders of the family.

The way in which members of the older generation actively engage with memories of life in Bangladesh in order to explain (or at least make some sense of) their currently less favourable situation in the diaspora results in the kinds of representations that Salman Rushdie (1992) calls 'imaginary homelands'. Imaginary homelands are created when personal experiences, memories of specific episodes and sense impressions from everyday life in the country of origin are transmitted from the first generation, who had the experiences, to the second generation, who have no such experiences. Similarly, the narratives and nostalgic memories of the first generation of migrants in Denmark tend to make of Pakistan an 'imaginary homeland', where the hard everyday life and limited possibilities of the past have become less important or have simply been forgotten. This nostalgic image of Pakistan contrasts with shared experiences of Denmark as a place where family values are changing, and losing importance. Everyone has examples from their own families or networks of friends, business partners or neighbours that seem to confirm the tendency that the formerly stable family institution is subject to change. I give four brief examples of this disturbing tendency.

1. **Authority.** In the villages where the majority of first-generation Pakistani migrants grew up, the right to make crucial decisions in relation to the public sphere was often a prerogative of the oldest male family members, while decisions in relation to the domestic sphere were managed by the senior women of the family (see Eglar 1960; Lefebvre 1999). In Denmark, however, seniority does not automatically lead to this kind of privileged position. Many older Pakistanis today have left, or are about to leave, the labour market. Some live on welfare benefits or pensions, due to unemployment or early retirement resulting from severe health problems (diabetes, osteoarthritis, etc.). In the first generation there are also many – especially women, who have been taking care of the domestic sphere and raising the children – who struggle to speak and understand Danish. They often have to rely on their children as translators, which can disturb or even reverse the parent-child relationship – a circumstance that undermines the authority of the first generation.

2. **Gender.** Traditional gender roles are being challenged by the upcoming generation. Many women in the second generation prefer to have a career rather than be a housewife dedicated solely to taking care of husband, children and parents-in-law. In their own upbringing, members of the second generation have attended day-care institutions (*vuggestuer/ børnehaver*), public schools (*folkeskoler*) and higher educational institutions,

and they have also been actively engaged in leisure-time activities outside the household, such as sports clubs or political and religious youth organisations. All these institutions have provided the second generation with numerous possibilities to mingle with representatives of the opposite sex outside the protected sphere of the household and the controlling gaze of family members. Due to differences in the upbringing of the first and second generations, every Pakistani family must renegotiate gender roles and decide to what extent and in which situations they will observe *purdah*, the code of gender segregation, or for instance, to what extent it is acceptable for the second generation to have friends of the opposite sex.

3. **Marriage and divorce.** One thing, however, that both first- and second-generation Pakistanis seem to agree on is that the institution of marriage is going through a radical and disturbing change. As discussed in Chapter 3, the institution of the arranged marriage is being challenged by the trend towards love marriages. Another problematic aspect is the growing number of divorces. The latest figures on divorce, dating back to 1999, show that six to seven per cent of Pakistanis in Denmark aged 30–34 are divorced (Schmidt and Jakobsen 2000: 132). It is my impression that divorces today have become much more common. When discussing the issue with my interlocutors, they also explain that there are more divorces today than just ten years ago – and that compared with the number of divorces their parents experienced in their youth in Pakistan before coming to Denmark, the numbers have exploded! Today it is not uncommon for the second generation in particular to divorce, if marriage does not fulfil individual expectations. As Naem, not married back then, said with a smile: 'Maybe we Pakistanis are actually becoming Danish!'.

4. **Age.** Many older Pakistanis are concerned about their old age and whether or not their offspring will take care of them in the future (Mølgaard and Lindblad 1995; Moen 2002; Mian 2007). In the patrilocal household, it is traditionally the duty and obligation of sons and in-married wives to live with and take care of aging parents, but many Pakistani parents do not have living accommodation of sufficient size for their sons and daughters-in-law to live with them. Others have to accept that their sons and daughters-in-laws simply do not want to live with them, but prefer to have their own place (see Chapters 3 and 9). Available figures show that only fifteen percent of Pakistanis in Denmark actually live in households consisting of a married couple and one of the partner's parents (Schmidt 2002: 66).

These four tendencies regarding authority, gender, marriage and age contribute to the disturbing experience that the family institution has started to fall apart. In sharp contrast to the growing disappointments of everyday family life in Denmark are the glorious memories and anecdotes of Pakistan. In this way, an idealised image of the extended family is given a central position in the vision of the 'imagined homeland' that is remembered, narrated and circulated in the migrant community. The *desh* of Pakistan is reconfigured as a morally uncorrupted place, where family members, regardless of age and gender, have the necessary resources of time, economy and physical space (in terms of living accommodation) to care for one another both practically and emotionally. In this respect the imagined homeland of Pakistan is associated with an idealised family life, in contrast to the disappointing real-life experiences of Denmark.

In the following sections I will turn to Pakistan, and discuss some of the numerous difficulties that have confronted returnees of the first and second generations in their quest for the 'imaginary homeland' and idealised images of family life.

His father's son

When I visited Kazim in 2004, he had just finished building his father's house in their village near Jhelum. At that time Kazim had been living in Pakistan for five months with his wife and their three children aged 11, 10 and 5. Even though the house was on a narrow gravel road, it looked palatial. It had three storeys with tiles, expensive furniture, a satellite dish and air conditioning, and was surrounded by walls and guarded by an armed watchman. The house was built on a piece of family land that Kazim's father had inherited from his father, and was close to where his father's aging siblings lived with their families.

Originally Kazim's parents came from villages in Punjab, but years ago they moved to Rawalpindi when the father was offered an appointment as a schoolteacher. This was where Kazim was born. When he turned three, his father emigrated, and Kazim, his mother and siblings were left behind. Their father quickly succeeded in finding a job in Denmark. The money he made enabled his wife to send the children to an English private school, instead of the public school. The remittances meant that the household was equipped with luxury articles like a refrigerator, a colour TV and a bicycle for Kazim. The living standards of the family were better than all the others in the street, and once a year the father returned to visit his wife and children.

In Denmark, Kazim's father was engaged in helping his fellow countrymen. Educated as a teacher, he had a good basis for learning Danish quickly, and his ability to speak and read the language soon became a competence that many migrants benefited from in the newly established and growing Pakistani community. Over the years he cultivated a large network of friends in the Copenhagen area. In 1984 the father applied for family reunification for his wife and four children. Approval was given, so Kazim arrived at the age of seventeen with his mother and siblings and moved into a small apartment in Vesterbro, where they had to learn to live with their father. Kazim started at a language school and attended a shorter period of education, which he never finished because he was unable to find an apprenticeship. Instead, he had different jobs cleaning public buildings or delivering newspapers. Later he started driving a taxi. Kazim nurtured the friendships he established in the language school after arriving to Denmark, and he also became friends with several of the Pakistanis who visited his father, but he never made any Danish friends.

In his narrative, Kazim presented himself as a man with little success in his career or social life. The less favourable representation of his own merits was contrasted with his accounts of his father and his younger brother, who had become a successful IT worker with a large Danish company. Kazim's decision to return to Pakistan was therefore made out of a combination of resignation in relation to his marginal position in Danish society and his longing for the Pakistan where he grew up. So in 2003 Kazim decided to return.

But Kazim was no longer alone. In 1992 he had married a cousin in England and was blessed with three children. The marriage was arranged by his father and uncle. His wife, who had also lived part of her childhood in Pakistan, strongly objected to the idea of moving back.

> Moving back to Pakistan was a tough decision because I was the only one who wanted to return. Even my wife objected. We talked about it for hours. What are we supposed to do down there? What shall the children do? How are we going to support ourselves? What about the heat in the summer? Which school should we send our children to? And what about our economy? Why leave Denmark? So it was a really tough decision [Kazim].

But Kazim had made up his mind. In order to explain to me (and maybe also to himself) why it was so important for him to return to Pakistan, he made an explicit comparison between himself and his brother:

> My brother is typically Danish: he does not want to live in Pakistan, but only wants to visit on holidays. He was only six when he came to Denmark. I was seventeen – that makes a difference. I have discussed it [returning to Pakistan] with him, but he does not want to come here. He speaks Urdu, but can neither read nor write it … I, on the other hand, was born in Pakistan – that is why I miss it more than my brother. He was born in Denmark [during one of their mother's visits], and that is why he does not miss Pakistan. Of course we talk about Pakistan. And I am perfectly aware of the many ugly things, like the traffic, the corruption, the noise, the uncertainty, but I miss Pakistan nevertheless – otherwise I would not be here [Kazim].

Kazim's explanation captures a general tendency in most of the interviews I have conducted with returnees in Pakistan. It was very common for them to miss Pakistan while they were in Denmark: it was almost as if they lacked an important part of themselves. But when they returned to Pakistan, they soon realised that they now missed aspects of life in Denmark. In their ambivalence and in their physical and imagined movements between Pakistan and Denmark, migrants embody a restlessness, an inability to be 'at home' (Gardner 2002: 210). The two countries fulfil different functions and needs, and migrants may simultaneously be drawn to and repelled by both.

Intractable parents

The disagreement between Kazim and his wife and brother illustrate how individual family members may have different preconditions and motives for preferring a life in either Denmark or Pakistan. These kinds of differences are also to be found between adult children and aging parents, or between parents and non-adult children.

I visited Nadeem and his family in Islamabad. They lived in an extended family consisting of Nadeem, his wife and four children, and his parents and three minor siblings. Nadeem was born in Pakistan, but moved to Denmark in 1971 with his parents. While their children were young, his parents, Mr and Mrs Butt, tried a couple of times to return to Pakistan, mainly because they did not want their children to grow up in Denmark as immigrants, as had Nadeem's father during his own childhood as an immigrant from Kashmir living in the Punjabi lowlands. Despite these attempts, the family returned to Denmark, the first time because they did not have the economic means to maintain the same living standard in Pakistan as they had in Denmark, the second time because Mr and Mrs Butt recognised that the best educational options for their children were in Denmark. However, the third time they were lucky. As a trained medical doctor from Denmark, Nadeem had a well-paid job at a hospital in Norway, where he worked intensively for a week or two every month. The rest of the time he lived in Pakistan with his family. Because of this 'mobile livelihood' (Olwig and Sørensen 2002), Nadeem, his wife and parents had the economic means to realise their dream of living together as an extended family, at least most of the time. However, life in Islamabad was difficult for the parents, who preferred to stay in their less luxurious house back in the father's village near Jhelum, close to old friends and relatives. According to Mr Butt, living in Islamabad was 'just like living in Denmark': people stayed inside their big houses and kept to themselves. The only life in the streets was provided by the guards, who stood in front of the houses in the neighbourhood, smoking and gossiping.

In the same way, Kazim also had to realise that his parents did not share his dream of returning to Pakistan unconditionally:

> Kazim: I would like for my parents to move to Pakistan. They have worked enough. My father is more than sixty and my mother more than fifty. In two years my father will get his pension. I have discussed it [returning to Pakistan] with him, but all he says is: wait two years! I want to bring him to Pakistan, even though he does not want to. I want him to move back to Pakistan because this is the place where his brother and sisters live. He has been away from them for so long, and now he has only little time left to be with his family. The main reason for building this house was that his [the father's] siblings could come and visit him …
>
> Mikkel: (interrupts) Does your father not want to go back?
>
> Kazim: No, he does not want to. He prefers to stay in Denmark. I will wait for two years, but when he turns 65, he has to come. We can make him move to Pakistan.

Apparently Kazim's father does not share his dream of return. He has his own life, including a job, a wife, three children and grandchildren and most of his social network in Denmark. He is not willing to give all that up just to comply with the wishes of his oldest son.

The two cases of Kazim and Nadeem illustrate how the formal authority to define what is best for the family is being transferred from father to son within the family structure. Nadeem's parents have already given their economically successful son the right to make many family decisions. They just wish to stay for a period each summer in the house in the village. Kazim, on the other hand, has to be patient and wait for his father to reach pension age before he can make him come to Pakistan and complete the ideal of a happy extended family that motivated Kazim to return in the first place. Bringing his parents to Pakistan, however, is also a strategy to overcome the loneliness he and his wife and children experience in the isolated house in the village. Kazim does not really have any relations in the village. All his personal memories and social networks are connected to his upbringing in Rawalpindi; so they seldom leave the house, but stay inside behind the tall walls.

The two cases emphasise that Pakistan is a contested site, and a space ascribed different meanings. The migrants are not only transnationals belonging to Denmark and Pakistan; they are also to a large extent translocals, as it is very specific local sites in Denmark and Pakistan that they are related to (cf. Pedersen 2009: 6). When Pakistan is constructed as an 'imaginary homeland', it is on the basis of more or less concrete, but always absolutely personal memories and experiences of 'home' and belonging. For Nadeem's parents this is not Islamabad, but the house and everyday life among friends and relatives in their native village. For Kazim, it is his childhood memories of Rawalpindi.

The mutiny of the children

My fieldwork suggests that children in particular find it difficult to move to Pakistan. Children are formally subjected to the will and decisions of their parents. When migrant parents decide to return, the children are removed from their well-known environment and taken to another part of the world, where everyday life is organised in new ways. This sudden replacement can result in dissatisfaction or grief (cf. Anderson 1998; Olwig 1998). Kazim's children objected in different ways to their father's decision to move the family back to Pakistan:

> Mikkel: you have three children. Two of them go to school in Denmark ...
>
> Kazim: (Interrupts) Yes. They do now, but they will not continue to do so ... we came down here five months ago. I will not put pressure on my children and force them to live in Pakistan. They were happy here the first three or four weeks, but as time passed by, they started to miss Denmark, and they only spoke in Danish to each other. They had no playmates here. They just sat passively and were bored. They did not want to stay in Pakistan, even though I gave them everything they asked for – they had a computer, Playstation, internet, DVD, etc. I gave them everything, but they were not happy about living here.

Kazim and his wife therefore decided to send the two oldest children back to Denmark to live with their grandparents. The youngest daughter at five still lived in the house; she did not have the same resources or capital as her elder siblings to formulate her wish to go back to Denmark. Nevertheless, Kazim was well aware that she missed Denmark, because every day she talked about the teachers and the children from her kindergarten.

Migrants like Kazim and Nadeem move their family back to Pakistan in order to cope with their restlessness and feelings of incompleteness. Return migration is a strategy to overcome years of alienation in Denmark. However, by moving to Pakistan they risk passing on the same feelings of restlessness and incompleteness to their children. The case of Kazim shows that, even though his children might be considered strangers or aliens in some situations in Denmark because of their immigrant background, it is nevertheless where they have their primary experiences and references. In Pakistan, on the other hand, returnees are often looked upon as 'Danes' by neighbours and relatives. For various reasons children (of the second or third generation) do not always share their parent's conception of Pakistan as *desh*. They often see Denmark as their homeland.

When I returned to Pakistan in 2007, Nadeem had moved into a new house in an even more fashionable part of Islamabad with his wife and children. His parents and siblings lived close by in another new house. The splitting of the household and family had not been dramatic, and they still lived close together and continued to share time, meals and decisions. According to both Nadeem and his parents, it was a more convenient solution for everyone to live in two houses, and despite the split, their image of the extended family was still intact. Since my first visit, Nadeem's oldest daughter had blossomed into a young woman, and his latest headache was what he should do with the teenager in the future. He wanted her to have an education from a European university in either Britain or Denmark, but he would not allow her to go by herself. Instead he considered whether he, his wife or his younger brother should escort the girl to Europe, to keep an eye on her.

Kazim, on the other hand, had to realise that no one else in his family shared his dream of return. He had no job, and during the last five months they had been living on their savings, but now money had become scarce. Kazim's plan was to drive a taxi in Copenhagen in order to support the family. He estimated that after a year of hard work he could support the family for approximately four years. Still, he admitted that he had started to miss Denmark himself. When I came back in 2007 I did not succeed in finding Kazim, but I learned from one of his previous neighbours that his wife and daughter had returned to Denmark. Kazim himself had moved to Rawalpindi, where he was trying to start up a business with one of his friends. It seems that the first round of the domestic struggle to decide the future of the family had been won by Kazim's wife, daughter and aging father.

Pakistan as a new beginning

Pakistan has in recent years become a significant site in the global war against terror. The armed confrontations in the northern regions, along with episodes like the murders of the American journalist Daniel Pearl in 2002 and the former national leader Benazir Bhutto in 2007, the brutal clearing of the Lal Masjid (the Red Mosque) and the increasing numbers of suicide bombs in major cities like Islamabad, Peshawar, Lahore or Karachi have been intensely covered by the international media and have contributed to creating an image of Pakistan as a dangerous place governed by religious fundamentalists and sectarian violence. Pakistanis in Denmark are also concerned about this development. After Islamabad's fashionable Marriott Hotel was demolished by a suicide bomber in September 2008, many interlocutors related how they (or some of their local friends or relatives) had just been driving by earlier the same day or how they planned to go to the hotel for *iftar* a couple of days later. In this respect, the war against terror is no longer a virtual war in the media, or something that takes place in the remote northern areas: it has become a concern that migrants returning to Pakistan for holidays or longer visits have to take into consideration. However, the image of Pakistan as a place of religious extremism is also challenged – for instance by Mr Latif and his family.

Mr Latif, a middle-aged man, was born in one of the villages around Kharian and had seen most of his family migrate to either Denmark or Norway. The youngest of five sons, he had inherited the house in the village when his parents died within a few years of one another in the late 1990s. But he did not live there. Instead he rented a fashionable house in Islamabad (where we met), and only went to the village once in a while. According to him there was 'too much family in the village'. Back in 1986 Mr Latif came to Denmark, where he worked in a restaurant and a factory before opening his own corner shop. In 2003 he sold the corner shop and started working as a taxi-driver instead.

In 2005, Mr Latif returned to Pakistan with his wife, two daughters and a teenage son. He was well aware that it was very difficult for the children to return, because 'they are actually too old to make such a move'. The reason for their return was that his sixteen-year-old son had started to get into trouble in Copenhagen. Within a short period he had become very religious and had started to hang out with a group of 'Arab boys' involved in Hizb ut-Tahrir. In Denmark, this Islamist organisation recruits new members within the growing segment of frustrated young Muslims, both immigrants and converts. According to the ideology of Hizb ut-Tahrir, Islam is a consistent system, a total way of life providing guidance in matters of politics, faith, economics, health and everyday life in general (cf. Sinclair 2008). Enrolled members tend to be absorbed in the politico-religious ideology, and agitate at public meetings and seminars for what they consider to be a righteous Islamic way of life and for the re-emergence of the Islamic caliphate. It may have severe effects on local family life when young people suddenly become 'new-born religious' and absorbed in the ideology of the organisation. The politician and medical doctor, Ikram Sarwar, has publicly related how his family became divided because his two younger brothers joined Hizb ut-Tahrir (*Politiken*, 10 February 2008).

Not particularly religious himself, and well aware of all the problems that devoted Hizb ut-Tahrir members may cause in their families and surroundings, Mr Latif decided to move to Pakistan. The object was to remove his son from what he considered to be a problematic fundamentalist environment, and to take him to Pakistan, where he could learn about his background, heritage and culture. Even though Mr Latif wanted his son to finish his education in Pakistan, he acknowledged that as a Danish citizen he could move back to Denmark as soon as he turned eighteen. Mr Latif's strategy to return to Pakistan in order for his son to be less religious contradicts dominant assumptions both about Pakistan as an Islamic nation-state and the explicit motive of many returnees: to move to Pakistan in order for their children to have a proper religious upbringing in an Islamic society. Nonetheless, Mr Latif saw Pakistan as a chance to bring his son back on the right track.

Strategies of old age

Aging, and old age as such, is a stage at the end of life that people prepare for, one way or another. While the Danish welfare state provides nursing homes for older citizens in need of care, older Pakistanis often call this option their worst nightmare. It would not only be physically and emotionally difficult for them to live alone, away from their children and grandchildren, but also extremely embarrassing to be abandoned by your own family. Nonetheless, in her study of older Pakistani immigrants in Denmark, sociologist Saira Latif Mian finds that men tend to have a more realistic (or cynical) perspective, as they prefer to end up in a nursing home rather than become a burden to their adult children and family in general (2007: 76ff.). Another option in old age is to return to Pakistan.

Building on the migration history of Pakistanis in Britain, Kaveri Harriss and Alison Shaw identify four distinct phases of migration: 1) the *male labour migration* in the 1950s, 1960s and 1970s; 2) the phase of *family reunion* that occurred from the mid-1960s through to the 1980s; 3) the phase of *marriage migration*, beginning in the 1980s and continuing throughout the 1990s; and 4) a fourth phase of *migration for family care*, which entails long- or short-term migration for the care of elderly kin (Harriss and Shaw 2009). In another article, Shaw introduces the term 'de facto childless' referring to aging migrants who cannot rely on their children because relationships have broken down or because the children have physical or mental disabilities, lack the resources to offer support or have moved away (Shaw 2004: 208). The two scenarios of 'migration for family care' and of being 'de facto childless' informed Ms Khan's decision to return to Pakistan. Ms Khan is a woman in middle age. She came to Denmark in 1975 through family reunification after her parents accepted a *rishta* from the family of a male migrant who was already living and working in Denmark. But the marriage was never happy, partly because Ms Khan and her husband never succeeded in having any children, and partly because her husband, according to Ms Khan, treated her disrespectfully and had several extramarital affairs. In the end Ms Khan demanded a divorce and has lived alone ever since. Today she has returned to Pakistan in order to take care of her widowed father and to prepare for her own old age. As a childless, single, middle-aged woman, Ms Khan has accepted that she will never have any children, and that she therefore has to accept the position of an – at best – respected and beloved 'auntie' in the family system. Therefore she dedicates some of her remaining time and money to charity:

> I want to spend my savings on humanitarian work in Pakistan. My mother is dead, my father does not need my money and all my siblings are abroad. I have no children, so no one will inherit my possessions. Instead I will use all of my money in setting up a health clinic in my village. I have already found a piece of land. I plan to call it *Nordic Trust* [Ms Khan].

Another reason for returning to Pakistan is Ms Khan's concerns about her old age. Who will take care of her in her last years, and who will say *dua* (prayers) at her grave when she is dead?

> I want to die in Pakistan. Among us [Muslims] it is a religious question – when we die, we believe that if you are buried among fellow Muslims, that you have the blessing of God, and that our family members will come and pray for us and our Sunna. But if I am buried in Denmark, no one would ever come by. That is the reason why I return to Pakistan. It is both for emotional and religious reasons [Ms Khan].

Beside the religious motivation to give and to share her wealth with people in need, Ms Khan not only wants to make a difference in the local area, but also hopes to make an impact on her relatives and the people around her, so that some of them will take care of her later in her life and commemorate her and pray for her after she is dead.

Finally, I return to Mr Shah, whom I quoted at the beginning of this chapter, in order to show how strategies of old age may also involve the creation of new family-like relations.

After Mr Shah sold his business in 1990 and returned to Pakistan with his wife and two sons, he succeeded in starting up a factory that produces and distributes the colourful tiles that are used to decorate the numerous migrant houses. When Mrs Shah moved to England shortly afterwards, she settled close to her own parents and siblings, where she has lived with her two sons ever since. However, they frequently visit Pakistan, and Mr Shah has been to England.

Today both sons are adults, and Mr Shah will soon retire. He would like to bring his family permanently to Pakistan and see his sons take over his business, but neither of the two sons share that dream. They have been raised and educated in England and are extremely bored when they occasionally visit their father in Pakistan. Even though neither of his sons is interested in the business, they have agreed on a compromise: the two sons will take turns going to Pakistan, where they can learn about the production process and the business in general. Later the plan is to start a second company in England, and then they will take turns, one year at the time, one of them in England and the other in Pakistan.

Mr Shah and his nineteen-year-old son Farouk, who was in Pakistan at the time, explained these plans to me over dinner the first time I visited. Later the same evening, after Mr Shah and his wife left for a social visit to some relatives in the village, Farouk disclosed an alternative plan that he and his brother had been working on. They wanted to reunite their parents in England as soon as their father stopped working. For the moment they were just pretending to go along with their father's plans in order to please him. In this respect, Farouk and his brother had two strategies. First of all, they pretended that the plan to set up two companies was acceptable to them, which gave them time to set up a profitable business in England. Secondly, they had managed to convince their father to invest in a new house in England, as a way to reaffirm their relatedness to the city and neighbourhood where they grew up.

However, Mr Shah was not naïve. He was well aware of his sons' lack of enthusiasm about the factory and about Pakistan in general, so he initiated a couple of counter-strategies. First of all, he and his wife arranged a *rishta* between their eldest son and a girl from one of the local families in the village. Such a marriage would connect the son forever to the village. Secondly, Mr Shah had found a protégé at the factory, a young man from the area who displayed all the interest and enthusiasm about the business that his own sons lacked. Independently of each other, they both explained to me that their relationship was very close, just like that of father and son. Maybe in time the young protégé will assume the position of the biological sons and not only take over the business, but probably also the responsibility of taking care, practically and emotionally, of the aging Mr Shah.

Conclusion: beyond 'the point of no return'

This chapter has discussed the numerous difficulties that Pakistanis encounter whenever they attempt to return. Very often returnees' prior expectations and fantasies of the 'imagined homeland' have to be re-examined when they are challenged or proved to be wrong by everyday life in Pakistan. One common motivation for return is the attempt to recreate the moral order of family life. However, back in Pakistan many learn the hard way that it is never as easy to establish the ideal family as it is to dream about it. The general difficulties in living in the social, legal and cultural environment in Pakistan, along with all the problems of being reintegrated into the local family, challenge the idea of Pakistan as a morally good place. Confronted with the circumstances of life in Pakistan, the numerous problems, disappointments and moral corruptions that seemed to characterise family life in Denmark may not be so bad after all.

The different life stories presented in this chapter emphasise that my distinction between the first and second generations is merely analytical. Individual trajectories and family histories show a much more complex and blurred picture when it comes to describing where people are born and raised and where they feel they belong.

Finally, the chapter also illustrates that aspirations for return migration are influenced by age, life courses and family cycles. In the 1970s and 1980s, the first generation of male labour migrants and their wives were captured by the myth of return: some sent their children back to Pakistan to live with relatives or attempted to return as entire families. Most of them ended up in Denmark again. Today, when the first generation has retired and their children in the second generation have become adults and parents themselves, new lines of affiliation and belonging are informing the dreams and aspirations of return. Many in the older generation would like to live the rest of their lives in Pakistan, surrounded by their families, before they die, and often prefer to be buried in Pakistan. Many from the second generation, on the other hand, are considering settling – or have started to settle – in Pakistan in order for their children to have a proper religious upbringing in a society in which they are not second-rate citizens and not the targets of racism and Islamophobia. In the broader perspective of the entire migration history of Pakistani migrants in Denmark, it becomes clear that ideas and aspirations of return change over time in individual life courses and as result of family transitions. Furthermore, the intense focus on Pakistani Muslim immigrants following September 11 plays a significant role in current discussions and plans about leaving Denmark. In this respect, the presented life stories substantiate the argument that Pakistan and Denmark, *desh* and *pardesh*, are places in a transnational social field that will be ascribed new meanings over time by different agents in various contexts. No matter what, returnees have to accept that the Pakistan they have been thinking, talking and dreaming about for decades is nowhere to be found. The tragic truth about 'imagined homelands' is that there is no way back.

Chapter 7
An imagined return

Negotiations of identity and belonging

Whereas Chapter 6 discussed the problems migrant families face in Pakistan when they attempt to return, this chapter takes us back to the Danish setting and presents an 'imagined return', in the form of a stage play, written and performed by members of the Organisation of Pakistani Students and Academics (OPSA) to celebrate the fifty-fifth anniversary of Pakistan as an independent nation-state. In brief, the plot was about a migrant family who return to Pakistan for the summer holidays, to be confronted by their relatives, their origins and their common national history.

By presenting the characters and actions of a fictional family, the play launched a public, intergenerational critique that could not easily be articulated or accepted within a Pakistani family structure informed by the values of parental respect and authority. The stage play addressed the unfortunate fact that the first and second generations of Pakistanis in Denmark often do not share well-defined ideas concerning who they are and where they belong. On the contrary, notions of identity and belonging tend to become sites for intergenerational conflict and challenge in many families. Disagreements between generations are sometimes articulated in terms of national categories or discourses (for example, whether family members should be more or less Pakistani or more or less Danish), but they can also be experienced through other ascribed markers, such as ethnicity, religion or place of origin. Due to their post-colonial repertoires of identity (see Introduction) and of engagement in a transnational social field, Pakistani migrants can imagine themselves as belonging to numerous different communities and configurations of identity. In this respect, the stage play not only made it possible for OPSA members and the rest of the audience to question the ways in which first-generation migrants have (mis)managed their Pakistani identity and cultural heritage while living in Denmark; it also made it possible for everyone present to imagine alternative notions of identity and belonging, as it offered the better-educated second generation a possible means of reconciliation with Pakistan. In this chapter I analyse the representation of characters in the OPSA stage play in order to discuss how and why the repertoire of identity is managed and evaluated so differently by older and younger members of Pakistani migrant families.

Family life, authority and respect

As already noted, the demographic constitution of the Pakistani migrant community in Denmark is changing. The structural transitions in the second generation from 'child' to 'parent' or from 'parent' to 'grandparent' involve processes of self-reflection in which the young contrast their own values, expectations of life, relations with family and kin and hopes for the future with those of their parents. This repositioning within family cycles often forces latent disagreements and differences into the open. In her study of Pakistanis in Oxford, Alison Shaw discusses the structure and dynamics of migrant families:

> The ideals governing relationships between family members, generally expressed by all, but sometimes challenged by the younger generations, include a formal hierarchy within which each person has a clearly defined role, determined by age and sex, in relation to other family members ... Communication between men is formal and men are not supposed to smoke, talk freely or joke in the presence of their older brothers or father: they should always be respectful and deferential (Shaw 2000 [1988]: 93).

This resembles the code of conduct found in many Pakistani families in Denmark. The claim of respect for the family, for parents and older people in general is part of Islamic tradition, and is therefore often reproduced as an unquestionable part of what it means to be Pakistani and a good Muslim (Østberg 2003: 157). The hierarchy and claim for respect often create a distance between grown-up children and their parents. Many youngsters, for instance, find it extremely difficult to discuss personal problems with their parents, especially with their father. Instead, young people may consult their mother, a trusted uncle or perhaps an older brother or sister.

An important aspect of the code of conduct is not to criticise the opinions or actions of one's parents in public. Impudent or bold behaviour by a son or daughter will often be interpreted as a sign of a failed upbringing, questioning the ability of the parents to raise their children properly. Stories of disrespectful youngsters are a major theme in the ongoing gossip within the Pakistani community. The family structure makes it very difficult for members of the younger generation to articulate any dissatisfaction they may experience with their parents or families or with their lives in general.

In social contexts solely composed of young Pakistanis, everyone is much more outspoken about parental values that seem silly, old-fashioned or exotic to them. It is not uncommon to joke about stubborn parents who do nothing but praise their *zaat* origin, tell anecdotes about life back in the village, gossip about their neighbours or discuss local Pakistani politics. This kind of joking relationship between youngsters is affectionate regarding the cultural idiosyncrasies of the parents, but it also exposes the gap between the two generational cohorts.

The Organisation of Pakistani Students and Academics (OPSA)

One site in which differences between older and younger generations have become salient is that of Pakistani associations and organisations in Denmark. The Organisation of Pakistani Students and Academics (OPSA) was founded in 1993 with the merger of two existing student associations, of Pakistani medical students (POM) and Pakistani students of engineering (SPI). The aim was to form an effective youth organisation for all Pakistani students in Denmark, one which could become an important actor in the local community and in the wider Danish society.

Since the early 1970s, there have been numerous Pakistani associations in Denmark focusing on politics, religion or cultural activities, and different 'societies' have recruited members from specific geographical areas or from certain *zaat*. From the outset, OPSA was different. First of all, OPSA was not oriented towards Pakistan. Instead, the explicit aim was – to quote former chairman Mazhar Hussain – to 'organise young Pakistanis and integrate them into Danish society'. Secondly, OPSA wanted to 'unite young Pakistanis, despite the political, social, cultural, geographical, ethnic and religious boundaries that divided the organisations and the generation of their parents' (OPSA-nyt 1999; my translations). These ambitions were met with great suspicion from the wider Pakistani migrant community, but for several years, OPSA succeeded in doing just that.

At its height, OPSA had more than 200 paying members, and reached many more by arranging public events. The organisation represented a 'free' space in which it was possible to reverse the negative stigma of being part of an ethnic minority, *the usual suspects* in Danish society. During its early years, OPSA held several public debates on politics, religion, education, health and employment issues, and for three years it published its own monthly magazine. In 2000, OPSA created a website where members and non-members could discuss shared interests in topics such as family, culture, marriage, Islam, Bollywood movies, poetry, etc. OPSA also successfully arranged a number of 'family shows' such as the one discussed in this chapter, which was held in August 2002 to celebrate the foundation of Pakistan as an independent nation-state.

'A Sunbeam of Hope'

The family show was held in the assembly hall of a public school in Ballerup, a suburb of Copenhagen. The announcement of the event as a 'family show' indicated that it was a social occasion at which nothing offensive, such as public dancing, would take place. As this was a public event and a celebration of Pakistan's national day, the approximately 350 guests were dressed up for the occasion in vividly coloured *shalwar kameez* or suits. The show lasted all afternoon and consisted of a quiz, a musical performance, and several speeches given by prominent members of the Pakistani community. During the interval, refreshments were served. Everyone in the audience was in high spirits, and expectations built up concerning the climax of the afternoon, the performance of a play written and performed by members of OPSA for this particular occasion. After a forty-minute break the audience returned to their seats, and there was a sudden hush as the lights in the assembly hall were dimmed.

The title of the play was *A Sunbeam of Hope*. Most of it was in Urdu and, as my understanding of Urdu is only fragmentary, I asked Hassan, an OPSA member in his early thirties, to be my interpreter. Hassan was no longer active in the organisation since he had finished his education some years earlier, had started working and had married a young woman from Pakistan. They were attending the show together with their two small children.

The narrative of the play was simple: A Pakistani migrant family goes on holiday to the father's native village in 'little Scandinavia'. There, in the village, they are confronted with family members they have left behind, and the two children from Denmark learn where they come from and begin to understand the importance of their national and religious heritage.

For artistic effect, each character was presented as a stereotype, reflecting the common dilemmas involved in migration and the difficulties of preserving family relations across distances in time and space. However, as enacted by OPSA members on stage, the stereotypes caused much amusement and laughter. I will present each character in the play separately to elaborate on their stereotypical features.

The father calls himself 'Charlie'. This is not the name he was given by his parents, but one he has been using for decades. According to Hassan, it was not uncommon in the parents' generation to take a new name when they first arrived in Denmark, as this indicates a change in personality, meaning that migrants present themselves as more Western or modern than before. Charlie is dressed in a multicoloured Hawaiian shirt, with a vulgar tie and large sunglasses, and money passes through his hands like water, virtually throwing it around. Charlie has made his fortune driving a taxi in Copenhagen. From his mode of dress and extravagance, the audience understands that Charlie sees himself as 'a man of the world.' Nevertheless he is the stereotype of a *nouveau riche*, a man with lots of money but no sophistication.

The mother has no name: she is just presented as Charlie's wife. In this subtle way, the playwrights question the gender roles of the older generation and the organisation of the patriarchal family in general, in which a woman may be defined through her husband. During the play, the mother repeats two phrases. The first is 'No problem, no problem.' The second is a jingle in

Danish: '*Dagpenge, børnepenge, masser af penge*', meaning 'Unemployment benefit, child benefit [awarded to all families with children in Denmark], loads of money.' This jingle is reiterated over and over again and sounds almost like a formula: 'unemployment benefit' plus 'child benefit' equals 'loads of money'. Every time the mother repeated the jingle, the audience doubled up with laughter. The mother also considers herself a lady of distinction. Hassan explained that her dress and haircut were recognisable signs of her trying to be a more distinguished lady in Denmark than she used to be back in her village in Pakistan. Her ambition for social mobility is also made clear to the audience when she pretends to come from a higher-ranking *zaat* than she really does. In one scene after the family has returned to Pakistan, the mother is confronted by her own brother who, in disgust, asks her: 'Who do you think you are?' She arrogantly replies: 'I am modern!'

The teenage boy speaks only Danish. He has never learned to speak his parents' native tongue, and he does not care to. He is dressed in a hip-hop outfit and has bleached his hair. He repeatedly complains about spending his holiday in the village, and wishes instead that he had driven to Spain with his friends in their big Mercedes.

Unlike her brother, *the teenage daughter* speaks a little Urdu. Still, at the end of the play she has a long monologue in which she expresses her regret that she does not know Urdu and therefore is not able to understand her grandparents. Both children know very little about their relatives in Pakistan before the holiday. This fact is revealed when the bewildered son confronts his father with the question: 'Why have you never told us about our family and your native village?'

Charlie's elderly father – *the grandfather* – is the teacher in the village. He is very surprised to learn that he has grandchildren, because he has never heard about them. This informs the audience of the kind of relations (or lack of relations) between the family in Denmark and their relatives in Pakistan.

The grandmother has no dialogue but just sits in a wheelchair, being pushed around the stage by some of the other characters. A male OPSA member plays the part of the old lady, making the minor part an important comic contribution to the play.

The maternal uncle is a proud and idealistic man who acquired a university education in Pakistan. Despite the opportunity to emigrate, he has chosen to stay and make an effort to help the country prosper. However, as this decision is more idealistic than realistic, he is therefore unemployed.

The play consisted of five acts and can be summarised as follows.

Scene 1

A chaotic scene in the international airport at Lahore. The family members from Denmark think they are being robbed of all their belongings, but it turns out that two porters are fighting to carry their luggage. After clearing up the misunderstanding, the porters are given generous tips by Charlie – there is money enough and tips for everyone.

Scene 2

The family arrives in the village, where we witness the reunion of Charlie and his aged parents. When his old mother sees him, she manages, despite a lot of difficulty, to get out of her wheelchair and go over to him to welcome her long-lost son. Charlie ignores the old woman because he does not recognise his own mother. Instead he approaches his father. This time the encounter is reversed and it is the old father who does not recognise his own son. However, the misunderstandings are cleared up and they all embrace each other.

Then the two teenage children enter the scene. Charlie introduces them to his father as mistakes – perhaps to excuse their Western attitude and language. The children are not in any way affected by meeting their grandparents for the first time. Instead, they comment on the village, which they find dirty and disgusting. When the old grandfather understands that these two grown-up kids are his grandchildren, he greets them in the traditional way. As a respectable elder approaching a youngster, he wants to put his hands on their head. The children, on the other hand, misinterpret his gesture and respond by giving the old man a 'high five'.

Finally Charlie's wife enters the scene. She deliberately ignores the greetings of her parents-in-law and acts in a demonstratively arrogant manner towards them while constantly commenting on the heat and the smell, suggesting that they should buy an air-conditioner and clean the house. All her adult life she has been living in Denmark as Charlie's wife, and through her bad manners and rude behaviour she deliberately violates the code of proper behaviour towards parents-in-law.

Scene 3

The third scene is built up around a series of monologues. First, the teenage son expresses his boredom at being in the village. Then the teenage daughter comes on stage, very upset at not knowing or understanding her own grandparents, and regretfully complaining that she apparently has nothing in common with them. We then see the old grandfather in despair as he no longer knows his own son. In his monologue, he relates the family story of how he was the one who, years ago, wanted his son to leave Pakistan in order to make money and provide for the extended family, so that all could be better off. Now he realises that emigration has its own consequences. The years in the West have changed his son: Charlie is no longer the son he used to be. Finally we see Charlie contemplate how difficult, maybe impossible, it would be for him to return to the village and to Pakistan. His life in

Denmark has made him a complete stranger to the simple life of his family and the village.

Scene 4

The mother's brother enters the stage. Despite his education, he has not been able to find a job in Pakistan. Charlie and his wife suggest that he should move to the West, and offer to help him. Nevertheless, he rejects the offer and insists that Pakistan is the place for him to live. National patriotism is more important to him than money. Provoked by their offer, he confronts Charlie and asks him what all his money is worth when he is obviously embarrassed by his own parents and has lost his pride in the family, his village and in being Pakistani. Without expressing it directly, the mother's brother poses the question: 'Does money make you happy?'

Final scene

We see the grandfather – the old teacher of the village – sitting on a rock. By his side is one of his students, a young girl from the village. She asks him to tell her the story of how Pakistan was created. He begins to tell the story of the struggle for independence, the mass movements of people between India and Pakistan, the violence and killings between Muslim, Sikh and Hindu during that period, and finally the partition and birth of Pakistan as an independent nation-state on 14 August 1947. As he tells the story, the two grandchildren pass by and are immediately captivated by what he relates, becoming absorbed by their Pakistani heritage, history and identity. The moral of the play is obvious: Charlie and his wife, representing the first generation, may have lost or deliberately distanced themselves from Pakistan, but their children, though born and raised in Denmark, can still learn a lot from their history, and should be proud of their Pakistani and Muslim background. The point is emphasised at the end, as the teenage son promises his old grandfather, in Danish, that he will return to Pakistan.

The curtain falls for the last time and the play ends.

Legitimate intergenerational criticism

The play met with a favourable reception. The audience laughed when they were supposed to, and applauded for a long time after the final curtain. Everyone seemed to be having an enjoyable afternoon, but despite the fun and laughter, the play had a serious moral at the end. During the last scene, when the teenage son reassured his old grandfather that he would return to Pakistan, Hassan looked at me and said: 'Boy, I don't know how you feel about this

… but I have goose bumps all over.' Judging by his reactions and the serious atmosphere in the audience, the narrative of the play made an impression.

Overall, the play levelled severe criticism at the parental generation, represented by Charlie and his wife, who had forgotten their past and who they were before they settled in the West. However, the play also contained a strong element of self-criticism, in that the playwrights used the parts of the two teenagers to question the younger generation's indifference to family relations, history and nationalist sentiments: a criticism mediated by the stereotypical nature of the characters. According to Phyllis Chock (1987: 348), stereotypes are 'filled with rich, socially evocative, and culturally transmitted content of images, forms, tropes, and in the case of tropes, structures of relations that they state and explore and that are stated and explored in them in turn'. The use of stereotypes made it possible artistically to explore collective experiences and dilemmas of identity and belonging. Everyone in the audience knew someone – a father, friend or neighbour – who was more or less like Charlie; some might even see aspects of him or some of the other characters in themselves. By turning each character into a stereotype, it became possible for both older and younger members of the audience to enjoy the performance and laugh at the characters, despite the fact that the play dealt with serious dilemmas from real life in many families.

The play became a medium for an intergenerational critique because – like a mirror – it reflected dilemmas and conflicts in everyday family life, while ignoring the conventions of privacy and delicacy when dealing with family problems. Normally it would be inappropriate at a 'family show' to violate the boundaries between the public and the private, or the code of respect between older and younger generations. Nevertheless, this criticism was accepted because it took place within the fictional setting of the play and on the specific occasion of the national day. In particular, the change in attitude of the two teenage children saved the day. At the beginning they are spoiled and indifferent to their grandparents and uncle, but gradually they become eager to learn more about their family and about Pakistan in general. Whereas Charlie and his wife might be lost, the next generation has a renewed longing to know about their family and heritage. The point is substantiated by the title, *A Sunbeam of Hope*, with its promise for the future. The strong nationalist sentiments filling the assembly hall at the end of the play meant that the provocative stereotypes and symbolic violations could be ignored.

To substantiate this interpretation, I will briefly mention an episode following the Eid show hosted by OPSA six months prior to the national day, at which a similar intergenerational critique was rejected. On this occasion, too, OPSA members had produced a play dealing with the controversial topic of arranged marriage. The stage was set up as a 'people's court', with a judge and two secretaries. In the performance, Amir, a young Pakistani man born and raised in Denmark, was accused of adultery. The duty of the court was to decide who was to blame for Amir's actions. The court called in a number of witnesses. First came the 'Don Juan'-like figure of Amir, who explained that he had only agreed to the marriage in the first place to please his parents. Next on the witness stand was his highly independent wife from Pakistan, who was not prepared to put up with his adultery. Then the court called his father, who merely focused on the fact that his son and new daughter-in-law were from the same *zaat*. Then Amir's loud and dominant mother was called, who was more than happy to get a daughter-in-law from Pakistan to do all the work in the household for her. Finally, the court called Amir's secluded and indifferent sister, interested only in her studies and her looks.

On this occasion, too, the audience was amused by the plot and the funny characters. After the witnesses had appeared on the stand, the judge asked for some reactions from the audience before reaching his verdict. Following his request, a few of the seniors present took the microphone and commented on the play and the actions of the characters. In this way, the audience was included in the play as a kind of jury. Finally the judge pronounced his sentence, in which he strongly advised both parents and children to discuss openly the sometimes conflicting desires of marriage arrangements in order to avoid unsuitable matches like Amir's in the future (see Rytter 2003b).

In the weeks following the Eid show, OPSA was subjected to a great deal of criticism in the Pakistani community for bringing the topic of arranged marriages out into the open at a public gathering. It was not the sensitive topic of marriage or the stereotypical characters of the play that resulted in the critical reception afterwards, but the fact that the Eid show went beyond the physical limits of the stage by directly addressing the audience. In doing so, the boundaries of acceptable intergenerational criticism had been violated. The play transformed the relationship between the actors and the audience into an open dialogue between the first and second generations, addressing the sensitive and private topic of marriage on a public occasion. This was not acceptable to many members of the older generation. Learning from this previous experience, OPSA abandoned the idea of having a discussion with the audience following *A Sunbeam of Hope*, instead letting the moral and critical remarks in the play speak for themselves.

Managing identity

As suggested in the Introduction, Pakistani migrants share a historically defined range of possible identities but, as the play suggests, the evaluation of these potentials differs between generations. OPSA used the performance of different stage plays to discuss the basic existential question of 'Who are we?' with their parents.

Both plays were sites for experimentation and for the contestation of identity and belonging, where the audience was confronted with characters lost to *Danish* and *Western* values and attitudes, such as the indifferent children with no interest in Pakistan nor fluency in their native tongue, the promiscuous Amir and his vain sister, Charlie with his conspicuous consumption, or his wife and her disrespectful treatment of her parents-in-law. These manners and values were in sharp contrast with the piety and knowledge represented by the old grandfather or the patriotism reflected in the uncle's decision to stay in Pakistan and help build up the country. The OPSA playwrights used the opposition between values considered *Danish*, *Western* or *modern* and those considered *Pakistani* as a means to urge the audience to manage their lives and identities carefully.

However, the most important assertion of identity was the division between identity configurations based on *zaat* and those grounded in Islam. The *zaat* identity was represented and ridiculed in Charlie's wife, who has aspirations for *zaat* mobility, or by the comical character of Amir's stubborn father. The religious identity, on the other hand, was emphasised by what happened to the two teenagers, who, listening to their grandfather's narrative, become absorbed in the national history of Pakistan, and gain an understanding of their destinies as the children of a great Muslim nation-state, and as brothers and sisters within the global *umma* of Islam.

Zaat, the patrilineal clan, has been a widespread principle of social organisation and stratification in rural Pakistan. Each *zaat* has a distinct historical and socio-economic status and, even though the migration process has in many instances turned old hierarchies upside-down, some of these connotations still persist in how members of these different groups view themselves and are viewed by others (Shaw 2000: 115). But due to the relatively small number of Pakistani migrants constituting the village-like community in Denmark, the situation seems different from that in the United Kingdom. Whereas networks of relatives, fellow-villagers or *zaat* members were significant agents in facilitating the process of chain migration in the early 1970s and the establishment of businesses in the 1980s (see Chapter 2), Pakistani families also mixed with each other as neighbours, colleagues or friends in spite of *zaat* differences. As large groups of second-generation Pakistanis grew up and became ready for marriage in the 1990s, this changed. *Zaat* suddenly became a highly relevant feature of identity and a way to distinguish between families, as it was reintroduced by the parents' generation as a prescriptive boundary in marriage arrangements. As Nadeem, a former chairman of OPSA explained: 'It is not us [from the second generation] who think of *zaat*. That is simply a domain of the parents. It is their privilege or destiny to think this way'.

In discussing what he calls the post-traditional society, Anthony Giddens (1994) distinguishes between different knowledge regimes: 'experts of knowledge' and 'guardians of truth'. Where the first of these regimes is a non-local, de-centred and contingent way of knowing that can be mastered by experts, the second obtains authority and legitimacy from formulaic notions of truth which are the prerogative of the guardians alone. Traditionally, the composition and significance of the *zaat* system has been a prerogative of the parental generation: they are the ones who know how to navigate it, understand why it should be considered important and will confide what will inevitably go wrong if youngsters decide to transgress the prescriptive boundary of the *zaat* in marriage.

The religious revivalism of the younger generation can be seen as a counter-strategy to the formulaic truth regime of the parents' generation. In studying the Quran and the Sunna, they see no justification for dividing Muslims into different *zaat*. Often a person who falls in love with someone and wants to marry will seek Islamic arguments to convince their parents that this kind of marriage is a religious right (Shaw 2000: 193; Jacobson 1998). The second generation have increasingly become 'experts in Islamic knowledge', a resource which they use in intergenerational negotiations with their parents.

OPSA has always been a significant player in the ongoing process and in distancing the second generation from ideas and practices related to *zaat* identities. In this wider historical context, it is no surprise that *A Sunbeam of Hope* ended by advocating community solidarity, and commemorated the encompassing identity configurations of being *Pakistani* and of being *Muslim*, which were shared by everyone in the audience.

Interestingly, the second overall objective of OPSA – 'to integrate Pakistani youth into Danish society' – was totally absent on this day in August 2002. Following September 11, many OPSA members were ambivalent about the original ambition, as they did not feel accepted or recognised for their efforts by the wider Danish public or society. A crucial turning-point was when anonymous contributions celebrated the terror attack in New York on the OPSA website. Suddenly the homepage and the organisation were accused in national newspapers of being a site for the discussion of extremist viewpoints. In the following year, several committee members suspected that they were being monitored by various, never identified, authorities. In retrospect, September 11 changed the organisation and its members' attitudes. Thereafter, the ideals of the OPSA founders – 'to integrate Pakistani youth into Danish society' – were no longer salient: instead the value and importance of being *Pakistani* and *Muslim* were stressed.

An imagined return

Finally, *A Sunbeam of Hope* can also be interpreted as an imaginary return, one where the actors and the audience were offered an opportunity to imagine what it would be like to return to Pakistan and meet long-lost family members.

As discussed in Chapter 6, over the years many families have tried to return and resettle in Pakistan, but the vast majority have moved back to Denmark again, realising that the homeland they longed for no longer existed. Despite the shared experiences of disappointment and disillusion, the possibility of return is still discussed in some families. Global events and developments in national politics have changed the political climate in Denmark since the beginning of the new millennium. Some argue that this altered political climate has resulted in a certain ethno-nationalism (Gullestad 2006: 302), where it becomes difficult for the children of immigrants – even those who were born and raised in Denmark – to be accepted as law-abiding fellow-citizens who contribute to the welfare state though their educational achievements, work, taxes, political participation and so on. Instead, they are met with suspicion. This recent socio-political development has made many Pakistani families seriously consider the possibility of leaving Denmark and instead moving to the United Kingdom, Canada, Sweden or back to Pakistan. In this way, the idea of return has been revived.

One of the highly educated members of the younger generation who has reacted against the new political trends in Denmark is my interpreter, Hassan. In 2005, he moved his business and his family, consisting of his wife, two children and mother, permanently to Lahore. He did this partly to oblige his homesick Pakistani wife and mother, and partly because he did not want his children to grow up in a Danish society in which they would always be second-class citizens. Knowing now that three years after we sat together in the dark assembly hall enjoying the OPSA performance, Hassan would move his family to Pakistan makes it understandable that he should have 'had goose bumps all over'. Maybe the idea of leaving Denmark and returning to Pakistan had already taken shape in the back of his mind.

In the context of a homeland that has been handed down from generation to generation and the current socio-political environment in Denmark, *A Sunbeam of Hope* can be interpreted as an imagined return, and a possible reconciliation with the past. The play urges families to see Pakistan as a serious alternative to life in Denmark. No matter how distanced or alienated the old and young generations may feel towards people and places in Pakistan, it is still possible to recreate strong ties of emotion and solidarity. In this respect, the message of the play seems to be that, despite everything, there is hope for the future.

Concluding remarks: negotiating family relatedness

Among migrants, notions of identity and belonging are highly political and contested topics. This is not only the case in national political discourses on immigration, but also in the micro-universe of the family. Young people especially may find it difficult to formulate a legitimate opposition to established values and ways of living within the family. This chapter shows how members of a Pakistani youth organisation were able to use artistic expression as a means to address some of the problems they share in relation to their parents' generation. In doing so, they succeeded in turning delicate private matters into topics of public discussion.

A Sunbeam of Hope illustrates how second-generation Pakistanis might have very different ideas of how to evaluate the range of identities they share with their parents due to their common history as immigrants in Denmark.

The case exemplifies the growing gap between the generations when it comes to definitions of who they are and where they belong. It is far from obvious how identity and belonging are negotiated within transnational families, or whether these negotiations will result in continuity or radical changes of intimate social relations.

Today, after several years of declining membership, OPSA is no longer an active organisation. One reason for this is that many members finished their studies, started work and got married, leaving little spare time for voluntary work in a student organisation. Those who remained active in the organisation experienced severe disillusionment, not feeling that their efforts made any difference in either the Pakistani community or the wider Danish society. Finally, OPSA has had a hard time competing with the numerous new youth organisations that have emerged in Denmark, recruiting young Muslims and offering them membership of associations based on religious instead of national criteria. As a consequence, it was decided at the annual general meeting in 2007 to suspend the activities of the Pakistani student organisation.

Chapter 8

The Kashmir earthquake

Dynamics of intensive transnationalism

In Chapter 6, I discussed how Pakistani families over the years have attempted more or less successfully to return to Pakistan, and, in Chapter 7, how a stage play at a family show came to constitute an 'imagined return' to the actors and the audience. In this chapter, I go on to discuss how a catastrophe like the Kashmir earthquake of 2005 can make Pakistan stand out as an obvious homeland to migrants in diaspora – but only for a while. In this respect, the disaster made Pakistan become a 'momentary homeland' to many Pakistani migrants in Denmark.

In October 2005, an earthquake hit the region of Jammu and Kashmir in the northern parts of Pakistan, killing 75,000 people. Even more were injured; almost three million lost their homes. This natural disaster, in a single moment, turned life upside-down for thousands of families in the affected mountain region. But the event also had consequences in Pakistani communities around the world. In Denmark, the period following the earthquake was one of immediate activity, which saw people in the migrant community striving to provide emergency treatment for the many victims in Pakistan. Such liminal periods, which suspend regular, everyday life and mobilise people to help victims of disasters in other parts of the world, have been called 'intensive transnationalism' (Holm and Fabricius 2008: 87). One significant development in the aftermath of the disaster was the ad hoc establishment of an association consisting mainly of second-generation Pakistani medical professionals, calling itself 'Medical Doctors in Assistance to the Earthquake Victims in Pakistan' (*Læger til hjælp for jordskælvsofrene i Pakistan*). In the following months, this association sent trained medical staff to the disaster area. In this chapter, I discuss the origins, developments and impacts of the doctors' initiative both within and beyond the migrant community in Denmark, and how, for a while, the disaster made Pakistan stand out as an indisputable 'homeland' for everyone in the community. I suggest that the earthquake enabled the doctors to relate to the homeland of their parents, and that the event was used by the doctors to consolidate their position as a rising successful elite in the migrant community.

In approaching the Kashmir earthquake as an event with numerous unforeseen consequences around the world, I am inspired by Max Gluckman and other scholars of the Manchester School, who, early in the history of modern anthropology, emphasised the importance of connecting local ethnographic data (mainly from Africa) to broader historical processes, economical conjunctures and global regimes such as imperialism and colonialism (e.g. Gluckman 1940; Evans and Handleman 2006). The Manchester School scholars' awareness of local–global interconnectedness stimulated a shift away from the conventional focus on 'society' to develop a much more flexible notion of 'social fields' (Gluckman 2006 [1961]: 20). In this respect, the study of local social situations was never analytically restricted to what was immediately observable. Clyde Mitchell (2006 [1983]: 27) emphasises this point when he defines the social situation analysis as 'a detailed examination of an event (or series of related events) which the analyst believes exhibits (or exhibit) the operation of some identified general theoretical principle'. Nevertheless, I suggest that the analytical approach of social situational analysis needs to be updated so that it can cope sufficiently with the challenges of contemporary ethnography in the twenty-first century.

One of the most obvious challenges since the heyday of the Manchester School has been the appearance and expansion of advanced communication technology – an imprint of late modernity itself. Different media have not only conquered our local worlds and intimate spheres of life, but also enabled the creation of bonds between people, places and spaces around the globe in ways never before seen or imagined. Currently, we are subjected to the experience of time-space compression (Harvey 1989) and simultaneity (Levitt and Glick Schiller 2004) as shown, for instance, by the fact that an event in one local site can and often will become the topic of discussion and motivate people into action in different settings around the world. Critical local events are often communicated worldwide by international television news or radio broadcasts, or through more idiosyncratic and less controllable channels such as internet sites, Facebook, blogging, Twitter or chains of SMS communication. The Rushdie affair of 1988–9, September 11, the cartoon controversy of 2005–6 or the democracy movement in the Middle East in the spring of 2011 are all examples of how local events can spread worldwide, via chaotic networks of networks, and bring about unpredicted outcomes as the event generates new configurations of identity and imaginaries, creating spaces for political action that were not accessible or even thinkable before.

The Kashmir earthquake became just such a global, media-borne event. This chapter analyses some of the effects of the earthquake among Pakistanis in Denmark, and especially how it motivated the rise and fall of the association 'Medical Doctors in Assistance to the Earthquake Victims in Pakistan'. Almost as an inevitable consequence of the earthquake turning into a media event, this initiative became a kind of reflexive performance through which second-generation Pakistani doctors enacted, fulfilled or disappointed the expectations and promises of their profession. The significance and impact of the organisation will be explored in three interconnected contexts: the migrant family, the Pakistani community and the arena of national identity politics.

The disaster

On the morning of 8 October 2005, the city of Muzaffarabad, situated in Pakistan-administered Azad Kashmir, was hit without warning by a huge earthquake estimated to measure 7.6 on the open Richter scale. In the beginning, there was no exact information about the damage. Initial reports from Islamabad, the capital of Pakistan situated a couple of hundred kilometres south of the earthquake's epicentre, stated that the Mangla Towers, a high-rise block of apartments, had collapsed, killing nearly 100 people. It was not until national and international media entered the mountain regions that people in Pakistan and around the world realised the full extent of the damage and human casualties that this natural disaster had caused.

Many Pakistanis in Denmark followed the course of events on Pakistani television channels, the BBC, CNN or the internet. Migrants with relatives or friends in Islamabad, the neighbouring city of Rawalpindi, or the northern areas telephoned Pakistan to make sure that their loved ones were safe. As most Pakistanis in Denmark originate from the lowlands of the Gujrat district of Punjab, only a few families actually lost relatives as a result of the earthquake. Pakistanis who had settled in the United Kingdom were much more affected by the disaster, as more than eighty per cent are Kashmiri and originate from Azad Kashmir (Rehman and Kalra 2006: 311).

When Pakistani and international teams of relief workers finally entered the mountain region, the reported number of casualties shot up dramatically. Every hour of every day brought new and higher figures. During this critical period, Pakistanis in Denmark suffered and identified with the many victims with whom they were confronted in the media. Three circumstances intensified the immediate identification and emotional connection with the victims. First, the earthquake hit ordinary people and families, who, for the most part, had lived lives very similar to those of the first generation of migrants before they moved to Denmark approximately forty years earlier. Secondly, the disaster happened in the month of Ramadan, a time where everyone is focused on helping those in need by giving *zakat* (alms), a religious duty for Muslims. Finally, it was significant that the earthquake hit the Kashmir region, which since the independence of Pakistan in 1947 has been very important for Pakistani national identity and imaginary. During the last sixty years, Pakistan and India have fought several wars over the disputed territory. As recently as 2002, the unresolved Kashmir conflict put these neighbouring countries on the edge of a nuclear confrontation.

After the extent of the earthquake's damage was revealed, discussions started within the Pakistani community in Denmark on how people could contribute to helping their needy 'brothers' and 'sisters' in Kashmir. Due to a general mistrust among Pakistani immigrants of both Danish and Pakistani NGOs and relief agencies, within a few days several collections had been organised in order to assist and support the earthquake victims. Money was collected mainly in different mosques and 'societies', associations that cater exclusively to Pakistanis who share similar *zaat* or originate from the same city, such as Lahore or Sialkot. Clothes were collected, packed and shipped to Pakistan, and people used the internet or SMS to donate generously to the different collections. The Pakistani embassy soon set up a fund that in few weeks had collected $382,000, and an NGO titled 'Muslim Aid' collected no less than DKr 2.1 million (Holm and Fabricius 2008: 91). The willingness of people to donate through such ad hoc initiatives reflected a strong sense of intimacy with and relatedness to the victims among migrants: these should not be seen as individualised, impersonal relief contributions (Rehman and Kalra 2006: 313).

Pakistani medical doctors in Denmark began discussing what they could do to help the victims and how to mobilise their efforts. A few days after the earthquake, a group of doctors met to develop a strategy. First, they wanted to mobilise a larger network of Pakistani doctors who were willing and able to help. Secondly, they would search for sponsors to cover the costs of travel expenses and necessary medical equipment. Thirdly, they realised that they had to plan logistically for doctors to be flown into the disaster region. Finally, they discussed how they should handle the media so that their efforts would be both visible and politically effective in placing the earthquake on the public agenda in Denmark.

After a few days, more than forty Pakistani doctors had volunteered to help. Looking back at the event, a doctor from the first team sent to Pakistan related to me in an interview how one evening he had been sitting at home on the couch, watching images of the disaster on the television, when his wife angrily yelled at him: 'You're a doctor, and yet you just sit here and watch television! Do something!' Common to everyone in the ad hoc network was a wish to take an active role in order to make a difference.

The group who initiated the network succeeded in persuading the medical company Pfizer to donate DKr 100,000 in support of its efforts. In order to accept a gift of that amount from a corporate sponsor, the informal network was turned into a formal association. Thus the non-profit organisation Medical Doctors in Assistance to the Earthquake Victims in Pakistan (referred to hereafter as MDAEV) came into being, with the single aim of sending doctors to Kashmir. The statutory general meeting was held twelve days after the earthquake hit, but already on the previous day a team consisting of four doctors had been sent to Pakistan. This was the first of what turned out to be six teams of doctors who would go to Pakistan in order to help with disaster relief.

All six teams of doctors stayed in the disaster area for from five to ten days. The first team arrived shortly after the disaster and worked in local hospitals or at temporary emergency clinics, treating both earthquake victims and regular patients in need of medical care. While the first couple of teams worked under primitive circumstances, the later teams faced more orderly conditions. The last teams, consisting of both doctors and physical therapists, focused mostly on rehabilitating patients. In this way, the doctors from Denmark became part of an estimated 200 medically trained overseas Pakistanis who travelled to the Kashmir region from Europe and North America in order to offer their help and assistance (Rehman and Kalra 2006: 314).

The rest of this chapter discusses the significance of the doctors' association and the impact of their performance on the Pakistani families, the community dynamics and on the identity politics of the Danish nation-state.

Family objectives and social mobility

In the previous chapters I have discussed how the trajectories and family histories of the migrant community are intertwined, creating the idea that 'everyone knows everyone else'. In such a relatively small, close-knit, village-like community, people watch over each other and discuss other families' affairs. Everything from businesses, health problems and the upbringing of children to marriage problems and wider family conflicts is discussed in these informal gossip networks. Whether or not a migrant family is considered to have been successful and to have done well is assessed using different criteria, such as economic, cultural and symbolic capital (see Chapter 2). Currently, an important asset in these ongoing evaluations is the cultural capital of education, that is, whether the family's children among the second generation have been able to complete higher education. However, following the logic of community competition, education is never *just* education; it constitutes a hierarchy of uneven status and prestige, where studying medicine and becoming a doctor is often considered to be the highest achievement in the hierarchy – the best you can do for yourself and your family. Both in Pakistan and within the Pakistani community in Denmark, the medical doctor is seen a figure of esteem and status, one who should be approached with respect.

In telling their life stories, many elders relate how they themselves left Pakistan years ago because they did not have access to a university education or could not afford the tuition fees. Instead, they have put their own (and sometimes even their parents') dreams and ambitions aside in order to emigrate and work as semi- or unskilled workers in Denmark all their lives. Now it is up to their children, who have been born and raised in Denmark, to fulfil these family ambitions (cf. Østberg 2003: 172). The intense focus on education and the significance of academic achievement is evident in many migrant families, and becomes manifest in the overwhelming interest – some might say pressure – on children's homework and study habits. As Sheraz, a young medical student, briefly summed up his upbringing: 'Study, study, study! That was all that mattered when I went to school.' This strong focus on education can, however, be difficult to handle when youngsters do not have the intellectual abilities, or simply have other plans for their future.

When a young Danish Pakistani man or woman finally succeeds in becoming a doctor, this is not just an individual career move, but an achievement that affects the entire family, improving its symbolic capital within the community. It gives meaning to the migration process and to the loss and deprivation that the first-generation parents suffered in Denmark during four decades of hard manual labour, limited contact with parents and relatives in Pakistan and the 'loss' of a homeland (see Chapter 6). It means nothing less than that the goals of parenthood, the family's legacy and very meaning of life are at stake in the school performance of the second generation.

All in all, doctors are ascribed a range of different positive attributes within the Pakistani community. This has become especially salient in recent years, as more and more young people of the second generation study medicine and become doctors. In its own tragic way, the Kashmir earthquake provided the new elite of young Pakistani doctors with an opportunity to fulfil some of the promises of their profession by using their medical training to give something back to those in need in Pakistan. The disaster enabled the doctors to create or recreate bonds of relatedness between themselves and the people and places in Pakistan that are an essential part of their common backgrounds and family histories.

One illustrative example of this process is the case of Adeel, one of the founders of MDAEV. When he was younger, he was sent to live with his uncle in Pakistan and attend medical school in Lahore. He was sent away so that he could focus on his studies and not be distracted by the parties, alcohol and women that might tempt and distract a young student in Denmark. Later he returned, and started working at one of the major hospitals in Denmark. Adeel was active in forming MDAEV, and volunteered for one of the first teams to go to Kashmir. When I met him, he related that it had made his parents very proud that he had decided to clear his busy calendar and immediately travel to Pakistan to offer his help and services. Adeel's participation in the medical team proved to his parents, as well as to the rest of the Pakistani community in Denmark and his family in Pakistan, that despite all the problems his parents had had with him earlier on, the upbringing they had given him had proved successful after all. Adeel had managed to become a doctor just as they had wished, and now he was using his abilities to help the people of Pakistan.

Community effects

In the days following the earthquake, after the first team of doctors had left for Pakistan, the number of casualties kept rising. Journalists posted ongoing reports from the area, and television broadcasts and internet sites provided images documenting the alarming proportions of the disaster. In the meantime, both Pakistani and international NGOs were flocking to the area. Within the Pakistani community in Denmark, the earthquake had a series of local effects. Whereas in the beginning the general reaction to the doctors' initiative was primarily one of pride and enthusiasm, MDAEV was later criticised for various reasons. To explain this change, it is convenient to divide the period of intensive transnationalism following the earthquake into two different phases.

The first phase covers the period just after the earthquake, when everyone closed ranks and worked together. The disaster created a mutual feeling of community, in which everyone suffered with the victims in Pakistan and tried to contribute in order to help them. As one of the doctors explained in an interview after the event:

> In the first period [after the earthquake] everyone wanted to help – and could help. Besides the teams of medical doctors who travelled to Pakistan and provided medical help in the disaster areas, this was also a time when money was collected. Organisation was needed, funds were applied for, some had to talk to the media and so on. Everyone contributed: the truck driver loaded the goods, taxi drivers drove around with messages and packages, engineers worked with the logistics … all good forces worked together. And everyone was equal within the framework of the common project: to help the earthquake victims in Pakistan.

This description resembles a study of philanthropy in the Pakistani-American diaspora, in which Adil Najam (2006) found that transnational activity was a latent resource that can be mobilised in certain critical situations, where people join forces and work together for a common cause. However, the communality of the first phase was succeeded by the splits and competition of the second phase.

Soon after the first pair of medical teams had left for Pakistan, the perception of the doctors' initiative began to change within the migrant community. This happened as the character of the disaster itself underwent change. After a few weeks, the Pakistani authorities and international NGOs had gained some control over the situation, and there was no longer the same urgent need for foreign medical professionals. Rather, the greater need was for professionals to assist with the rehabilitation of the injured and for help in reconstructing the area in general. The major, unambiguous disaster that had initially united the migrant community began to fade out of sight.

Meanwhile, a number of different relief initiatives and well-coordinated collections of money, sleeping bags, blankets and clothes were started in Denmark. Three Pakistani brothers, soon referred to simply as 'the Ahmad brothers', managed to arrange a big concert in the *Cirkusbygning* (circus building), a well-known concert hall in the centre of Copenhagen. Numerous artists performed for free, and all profits were donated to the earthquake victims. The Ahmad brothers received a lot of attention in the national media and ended up going to Pakistan, followed by a camera crew and television journalists who documented how they handed over the more than one million Danish kroner the concert had raised. Another far-reaching initiative was undertaken by a group of Pakistani teachers, who set up a transnational NGO, Help Education, to support the schooling of children in the disaster area. But the most effective NGO at the time was Muslim Aid, also with second-generation Pakistanis in leading positions, which had not only a good reputation within the migrant community, but also the necessary local connections in Pakistan to get their help out to the disaster area.

The point in mentioning a few of the numerous initiatives within the Pakistani migrant community is not to emphasise some at the expense of others. Rather, the purpose is to illustrate the different kinds of initiative that arose during this period of intensive transnationalism, and to suggest that the two phases following the earthquake were shaped by well-known community dynamics in competition for symbolic capital. In the first phase immediately after the disaster, all the hierarchies and differences that are normally present in the Pakistani community became insignificant, but after a while, in the second phase, they returned with a vengeance. In the beginning, there was a general consensus within the migrant community that the doctors were the ones with the professional skills and backgrounds to help the victims in the best and most effective ways. This consensus ceased when the situation changed and it became apparent that other kinds of assistance were needed. In the second phase, it was legitimate to question the contribution and effort of the medical doctors and to start working on other initiatives.

The many efforts to help the earthquake victims turned into yet another arena of competition for status and recognition within the Pakistani community – and this became the Achilles heel for MDAEV. Representatives of Muslim Aid, in particular, questioned the way the doctors managed the gift they had received from their sponsor Pfizer, asking whether it was reasonable for the money to be spent on clothes and trekking equipment for the doctors, rather than being given directly to the victims. Some pointed out that it would have been more efficient to use the money to hire doctors from, for instance, Karachi and pay them to work for a longer period in the disaster area, rather than to send doctors all the way from Denmark into the area for a few days at a time. Local doctors would have the linguistic and cultural competence, and hiring them would be a less expensive solution. Most critically, certain key figures in the doctors' association were portrayed in the gossip that circulated as primarily interested in promoting themselves in the media at the expense of their colleagues and the common cause of helping the victims in Kashmir. This also soon became a key issue within MDAEV itself, as the doctors started accusing each other of being 'earthquake tourists', insinuating that some were primarily interested in 'the experience' of going to the disaster area and in making impressive video recordings to show back home. As a result of various controversies, several doctors left the association and went to Pakistan on their own to help in different ways.

The point is that MDAEV soon became yet another arena of competition for symbolic capital in terms of status and recognition. This was true not only internally in the association, but also within the Pakistani community more widely, in which the MDAEV was just one among many initiatives set in motion to help the people of Kashmir in the best and most efficient ways. Many actors involved in the second phase after the earthquake had a double agenda: to help the victims, and to promote themselves within the migrant community. In this way, the impact of the Kashmir earthquake on the Pakistani community was structured according to an already existing grammar of identity, consisting of an ongoing dialectic between equality and hierarchy (Werbner 1990: 83), as well as the continued competition for symbolic capital in terms of status and prestige (see Chapter 2).

The developing dominant cleavage

So far, I have discussed how the Kashmir earthquake changed from being a local disaster in Pakistan to becoming a global media event with numerous effects. How the disaster affected the Pakistani community is just one issue. Another is how the event influenced the relationship between the migrant community and the wider society: that is, how the disaster in Kashmir affected the relationship between minorities and majorities in Denmark.

The reaction to MDAEV and its efforts to help was generally positive among the Danish media and public. When the first team of doctors returned from Pakistan, the association hosted a well-attended press conference at the Rigshospital, the national hospital in Copenhagen. Afterwards, the doctors received a favourable press, and some of them were invited to participate in various radio and television shows. Nevertheless, both the doctors and the migrant community at large were frustrated that the Danish government had not made a more significant economic contribution to the earthquake victims. The frustration intensified as weather forecasts for the Kashmir region warned of the approaching winter. Now it became even more urgent to send blankets, tents, food and medical equipment to prevent homeless earthquake victims freezing to death during the cold winter nights.

The doctors' dissatisfaction took shape at a meeting and confrontation with Ulla Tørnæs, then minister of development in the Liberal-Conservative government. Members of MDAEV criticised the government for not using the mobile field hospital that forms part of Danish preparations for national and international disasters. The lack of political will to help was interpreted as a unmistakable sign that Muslim lives in Pakistan were considered less valuable than the lives of Danes who were killed when the tsunami ravaged the beach and tourist resorts of Thailand (along with the coastlines of Sri Lanka, India and Indonesia) on 26 December 2004. Within the Pakistani community, it was forcefully pointed out that official Danish economic assistance to Pakistan was only a quarter of the amount spent following the tsunami.

In an open letter, central figures in the MDAEV urged Prime Minister Anders Fogh Rasmussen to mention the earthquake victims and their families in his New Year speech, to be transmitted on national television on the first day of January. The doctors drew attention to the fact that, the previous year, Rasmussen had spent most of his speech expressing his grief over the loss of Danish lives and extending his deeply felt commiserations to families bereaved by the tsunami. Furthermore, they explicitly referred to the way that the earthquake had been handled in Norway, as follows:

> How serious the present situation is, also to people living outside Pakistan, has been recognised in other countries. For instance, the Norwegian Minister of Development, Erik Solheim, has proved that official Norway knows and recognises that many Norwegians (with a family history related to Pakistan) are personally affected by the disaster, and by doing that he has recognised the loss and grief of his fellow countrymen and thereby included them in the national community of Norwegian citizens.
>
> Signed H.L. Butt, W. Ahmad and M. Iqbal

The correspondents appealed for a similar recognition of themselves as Danes and for an acknowledgement of the grief they had suffered after losing friends and family members as result of the earthquake. However, the Prime Minister ignored their request.

The experience of not being recognised as 'real' Danes (see Chapter 5) by officialdom in Denmark, and the suspicion circulating that the lives of Pakistani Muslims were seen as less valuable than those of Protestant (or atheist) Danes, once again changed the meaning and content of the disaster within the migrant community. It became yet another example of the more encompassing structural pattern dividing Danes from immigrants that has gained ground in Danish society in recent decades – a pattern in which Muslims have acquired a dubious status and are met with general suspicion.

In *Analysis of a Social Situation in Modern Zululand*, Max Gluckman (1940: 68ff.) introduced the concept of a 'developing dominant cleavage' and used it to discuss the relationship between blacks and whites in Zululand during the 1930s. This analytical concept stresses the social and·historical processes in which uneven distributions of power stimulate the creation of a cleavage, instead of focusing on the two groups that are separated by it. According to Gluckman, historical developments in the region – namely, colonialism, racism and the British organisation and administration of society in general – generated and strengthened a developing dominant cleavage between blacks and whites that was significant in every relationship and interaction between them (see Macmillan 1995: 51–2). A similar dominant cleavage is taking form in Denmark between Danes and Muslim immigrants (see Chapter 1).

Applied in the Danish context, the developing dominant cleavage captures the image of a social division between segments of the population along lines of race, ethnicity and religion that sometimes becomes salient in the everyday, lives of Pakistanis (and other minorities) in Danish society. The cleavage is neither tangible, nor an officially sanctioned division between segments of the total Danish population. Rather, it constitutes a reservoir, a potentiality of power that can be mobilised in certain situations either by the majority, who claim that they have a legitimate right to decide and define specific social situations, or by the Muslim minorities, who point out that they are being treated unjustly. In general, national identity politics have intensified in recent decades, and have increased the dominant cleavage between 'real' Danes and Muslim immigrants, regardless of the actual citizenship of the latter.

The doctors of MDAEV learned this lesson the hard way. They had done everything right. Their appearances in the national media showed them to be well organised, articulate and determined. Connected with Pakistan but nevertheless speaking perfect Danish, they constituted a group of immigrants who so far had been absent from the Danish debate on Muslim immigrants. The doctors contradicted the stereotypes of Pakistani immigrants as criminals, violent gang members, taxi drivers or proprietors of corner shops. Instead, they came forward and presented themselves as a group that, through education and social mobility, had risen above the crowd of 'regular' immigrants and the ongoing controversies between minorities and majority. Within the Pakistani community they were respected for their educational achievements, while for the Danish majority they stood out mainly as doctors, that is, impersonal medical professionals who are expected to provide their services regardless of personality, religion or skin colour. The doctors had a unique position, as they were respected and able to navigate on both sides of the cleavage. In this respect they were special.

However, the hesitation of the Danish state in helping the victims of the disaster, and its failure to acknowledge publicly the Pakistani community's grief over lost friends and family members, mobilised the dominant cleavage. From the very beginning, the doctors imagined that they could put the disaster onto the public and political agenda and, among other things, make the government send the mobile field hospital to Kashmir. The doctors worked on both sides of the cleavage to fulfil these ambitions. But as they failed, this was interpreted as yet another proof of how badly they, their families and Muslims in general are treated in Denmark. The doctors had to realise that, despite all their efforts to contribute to Danish society by using their higher education and working as medical professionals, they were not recognised as 'real' Danes after all.

Conclusion: momentary homelands

Today MDAEV no longer exists. The association had a specific purpose, and once it was achieved, the organisation simply dissolved itself. In the overall picture of the Kashmir earthquake, the Pakistani doctors from Denmark played a minor role, although undoubtedly an important one to those they treated. It should also be emphasised that the efforts of the doctors still command respect when the topic comes up in my conversations with Pakistani interlocutors, regardless of profession, gender or age.

At the outset of this chapter, I argued that the current state of globalisation – characterised by time-space compression, simultaneity and an accelerated diffusion of uncontrolled information – presents a challenge to contemporary ethnography. Events can no longer always be characterised as they used to be. These relatively new conditions for human interaction, and the creation of alternative social formations, compel anthropologists to explore and theorise the relationship between locally situated events and their chaotic patterns of unpredictable global effects. Our challenge is to understand the character and scope of these types of events, showing how they create new imaginaries, hopes, and fears and how they motivate people into political action around the world. In this project, an updated 'version 2.1' of the social situational analysis approach seems very fruitful. The discussion of how the Kashmir earthquake affected the Pakistani community in Denmark can be seen as constituting a humble beginning in this endeavour.

I have shown how the disaster presented an opportunity for doctors to fulfil some of the promises of their profession, to meet the ambitions of their families, and to help in the 'momentary homeland' of Pakistan. Their contribution soon became incorporated into a pre-existing logic of competition for symbolic capital within the migrant community, however. From a transnational perspective, the doctors were at short notice deeply involved in the activism and intensive transnationalism that characterised the transnational field after the catastrophe. It could also be argued, however, that the Pakistani doctors were never really part of an international social field and reality, but that their orientation was defined and determined by the structures governing the Danish context in which they acted. Even when reaching out to help the earthquake victims, they were also preoccupied with their own performance, and with how it would be evaluated by real and imagined audiences of family and kin, community members and the Danish population in general. All along, many of the doctors involved had alternative agendas, besides aiding the victims of the disaster in Pakistan.

The effects that the Kashmir earthquake occasioned among Pakistani migrants in Denmark reflect a pre-existing national and international structure, but they were also part of a process of reorientation, whereby new horizons might begin to take shape. From one perspective, the intensive transnationalism that followed the earthquake was a highly innovative period in which new modes of action and imagination came into being. But from another perspective, all of these inventions were grounded in well-known categories and in the already existing grammar of identity that is salient within the competitive Pakistani community. Perceived as a critical event, the Kashmir earthquake and the subsequent initiative by the doctors' association actually did have the potential to make a difference – not only for the victims in Pakistan, but also as a way to restructure relations and dynamics between families in the migrant community, and to alter stereotypical images of Muslim immigrants among the wider Danish public. Still, this potential was never realised. One important reason was that the Kashmir earthquake was subordinated to September 11, which has turned out to be the major critical event of the decade – one that continues to produce new local effects worldwide. Despite their intentions and efforts, the doctors of MDAEV ended up confirming the image and logic of the developing dominant cleavage between the national majority and the Muslim minorities living in Denmark.

Part IV
Afflictions

The fourth and final part of this book is dedicated to the religious life and conceptual universe on the basis of which Pakistani migrant families have reconstructed a moral and cosmological vision to support themselves in their new and all-too-often hostile Danish environment. In this endeavour, I could have focused on the public aspects of religious life, such as the establishment of numerous Copenhagen-based mosques that have served Pakistani migrants in different aspects of their lives over the years. But as my main focus is the migrant family, I turn my attention toward the specific religious ideas and practices that are used to form and contest relationships in the private spheres of households and family networks. More precisely, this fourth part presents and analyses the religious universe of *kala jaddu* (sorcery) as a specific arena in which problems and conflicts related to local and transnational family life are negotiated. Rumours and suspicions of *kala jaddu* constitute a specific allegorical arena which is used to reorganise and make sense of problematic family relations and changing moral orders. In this respect, *kala jaddu* constitutes what I will call a 'destructive–productive' force of family life, which not only tends to break up intimate relations and destroy common notions of what it means to be and to do family, but also enables the active creation of new affiliations and moral orders.

The question whether or not the phenomenon of *kala jaddu* belongs to 'real' Islam is a matter of controversy. In South Asian Islam, however, the Barelwi tradition does recognise some of the more mystical aspects of Islam that sometimes are rejected by revivalist and neo-fundamentalist religious groupings such as the Deobandi, Wahhabi or Salafi. The Barelwi tradition promotes a specific interpretation of the nature of God, and of the status of the Prophet Muhammad and of holy men or *wali* (friends of God), which can seem provocative to other branches of Islam (Lewis 2002: 40). Notions of *kala jaddu* are an aspect of South Asian 'popular Islam' defined as 'forms of worship that are not controlled by the *ulama*, but are not necessarily unorthodox. "Popular" does not refer to "lower"-class or rural populations; it concerns all social strata, as well as urban dwellers. Sufi orders are part of this popular Islam even if they do not oppose the *ulama* in general' (Roy 2004: 220; see also Werbner 2003). The chapters that follow will demonstrate that South Asian 'popular Islam' contains elaborate ideas of occult forces and interferences, including sorcery; they will discuss not only how this affects the private sphere and family relations among Pakistani migrants in Denmark and the diaspora in general, but also how suspicions of sorcery are related to wider complex historical and political processes within Danish society (cf. Kapferer 1997: 19).

Beliefs in and suspicions of *kala jaddu* are highly contested both within and between migrant families. Many of my interlocutors rejected *kala jaddu* as a manifestation of 'village mentality' (*landsbymentalitet*) or superstition when asked about it directly. However, both women and men in first and second generations of Pakistanis in Denmark who claim not to believe in *kala jaddu* can end up in critical life-situations or family conflicts where sorcery seems the only reasonable explanation. Whether it is legitimate to suggest the social diagnosis of *kala jaddu* as the explanation for a family conflict depends, to a large extent, on the context and the audience. Nevertheless, *kala jaddu* is an aspect of the common repertoire of identities between which Pakistani migrants can shift in different places and contexts.

In Chapter 9, I will discuss the marginal position of *kala jaddu* in Islam and in studies of Pakistani family life, as well as the problems of doing research on such a delicate subject. I present three extended accounts of Nazia, Shazia and Mrs Mian, who between them represent both first and second generations of Pakistani women in Denmark, and who fear that their everyday lives have been affected by sorcery committed by members of their transnational family networks. I suggest that suspicions of *kala jaddu* constitute a particular way to relate to one another and to renegotiate the moral orders of family obligations and relatedness, one that is especially relevant to those in vulnerable positions in their family structure and in the surrounding society.

In Chapter 10, I describe in detail the case of Tahir, a well-educated second-generation Pakistani man who tries to determine whether or not his brother-in-law is inflicted by *kala jaddu*. The masculine perspective challenges the widespread assumption that suspicions of *kala jaddu* are primarily to be found among women, and emphasises the feelings of ambiguity and uncertainty that second-generation Pakistanis face when they are suddenly confronted with day-to-day experiences that call for a social diagnosis of sorcery. The extended case study leads to a more general discussion of how suspicions of *kala jaddu* seem to have regained importance among the migrant community, partly as result of ongoing family transitions and upheavals, and partly as a result of the contested status of Muslim immigrants since 2001. There appears to be a connection between the external political attempts at social engineering, involving the securitisation of the Muslim immigrant family, and emerging uncertainty about, and suspicions of, *kala jaddu* within and between Pakistani migrant families in Denmark.

Chapter 9

In-laws and outlaws

Suspicions of local and transnational sorcery

Mrs Mian leaned forward and looked me straight in the eyes: 'I suspect at least one of my sons to be afflicted by *kala jaddu*!' Mrs Mian, a Pakistani woman in her mid-fifties and the mother of five grown-up children, has lived with her husband in a suburb of Copenhagen since the early 1970s. Before she revealed her anxieties about whether her son might be a victim of sorcery, we had already met a couple of times and talked about her life and family situation. Now, in order to convince me of her suspicions, she went through the circumstances that she regarded as critical evidence for the social diagnosis of sorcery: her son Bilal had always been such a good boy, had never smoked, drunk alcohol or done anything wrong, and had always respected his parents and seniors. After he married a young woman from Pakistan, however, he had started behaving in peculiar ways. Several times he had taken sides with his wife when she and his mother had been fighting over everyday incidents in the household, and he had accused his mother of lying. The most incriminating evidence, however, was that during her six-month stay in Pakistan – four months longer than originally intended – his wife had persuaded Bilal to buy an apartment of their own without even telling his mother. So that when the girl finally returned to Denmark, she went directly to the couple's new apartment without even visiting her mother-in-law. This was not normal. Bilal would never do something like that!

After this crucial incident, Mrs Mian decided to do some research on her own, using her networks in Pakistan, and she discovered that the mother of her daughter-in-law actually had a reputation in the local area in Punjab for practising *kala jaddu*. This convinced Mrs Mian that the daughter-in-law and her mother had performed sorcery on Bilal while she was in Pakistan.

Recovering from my bewilderment at the sudden turn in our conversation, I asked what she could do in response. Mrs Mian breathed a deep sigh of relief. All she could do now for Bilal in order to deal with the critical situation in her family was to pray and read the Quran. Using *kala jaddu* was not to be seen as a victory for her in-laws, but rather as their defeat. Mrs Mian would not use illegitimate powers to win Bilal back, and rhetorically asked: 'As long as I can work, then why would I steal?'

This chapter explores how and why Pakistani migrant families experience being targeted by *kala jaddu*, usually thought to be performed by members of the extended family in Pakistan. The three accounts of Mrs Mian, Shazia and Nazia, representing both first and second generations of Pakistani women in Denmark, will be used as prisms for the more general discussion of disruptive family and kinship structures, as well as of changing notions of relatedness within transnational migrant networks.

It is a common experience among Pakistanis in Denmark that the cherished institution of the family has been subject to radical change in recent years, as traditional structures of obligation, loyalty and responsibility between close relatives disappear or are rapidly reconfigured. The insecurity and uncertainty that follow correlate with the reappearance of *kala jaddu* in many families and personal narratives, as a social diagnosis that allows migrants in vulnerable positions to explain the inexplicable.

A starting-point in this analysis is that the practices of and belief in *kala jaddu* should not be dismissed as mere folk religion or superstition, but that they should be taken seriously as yet another way to do family. In line with recent kinship studies urging us to look at local idioms of relatedness and the various practices through which people construct lasting ties of emotion and responsibility (Carsten 2000), *kala jaddu* will be analysed as a particular way of pursuing family struggles and of relating to one another by supernatural means. The three cases of Nazia, Shazia and Mrs Mian involve in-laws in Pakistan, who are suspected of using illegitimate means to influence family affairs and to rearrange relationships within the Danish branch of the family. In this way, the three cases address the ambivalence within global kinship networks between consanguineous and conjugal families. Suspecting one's in-laws of *kala jaddu* not only suggests that they are deliberately trying to harm you, thus violating common codes of morality and decency; it also implies that they have definitively parted company with Islam. A critical social diagnosis of *kala jaddu* therefore reconfigures one's in-laws as outlaws.

A marginalised discourse

In anthropological terminology, *kala jaddu* falls under the category of 'sorcery', that is, a deliberate affliction directed at a specific victim. *Kala jaddu* should be confused neither with *nazar* ('the evil eye'), the innate and often uncontrollable witchcraft of jealous people (Spooner 1970; Sachs 1983), nor with autonomous and sometimes evil-spirited non-human creatures like *jinn*, *bhut* or *churail* that are occasionally reported as interfering with the everyday family lives of Pakistanis, both at home and abroad (Ewing 1997; Shaw 2000: 210ff.; Werbner 2003; Ballard 2006: 165; Khan 2006).

There are only a few empirical studies showing how *kala jaddu* affects family life. In her ethnography of the global Sufi cult of the then living saint Zindapir, situated in Ghamkol Sharif, Pnina Werbner (2003: 222ff.) gives examples of how malign spirits and sorcery can affect the lives of *murids* (followers) in Britain. In another article, she discusses marriage conflicts within a dispersed transnational *biraderi* network that resulted in accusations of intercontinental sorcery supposedly committed by relatives in Pakistan (Werbner 1999: 32). Werbner suggests that such 'demonic migrations' are the outcome of extended families and neighbourhoods being reconstituted in new environments in the diaspora, often creating new jealousies and anxieties (2003: 240). Similarly, Alison Shaw and Roger Ballard both emphasise several kinds of occult attack as part of ongoing power struggles within Pakistani migrant households, especially salient among female family members in less powerful positions (Shaw 2000: 209–10; Ballard 2011). In a South Asian context, several more traditional village studies (Carstairs 1983; Gardner 1995; Callan 2007; Varley 2008) and studies of various aspects of Sufi mysticism (Ewing 1997; Werbner and Basu 1998) have touched on the theme of *kala jaddu*. Finally, several studies deal with afflictions and occult attacks among migrants in the diaspora using a medical paradigm and with reference to discourses of healing (Sachs 1983; Hermansen 2005; Rozario 2009). Despite the extensive literature touching on *kala jaddu*, it is often mentioned only briefly as part of a more comprehensive cultural-religious universe. There has yet to be any sustained discussion in the South Asian literature of the sociological implications of sorcery (and witchcraft), such as has been debated in, for instance, the literature on Africa.

The marginal position of *kala jaddu* in the literature to some extent reflects the ways in which ethnographers approach issues of family and religion in Pakistan studies. Researchers may be too willing to accept their interlocutors' dismissive suspicions of *kala jaddu* within family networks as irrelevant folk religion or mere superstition, or when representatives of the 'new-born religious' second generation explain away such practices as leftovers of the 'cultural' practices and beliefs of their parents. This has led many scholars of Islam in the diaspora to focus on religious leaders and authorities, ignoring the popular practices as a pale and deviant shadow of what is supposed to be the true Islam (Ballard 2006: 162).

However, even though suspicions of *kala jaddu* tend to be reduced to a marginal discourse of family affairs, they are nevertheless a significant aspect of lived experience. According to Roger Ballard, magic is part of what he calls the kismetic dimension of religious life, a reference to those ideas and practices, such as visiting shrines and seeking the assistance of living and dead saints, that South Asians may use to explain the otherwise inexplicable, and having done so, to stop adversity in its tracks (Ballard 1999: 17). The kismetic dimension constitutes a folk theory of causality that provides reasons for misfortune, and enables counter-actions to be undertaken within the predetermined cosmic order of Islam.

Despite a growing interest in the kismetic dimension among Pakistanis in Denmark, *kala jaddu* continues to be a disputed aspect of family life, epitomising unresolved tensions in the community between notions of culture versus religion and tradition versus modernity. In her psychology-inspired approach to Sufism in Lahore, Katherine Pratt Ewing (1997) argues that her interlocutors encounter and relate to multiple discourses simultaneously. These 'shifting selves' explain how interlocutors from the upper middle classes cope with being intellectual, rational and modern, while at the same time being attracted to the emotional, mystical and traditional universe of Sufism. Ewing's ethnography emphasises that Islamic mysticism (or the kismetic dimension) is not simply 'traditional', as many religious reformists would have it. Rather, the notions of tradition and modernity are mutually constitutive, while the shifting self is a basic condition of post-colonial subjects, which enables them to navigate within and between supposedly contradictory discourses (Ewing 1997: 26). In this respect, Ewing's argument is in line with newer studies of 'occult economies' (witchcraft, sorcery, magic) in Africa. These transcend the dichotomy between 'traditional' and 'modern', and argue that, rather than leftovers from a previous traditional lifestyle, emerging occult economies with indeterminate meanings are highly modern phenomena, perhaps even constitutive of modernity itself (Geschiere 1997; Comaroff and Comaroff 1999; Moore and Sanders 2001: 12).

Following on from these insights, my etic analysis here goes beyond the emic descriptions of my Pakistani interlocutors, which often present *kala jaddu* as proof of the tough 'village mentality' (*landsbymentalitet*) found among 'cultural' people and 'traditional' families of rural origin. I argue, on the contrary, that the preoccupation with rumours and suspicions of *kala jaddu* must be understood as a thoroughly modern manifestation of the uncertainty and moral disquiet that result from ruptures in the institution of the family and from the contested status of Muslim immigrants in the Danish welfare state in recent years.

Navigating religious dimensions

When asked about *kala jaddu*, many interlocutors reply like Freha, a young second-generation Pakistani woman: '*Kala jaddu* exists. It says so in the Quran.' To convince a non-Muslim like myself of this fact, some will recite the *sura* on how the angels Harut and Marut brought magic into the world in the time of old Babylon as a temptation to test people, saying, 'We are merely a trail and a temptation, so do not disbelieve' (*sura al-baqara* 2: 102). Or they explain how later, during the lifetime and reign of the Prophet Salayman (Solomon), disbelieving *jinns* taught people how to use magic to estrange husbands from wives (Al-Sha'rawi 1995: 35). Others present evidence from the Sunna, relating the *hadith* of how the Prophet Muhammad himself was targeted by illicit magic on one occasion. The object that caused the harm was made from hair taken from a comb the Prophet had used, which had then been hidden in the well of Dharwaan. In a dream, the malicious object and the site where it was hidden were revealed to the Prophet. When the well was filled in, the spell was broken (Ameen 2005: 182). These stories prove the existence of *kala jaddu* within a Muslim universe: whoever denies this fact is a *kafir*, a non-believer (ibid.: 183). Reporting this evidence from the Quran and Sunna situates the existence of magic and sorcery within some of 'the primal scenes of Islam' (cf. McLoughlin 2009: 244) and within orthodox tradition. In this respect, *kala jaddu* is an ontological and cosmological fact that one has to deal with.

Some Pakistani interlocutors argue that the Prophet was the target of sorcery only because he was extraordinary in every way: that magic exists, but not among ordinary people. Others suggest that probably only a few diagnosed cases are actually *kala jaddu*. In this perspective, suspicions of *kala jaddu* are primarily a means for people to avoid taking personal responsibility for unfortunate events in their lives and families. Examples of arguments in this sense are that it is people's own fault if they get divorced, or that it is understandable if newly-wed sons and daughters-in-law wish to leave the patrilocal household in order to obtain some privacy. Diseases are a natural and inevitable part of life, and childlessness can have many other causes than sorcery committed by envious members of the extended family. This kind of 'rational' argumentation is common among well-educated second-generation Pakistanis, who think their parents and representatives of the first generation exaggerate the threat of sorcery and are too quick to conclude that misfortunes are caused by *kala jaddu*.

Still, many Pakistanis will seriously consider whether or not they might be victims of sorcery if they are struck by inexplicable misfortune and their lives suddenly turned upside down. Sofia, a married woman in her late twenties, explained that: '*Kala jaddu* is a means to make the life of someone else stop, for example, by causing them divorce, illness, childlessness or fire in their house.' Similarly Irfan, an unmarried man in his early twenties, explained: '*Kala jaddu* is when you are stuck – if you, for example, are a bright student doing well, and you then suddenly flunk an exam, and have to do the whole semester one more time. Then people start to suspect that something might be wrong.' And Irfan elaborates: 'You start to suspect *kala jaddu* when you suffer extraordinarily. It is not a single episode or unfortunate event, but when you see a pattern (*systematik*) of unfortunate circumstances in your life, then you start considering if this might be a case of *kala jaddu*.' In this way, suspicions of *kala jaddu* are related to critical moments of vital conjunctures where so far steady life-trajectories are suddenly challenged, and planned future horizons need to be reconsidered (cf. Johnson-Hanks 2002, 2006).

This was the case for Mariam, a young university student who was engaged to Hussain. Their match was the result of a crush, leading to numerous telephone calls, internet correspondence and secret meetings. Despite the reluctance of the families, the young couple were determined to get married and planned a controversial love marriage. Everything seemed fine, but just a few weeks before the wedding, Hussan broke off the engagement without any explanation. Mariam was devastated. What had happened, what had changed between them? She went through all the disagreements they might have had, without reaching a logical explanation for Hussain's rejection of her. Finally, she consulted a gifted friend who carries out spiritual investigations to find out whether Hussain had been struck by *kala jaddu* – perhaps by his mother, who did not approve of the *rishta*, or by a jealous aunt in Pakistan, who had her own daughter lined up for a marriage on the rebound if her nephew's engagement should be broken off. The friend concluded, however, that this was not a case of *kala jaddu*. Apparently, Hussain had simply changed his mind. Still, the case shows how Mariam, who would never normally have believed in or suspected *kala jaddu*, treated it as a reasonable explanation for the inexplicable change in her life-trajectory and future horizon.

Anyone can end up in a situation like Mariam, where one has to consider seriously the possibility of *kala jaddu*. Even though belief in *kala jaddu* is said to be stronger in the first generation than the second, and presumably more salient among women than men owing to the gendered organisation of public and private spaces (cf. Rasanayagam 2006; Ballard 2011), the kismetic dimension of religious life continues to be present as a reservoir that migrants can either mobilise or risk exposure to.

Studying *kala jaddu*

Within a village-like migrant community, where everyone protects their family's reputation, people are often reluctant to give an outsider access to the family sphere. This reluctance is all the stronger because Pakistanis have been negatively represented in the Danish media (see Chapter 1). It can therefore be difficult to study a sensitive topic such as *kala jaddu*.

First of all, *kala jaddu* is not something people talk about openly. Suggesting it as an explanation for misfortune is only done in the company of family or close friends – and definitely not to a non-Pakistani like myself, who is expected not to understand. One reason for this is that no one will risk being ridiculed for being 'superstitious' or 'backward'. Another is that you can never really trust anyone; because this kind of illicit magic is most often performed by family members, business partners or friends who envy your life, material belongings or success, you can never be sure that those with whom you share urgent anxieties about *kala jaddu* are not those responsible for it in the first place.

Secondly, Pakistanis commonly distinguish between three kinds of problems caused by *kala jaddu*:

1. *Personal illness*. Problems sleeping at night, sweating, dizziness or loss of appetite, along with more serious medical conditions such as heart problems, epilepsy, childlessness or mental illness such as depression or

schizophrenia are all examples of illness that can hit the individual and be interpreted retrospectively as the result of sorcery.

2. *Material environment.* You may start to suspect *kala jaddu* when apparently arbitrary accidents happen, such as a car accident, or if your house or personal belongings are damaged by water or fire.

3. *Social relations. Kala jaddu* is a sensitive topic because it deals with problematic family relations and domestic power struggles: for instance, when common expectations of the marital relationship between husband and wife are violated if one partner has an affair, or when a wife feels neglected because her husband is spending too much time with his friends or family instead of with her. It can also arise when siblings or *biraderi* members compete over resources, as in cases where one has more money, a more successful business, more sons, the biggest house, more land, etc. Structural inequality in transnational networks may result in envy, and may disturb the family relationship. Suspicions can also arise from conflicts between mother-in-law and daughter-in-law over power, authority, resources or love within the household, or when young people decide to leave the patrilocal household and get their own place, get involved in illegal activities, or have secret love affairs that end up scandalising the family. In such cases, the irresponsible actions of the second generation might be diagnosed as caused by *kala jaddu*.

Rumours and suspicions of *kala jaddu* are potentially disruptive and are treated with discretion. Finally, it is important to stress that anyone who performs *kala jaddu*, or makes others do so, will automatically exclude themselves from Islam (Ameen 2005: 202). Those who do so anyway are considered to be outlaws, living outside the moral order of decent people. In this way, knowledge of, or even the slightest interest in *kala jaddu* is highly suspicious. It is a topic one is not supposed to know anything about.

It is generally believed that *kala jaddu* is carried out in Pakistan by sorcerers who will charge money for their evil deeds. Interlocutors explain that it is always possible for migrants in Denmark to call someone in Pakistan who can go to a local sorcerer and have him or her perform the illicit magic. Apparently, occult attacks are not affected by the distance between Pakistan and Denmark. I have only a little anecdotal information on how *kala jaddu* is done in practice. Most often it is explained as the effect of a *ta'wiz*, an amulet that will affect you when, for instance, it is hidden in your house or garden. To be powerful, such a magical device should be made from the hair, nails or personal belongings of the victim, just as happened to the Prophet Muhammad himself. The *ta'wiz* can also be dissolved in water or hidden in food and then consumed by the victim. If the evil *ta'wiz* enters the body, the effect is supposedly much more devastating. Finally, some claim that *kala jaddu* is achieved by reorganising the words and sayings of the holy Quran. Just as the word of God is believed to have healing powers, so too it can have severely negative effects if it is mixed up in the right (or one might say wrong) way.

Having clarified how kala jaddu relates to both Islam and family life, I will now discuss the three cases of Mrs Mian, Nazia and Shazia in greater detail.

Mrs Mian's story

Mrs Mian, who was introduced at the beginning of this chapter, lives with her husband in a villa to the south of Copenhagen. The couple has been blessed with five children – three sons and two daughters – and five grandchildren. For many years they were self-employed, but today Mr Mian is retired and has handed over the business to his sons, and all the children have left the home. Mrs Mian regrets that none of her sons live with her, as the tradition of the patrilocal household prescribes. She feels very lonely.

After arriving in Denmark in the early 1970s, Mr Mian worked in a factory. As money was scarce, they had to rent a room in the flat of another Pakistani couple. After an accident in which Mr Mian suffered a complicated fracture, he lost his job, and they had to live on sickness benefits for almost a year. Therefore Mrs Mian and the two children were sent back to Pakistan, where for more than three years she lived with her mother-in-law and her husband's unmarried sisters. In 1976 she had to return to Denmark, because the family wanted her to have more children.

Once again Mrs Mian had to suffer the embarrassment of living in a rented room in the apartment of another Pakistani couple, but after a while they succeeded in finding a little apartment they could afford. Meanwhile the extended family's wishes were fulfilled when Mrs Mian gave birth to more children. In order to have a second income in the household, she later started working at various unskilled jobs.

Like many other Pakistani families, in the early 1980s Mr and Mrs Mian opened a corner shop, but they quickly sold it again after being harassed and racially abused by a gang of *grønjakker* (a local version of skinheads). Instead, they started an import company. The business soon became a financial success, so in 1990 they left their crowded apartment and moved into a big house with their grown-up sons and later the latter's newly arrived wives from Pakistan. This was when the problems began.

According to Mrs Mian, there are two types of daughters-in-law: those from Pakistani families in Denmark, and those from Pakistan. The first is brought up in day-care institutions and schools, has Danish friends and has learnt the 'Danish way' of not showing respect to teachers, parents and the authorities in general. Like many other migrant parents, Mrs Mian initially tried to overcome these problems by selecting *rishta* for her children in Pakistan, but today she has learnt better:

> Pakistani spouses are lazy and spoiled. They are brought up like hens in a cage in [often high-class] protective families, but when they arrive in Denmark, they suddenly become free birds. They do not know hard work or the value of money, and will not even take advice from their mothers-in-law. This is a real headache.

However, Mrs Mian does see differences between her daughters-in-law. Whereas Saima, the wife of her oldest son, is Mrs Mian's sister's daughter and came to Denmark when she was just seventeen, the wives of Bilal and his brother were in their mid-twenties when they arrived. They had been selected from the wider *biraderi* and came from influential families in Gujrat city. These girls quickly learned western manners. While Mrs Mian herself was a pioneer in Denmark and had to work her way up, her daughters-in-law arrived in established and well-off families:

> They come here with their Bollywood fantasies of what married life should be about, and suddenly they can become queens in their own little kingdoms. They have an urge to leave the house of their mother-in-law and get their own place to rule over.

After arriving in Denmark, the two daughters-in-law not only changed mentally, they also started dyeing their hair and wearing contact lenses. One of the girls even replaced her traditional dresses with jeans and revealing blouses. Mrs Mian asked her either to change her clothes or to leave the house. She felt that her 'daughters' should not dress like that in her home.

The conflicts went on until all three sons left the house. Two of them still have contact with Mrs Mian, but the connection with Bilal has effectively been broken. By using *kala jaddu*, Mrs Mian's in-laws have taken Bilal away from her.

Nazia's story

Nazia is a second-generation Pakistani woman in her early thirties. Together with her husband and their three children, she lives in a suburb of Copenhagen. She is just about to finish her training as a pre-school teacher.

When Nazia was a child, her father and mother had a very bad marriage, and they 'were never nice to each other'. Back then, her mother always told Nazia and her siblings that the marriage problems were the result of *kala jaddu* performed by her mother-in-law and sister-in-law, Nazia's grandmother and aunt in Pakistan. Their motives for trying to ruin the marriage were apparently envy of her mother's life and many opportunities in Denmark.

Today Nazia's siblings are married in Pakistan, but she herself is married to Jens, a Danish non-Muslim. Once, Nazia refused a suitor while she was on holiday in Pakistan. Her mother called from Denmark and asked Nazia's uncle to take a tuft of her hair and take it to 'the right people', in order to change her mind by using *kala jaddu*. Her uncle refused to do so, but the confrontation left Nazia with the disturbing knowledge that her mother would not refrain from using illicit powers in order to make her behave properly and obey her.

Years later, Nazia fell in love with her current husband, Jens, and they got married without the consent of Nazia's parents. This controversial move made the young couple the focus of inquisitive gazes and ongoing gossip in the local Pakistani neighbourhood, so Nazia and Jens decided to move to another part of Denmark. For years, Nazia had no contact with her family, except with one of her sisters. But then they decided to return to the city.

While living away from her parents, Nazia had at one time found what looked like flecks of blood on her wallpaper. A Pakistani friend had confirmed the findings to her as *kala jaddu* material. This made her worry that her mother might be using magic to get her back. The suspicion grew stronger after they returned to Copenhagen and Nazia started visiting her parents again in order for her children to become acquainted with their grandparents. After a while, Nazia and Jens had a big crisis in their marriage. Again she had to consider seriously whether this was the result of her mother's sorcery.

According to Nazia, her mother had from the very beginning interpreted Nazia's falling in love and marrying Jens as itself a case of *kala jaddu*, though presumably not inflicted by Jens or his family, who as Danes and non-Muslims would have no knowledge of it. Instead, she suspected that the love match and eventual marriage were the result of *kala jaddu* performed by her enemies in the extended family network in Pakistan. They obviously wanted to harm her, and did so by taking Nazia away from her.

Later Nazia learned from her sister that, at the time when she was not living in Copenhagen, the family found a bundle of bones buried in the backyard of the house. Each bone had one of the children's names inscribed on it. Immediately her mother concluded that family members in Pakistan had been trying to split her family up and take her children away from her. However, Nazia and her sister also discussed the possibility that it could have been their mother herself who had performed *kala jaddu* on the children in order to keep them nearby as an intimate part of her life. Even though Nazia tried to distance herself from her mother, she still played a crucial part in her life. This might indicate that magic was involved.

Shazia's story

Shazia lived with her seven-year-old son in a single-room apartment. After her divorce she had lived for almost a year with a lady friend and her husband, but then they threw her out and the municipality provided her with an apartment. Years ago, Shazia's parents were offered *rishta* by a Pakistani family in Denmark from the same village as Shazia's mother (see Fig. 5). Her parents accepted the marriage proposal and Shazia ended up living in Frederiksværk with her husband, a second-generation Pakistani immigrant (1). After six years they were blessed with a son, but soon afterwards they divorced, so in practice her former husband never really had a relationship with the child. Due to domestic conflict, Shazia was given custody of the child, and her ex-husband lost all rights to see the boy.

After the divorce, Shazia made the unconventional and controversial decision to live as a single mother and raise her son by herself. Shazia and

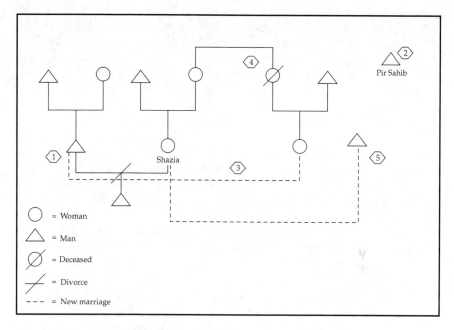

Figure 5. Illustration of Shazia's family relations

her son moved into an apartment in a block of flats where only the residents had keys to the staircase. Nevertheless one day she found a box of food and toys for her son outside the entrance to her apartment: 'It was a really nice box, just like those you can get at McDonalds'. Shazia asked everyone in the staircase if they had left the box outside her door, but nobody had. This made her really nervous, and she contacted an elder woman, a trusted 'auntie' in the Pakistani neighbourhood. She advised her to throw the box, the food and the toys out immediately. Even so, more packages with toys from McDonalds turned up on her doorstep. One time her son found one of the boxes. He was really disappointed when Shazia took it away from him and dumped it in the rubbish bin, instructing him never to touch or eat any delicacies he might find. Shazia would not have the packages in her house. According to Shazia, the most plausible explanation for all the packages placed on her doorstep in a locked staircase was illicit magic. She was convinced that the toys and food were a kind of love-magic, performed by her ex-husband and his family with the single purpose of taking her son away from her. She feared that if her son played with the toys or ate the food he would stop loving her and start to love his father instead.

In this period Shazia was very scared and had trouble sleeping at night. She discussed the happenings with her mother in Pakistan. In order to help her, Shazia's mother consulted the local Pir Sahib at a famous shrine in her native village (2), and asked him whether or not this was a case of *kala jaddu*. Pir Sahib confirmed the suspicion: this was *kala jaddu* initiated by Shazia's ex-husband's family, although he refrained from pointing out the actual perpetrator of the sorcery. The former in-laws' motivation for using *kala jaddu* was obviously that after the divorce Shazia had gained custody over the child. Several times her ex-husband had tried to get custody of the boy by legal means, but without success.

Now back in Denmark, Shazia decided to move away from Fredriksværk in order to remove herself from her old apartment (an address her husband and his family knew) and make a fresh start. In Copenhagen Shazia was given a secret address by the municipality so that her former in-laws could neither contact nor harass her. But as her ex-husband had remarried – to none other than Shazia's cousin (3) – and had moved to Albertslund, a suburb south of Copenhagen, she knew that it was just a matter of time before they would meet again.

After a while Shazia started to have nightmares. She was haunted in her dreams by her dead aunt (4), her mother's sister and the mother of her ex-husband's new wife. Every night her aunt came to her in her dreams and asked her forgiveness for the harm and evil she had caused Shazia. Once again her mother in Pakistan consulted Pir Sahib, who advised her to accept the apology, otherwise her dead aunt would keep visiting her. Shazia followed the advice, and it helped. Shazia learned that the aunt came to her to do penance for a misdeed. She was the one who had initially attacked Shazia and her husband with *kala jaddu* in order to split them up, since Shazia's ex-husband would then be free to marry her own daughter (Shazia's cousin) after the divorce. The cunning plan worked, and today her daughter had taken Shazia's position, as the cousin was married to Shazia's ex-husband and living in Denmark with him.

After her death the aunt apparently needed forgiveness for her evil deed, so she came to Shazia. In order to help Shazia get back on track, her aunt advised her in one of her dreams to remarry (5), and even suggested an unmarried man from the village as a proper match for her. Shazia followed her advice and married the young man, so even after her death her aunt had a big influence on her life.

Working and stealing

Shazia, Nazia and Mrs Mian all fear that *kala jaddu* has shaped their life-trajectories. The cases concern struggles for power and authority in the context of close relationships between husband and wife, parent and child or in-laws. Furthermore, they reveal the tensions and ambivalence that migrants may feel toward members of the extended family, especially in-laws in Pakistan. In this respect, the cases highlight important ideas of what it means to be and to do family in local and transnational migrant families.

Janet Carsten suggests that we take indigenous idioms of relatedness seriously in order to explore how family and kinship are produced and reproduced locally (Carsten 2000: 3). Recent studies have shown great variety and inventiveness in the means, ideas and practices that people utilise in order to relate to one another and to create lasting bonds of emotion and obligation. In migration studies, this perspective has been used to explore how transnational family networks are maintained or restructured over time (Bryceson and Vuorela 2002; Eastmond and Åkesson 2007; Olwig 2007; Pedersen 2009). Mrs Mian gives an important clue through which we may comprehend her current situation and anxiety about *kala jaddu* when she rhetorically asks: 'As long as I can work, then why would I steal?' Her question highlights a basic understanding whereby being and doing family are equated with a continued effort, while arrogating resources through *kala jaddu* is represented as an act of stealing. Basically 'working' means doing and being family in traditional ways, whereas 'stealing' becomes an act of reorganising relations, love and loyalty.

The idiom of work

In her study of the Pakistani community in Oxford, Alison Shaw (2000 [1988]) discusses a number of social and ritual practices in which families participate to stress the principle of fraternal solidarity. Most important is *lena–dena* (taking–giving), in which migrants exchange gifts at life-cycle events. On these occasions the amount of money that has been given is recorded, so that a gift can be returned on a later occasion (Shaw 2000: 227ff.). Moral expectations surrounding gift exchange are also an omnipresent principle in the social organisation of Pakistani families in Denmark. However, the patterns of exchange can take place on differing time-scales. While some gifts (in the broadest sense) are reciprocated within a short time, people sometimes spend years making financial and emotional sacrifices in order to receive a similar gift in the future.

One example is the 'intergenerational contract' between parents and children in the patrilocal family system (cf. Moen 2008; Whyte et al. 2008). In the Islamic religious tradition, and as a widespread practice in many Pakistani migrant families, it is the duty of parents to raise and nurture children in the best way possible and then to give them away in marriage. In return, sons are obliged to take care of their parents in their old age. Another similarly significant example is the expectation and moral obligation that in-married girls should show respect to the elders of the new family in the patrilocal household. Ideally the mother-in-law has the final say in domestic matters, as a result of the position she has achieved in the family hierarchy. A daughter-in-law should comply with her mother-in-law's desires and wishes, knowing that her own time will come to occupy the same position.

In both scenarios, 'working' means subordinating oneself to the structures and hierarchies of the patrilocal household. The personal sacrifice this may involve is widely accepted, as everyone knows that in time they will receive similar treatment.

Nazia related how, years ago, her older brother wanted to marry a wife from Denmark, but his mother pressured him to change his mind. Instead he ended up marrying the young Pakistani woman his mother had chosen for him. Nazia's decision to marry without the consent of her parents was a clear violation of the expectations and asymmetrical power of the parent–child relationship. Her action was condemned not only by the family, but also in the wider Pakistani community.

Similarly, Mrs Mian disapproved of how her daughters-in-law violated the basic moral principles involved in doing and being family: 'They show too little respect when they desist from living together, eating together, sitting, talking or praying together.' Unlike many Pakistani migrant women in Denmark, Mrs Mian had actually experienced being a daughter-in-law in the patrilocal household during her years in her husband's mother's house in Pakistan during the 1970s. After Mrs Mian was sent back to Denmark, she and Mr Mian were blessed with two boys. When her mother-in-law called from Pakistan, she greeted them first, then asked for one of the boys: 'You have two sons, and I have none. Let me have one of them.' So Mrs Mian had to send one of her babies to Pakistan to be brought up in the house of her mother-in-law. Crying, she explained that accepting the wishes of her husband's family was a sign of respect.

Mrs Mian's frustration with her daughters-in-law stemmed from the fact that she had always subordinated herself to the demands of the patrilocal family and worked hard to provide the financial and emotional support they required. She had done her duty and was now supposed to be enjoying the fruits of her efforts, but occult attacks had interfered.

The idiom of stealing

When Mrs Mian's daughters-in-law first arrived in Denmark, they all lived together in the same house as an extended family, but their everyday life was full of conflicts. According to Mrs Mian, the girls spent too much money and 'wasted time on make-up, ending up looking like dolls.' She had even seen them take money out of the family business's petty cash to go shopping, which led her to jump on her sons, who had just taken over Mr Mian's business, as irresponsible and incompetent. But worst of all, Bilal's wife had taken boxes containing different articles from the company's stock and taken them to Pakistan as gifts for her own family. The conflict reached its climax when Bilal bought a new apartment and left the parental household with his wife and daughter. Mrs Mian laments that, in the current situation, Bilal is giving all his love, time and affection to his beautiful young wife. She, in other words, is receiving the treatment to which Mrs Mian feels entitled. This is the real theft, the loss that led Mrs Mian to reach for the social diagnosis of *kala jaddu* as the explanation.

Nazia's and Shazia's stories also illustrate how different members of the extended family again and again try to manipulate or control each other by using *kala jaddu*. According to Nazia, the main motivation for her mother's suspected actions is the deep-seated fear that someone will take her children from her, just as she experienced when Nazia married Jens and then moved to another part of the country.

These three extended cases not only demonstrate domestic struggles over power and resources, but also the ambivalence that may arise towards members of the transnational family in Pakistan. From an analytical perspective, *kala jaddu* is a way of relating to others: not in a 'constructive' way, in which partners exchange symbolic and material objects in order to bring family members together and strengthen the moral connections and obligations between them, but as an abrupt way of reorganising families. In this respect, both suspicions and the concrete malicious practice of *kala jaddu* can be interpreted as a way to cut the network. In line with this, Bruce Kapferer explains:

> Magical practice and sorcery are major sites of innovation, and their methods of invention (a cosmology of invention) is to attack the very ways in which human beings routinely are seen or conceived to construct their realities ... they also do so by extending and adapting already available cosmologies, modes of constructing and patterning, to the pragmatics at issue, to the particularities of the case (Kapferer 2003: 21).

Kala jaddu is like a parasite that feeds off the conventional ways of being and doing family; simultaneously, however, suspicions and concrete practices of *kala jaddu* are also methods of invention that reorganise emotion and loyalty within the family, and thus the very morphology of the transnational migrant networks. In particular, the boundary between the consanguineous family and the conjugal family seems to be at stake. The widespread preference for endogamous, arranged marriages (Shaw 2001; Charsley and Shaw 2006; cf. Chapter 3) means that many transnational family networks have been woven together for generations. This preference, however, does not change the ambivalent status of conjugal families, highlighted when Mrs Mian explains the differences between daughters-in-law recruited from inside or outside the family, or when Nazia's mother insists that her daughter's life-trajectory and their mutual relationship are governed by her in-laws in Pakistan. When it comes to *kala jaddu*, in-laws are the usual suspects.

Conclusion: the family as an allegorical arena

According to Roger Ballard, circulating suspicions of sorcery and other afflictions constitute an 'allegorical arena' in which family conflicts can take place and relationships be negotiated:

Occult vocabularies of this kind serve to establish a powerful and sophisticated allegorical arena within which to explore, debate and contest the everyday stresses and strains of family life; and in addition to enabling those in distress to find their way to some degree of psychological solace, they also establish an arena within which to negotiate one of the most pressing sources of distress in familial contexts – a breakdown in interpersonal relationships such that a member of the group with limited bargaining power finds him- or herself pressed into an impossible position (Ballard 2009: 19).

Common to Nazia, Shazia and Mrs Mian is that they are in vulnerable positions during turbulent times of transition when their households are being reorganised and their local and transnational family relations renegotiated. Nazia has ambivalent feelings in relation both to her Pakistani family and her previous crucial decision of 'symbolic mobility' leading her towards a future in Denmark by marrying Jens without the consent of her parents. Shazia is vulnerable as a divorced woman and a single mother in Denmark without any family. Finally, Mrs Mian dreads what will become of her and her husband, now that her sons have left the household. Like many older Pakistanis, Mrs Mian suffers from arthritis and diabetes, and she represents a general concern among the older generation about what will happen to them later in life, now that their grown-up children no longer agree on what it means to be and do family 'properly'. Many feel deserted by their children, and fear ending up in residential homes, as is common for elderly Danes who are cared for by the welfare state.

The individual problems and life crises of Nazia, Shazia and Mrs Mian occur within the context of the emerging upheaval in the treasured family institution among Pakistani migrants in Denmark. As already discussed in previous chapters, the family is undergoing radical changes due to demographic shifts and economic and social mobility. At stake in this process of transition are not only the vertical relationships between generations of migrant families settled in Denmark, but also the horizontal relationships of the wider transnational family network, and additionally the notions of identity, home and belonging that they involve. The family, which used to be the firm foundation of life and existence, now seems to be crumbling away. Whereas everyone used to 'work' together, now they have begun to 'steal' from each other. Some see this reconfiguration of tradition and family relations as an opportunity to recreate their lives and future prospects; for others it is a disturbing development leading to broken illusions, uncertainty and solitude. Due to the destructive–productive qualities of suspicions of sorcery, local and transnational family relations and obligations break down, and this inevitably enables new moral orders and family formations to take form. In the context of family upheaval among Pakistanis in the Danish migratory context, *kala jaddu* seems to have regained its importance (see Chapter 10).

I end this chapter by returning to Mrs Mian. Whereas Evans-Pritchard's classic study of the Azande (1976 [1937]) dealt with the 'how' and the 'why' of witchcraft beliefs, recent studies suggest that witchcraft can be equated with a social diagnosis that not only allows people to explain how and why they are struck by misfortune, but also to act on their situation and move on (Whyte 1997). Reaching the social diagnosis of *kala jaddu* not only explains to Mrs Mian and her surroundings why her family is falling apart, it also makes it possible for her to take action against this. She might not get Bilal back in the near future, but she can work to change her situation, for example, by saying *du'a* (prayers) for him. Paradoxically, her current unfortunate situation has strengthened her position within the neighbourhood network of Pakistani mothers, where she has gained the reputation of someone who is familiar with the experience of troublesome sons and daughters-in-law and has been the victim of *kala jaddu*. The social diagnosis of *kala jaddu* not only makes sense of her loss, it also allows her to regain control over a world that is changing rapidly around her. She can start working in order to get her life back on track and re-establish a meaningful future horizon, despite the current critical situation.

Chapter 10
Demonic migrations

The re-enchantment of middle-class life

Whereas the previous chapter discussed how the destructive–productive qualities of suspected sorcery reorganise family relatedness and moral orders in transnational networks, this chapter discusses how the better-educated second generation of Pakistanis in Denmark deal with experiences categorised as *kala jaddu*, despite the fact that many regard it as a superstition, a 'cultural' phenomenon whose existence they doubt. Ambiguous encounters with *kala jaddu* not only urge the second generation to reconsider their religious beliefs and practices, but make them question their shared self-image as an educated, modern elite. Noman, an unmarried man in his early thirties, captured this paradox of the entire second generation when he explained: 'Many young people [of the second generation] do not believe in *kala jaddu*, but that does not mean that they cannot be affected by it!' Occult interference has become a social fact that Pakistanis in Denmark have to deal with one way or another.

In its focus on aspects of 'popular Islam', this chapter differs from many contemporary studies of Islam and Muslim communities in Europe, suggesting that second-generation immigrants have a radically different approach to religion than their parents. Following the emic discourses of young Muslims themselves, several studies distinguish between the so-called 'cultural' practices of the first generation and religious revitalisation among the second generation, who are attempting to rid Islam of the idiosyncrasies they identify among their parents (Jacobson 1997, 1998; Johansen 2002; Schmidt 2004, 2007). Analytically, the attempts of second-generation immigrants to strip religion of its differing national and cultural characteristics have been called the 'new Islam' (Kibria 2008). Common to these studies is a sharp distinction between the first and second generations and a focus primarily on the latter, typically represented by eloquent, unmarried young men and women in their teens or twenties. However, I suspect that if the researchers met the same informants ten years later, after they had married and had children, established their own households and had to deal with aging or dying parents, their religious ideas and practices would probably have changed.

Second-generation Pakistanis in Denmark seem currently to be confronted with numerous 'cultural' phenomena in their families and nearby surroundings that they would normally dismiss as superstition. When sorcery is suggested as a possible social diagnosis to explain why family loyalties and obligations are being neglected or ignored, it not only causes confusion, sadness or rage, but also makes counter-actions possible. This re-enchantment of middle-class life occurs as the second generation moves into new phases of adulthood and is confronted by a new moral landscape of expectations and obligations. Thus, even though the focus on generations might be relevant in migration studies, we also need to consider how people's perceptions of the world, and of themselves within it, change as they pass through different phases of life. A shift from 'generation' to 'life-trajectory' is one way to acknowledge that Islam is always subject to interpretation and negotiation, and that religious ideas and sentiments inevitably change during life courses.

This chapter presents and discusses the extended case of Tahir, a well-educated man in his mid-thirties, who ends up in a family conflict with his brother-in-law, Habib. As the conflict escalates, it is soon interpreted by those around them as a case of *kala jaddu* – but Tahir has his doubts. Even though beliefs about *kala jaddu* are an integrated aspect of the historically constituted identity repertoire embodied by Pakistani migrants (see the Introduction), *kala jaddu* nevertheless epitomises the 'cultural' beliefs and practices associated with the old life in rural Punjab that the second generation have actively tried to distance themselves from. I suggest that the differing but coexisting identity frameworks constitute a matrix, out of which Tahir and other second-generation Pakistani Muslims, as they move from being 'young' to becoming 'adults', must develop a more complex self-image and re-evaluate their ideas of what Islam is all about. Finally, the case leads to a more general discussion of possible connections between the resurgence of suspicions of *kala jaddu* in the Pakistani migrant community, and the external processes of securitisation that Muslim immigrant families in Denmark are currently subjected to.

Two generations of Pakistanis in Denmark

As explained in Chapter 2, most Pakistani families have settled in or around Copenhagen. The great majority of families originate from rural areas in the Gujrat district, while the rest come from larger cities such as Lahore, Rawalpindi, Sialkot or Karachi. In this respect, Tahir's family is special, as they come from Multan, a larger city in the heart of Punjab, where they lived after fleeing to Pakistan from India in 1947. Tahir himself grew up in a suburb south of Copenhagen, where he lived with his parents and three siblings. Due to his education in business, he has always seen himself as different from his parents. According to Tahir, the daily journey between his home and the business school was like travelling in time. When he was at home, it was like being back in Pakistan in the 1960s or 1970s, whereas his educational environment represented the progress and enlightenment of modern life in Denmark. Tahir explained several times how he saw it as the duty of second-generation Pakistanis to bring up and 'civilise' their parents, an ambition which emphasises the distance between the two generations and how parents, 'like children', often are unable to manage life in Denmark.

A significant feature of second-generation Pakistanis is their educational achievements. In the 1990s the rising second generation formed numerous youth and student organisations. One of these associations was OPSA (see Chapter 7), where Tahir and I first met in 2001. A common feature of all the youth associations was that they marked a distance between the emerging second generation and the 'village mentality' of the first generation, associated with the parents' emphasis on *biraderi* solidarity or *zaat* identity, honour and the patriarchal family institution (with marriages arranged by the parents, sometimes without the consent of the children). By contrast, the new youth organisations studied and discussed the wisdom of the Quran and Sunna of the Prophet Muhammad, invited religious scholars and arranged public meetings where crucial questions of Islam could be discussed. More recently, the internet has also been an important site for obtaining and exchanging a knowledge of Islam.

Over the years, second-generation Pakistani Muslims seem to have developed a specific variation of Max Weber's thesis that increased modernity and rationality will in time result in disenchantment of the world. In their version, the four decades of life in Denmark and the dramatic increases in literacy and education within the migrant community have initiated a process whereby Islam has become cleansed of cultural idiosyncrasies and national survivals. In this way the transition from first to second generation is believed by the second generation to constitute a process whereby the 'pure' religion has become separated from the 'messy' culture. This process is not unique to the local Danish context, but has been influenced by the religious-political Islamist projects that swept over the Middle East and Pakistan in the 1970s and 1980s, where Islamists successfully presented themselves as purifiers of Islam, fighting superstition and heretical local traditions, as well as the moral corruption of modernity and of western consumerism and lifestyles.

Based on this conviction of the correlation between education, rationality and 'true' Islam, much of the discussion in the newly established Pakistani youth organisations of the 1990s and 2000s was dedicated to seeking out the impact of Islam on one's everyday life: what is *halal* (permitted), and what is *haram* (forbidden)? How should the *hadith* and Sunna be interpreted and sharia understood? The basic question in these discussions was, how do we live as Muslims in Denmark? The emerging second generation used these discussions to carve out a space for themselves in relation to their parents and the religious landscape and imagination of the wider Danish public. This kind of religious activism, where they strategically worked to clear a platform for themselves as Danish Muslims, has been called 'proactive Islam' (*offensiv Islam*) (Simonsen 2001: 176).

Tahir was actively engaged in the movement of 'proactive Islam', but above all he was preoccupied with planning his upcoming marriage to Selma. Tahir made a point of selecting his wife himself. He did not want to marry the cousin his parents had lined up for him in Pakistan. Instead he chose Selma, a well-educated, second-generation Pakistani woman from a town north of Copenhagen. The only parental criterion they both agreed to comply with was the preference for *zaat* endogamy. As Tahir stated, mimicking his father: 'If it is not the same *zaat*, then forget it!' When they presented their marriage plans to their respective parents, neither family was happy about it. At the first meeting between the two sets of parents, Selma's mother, in order to spoil the plans entirely, even insinuated that Tahir's family were actually Indians due to their status as *mohajirs*, refugees from India after the partition in 1947. Maybe it was this insult, or some of the numerous problems they faced planning the big wedding, that doomed the idea of Selma and Tahir's mother living together even before Selma moved into the patrilocal household. Furthermore, Selma's ambitions of having a career proved incompatible with a demanding mother-in-law, so the newly-wed couple soon left the parental household and moved into their own apartment.

After a while Selma became pregnant and gave birth to a son. After maternity leave she started working in a telecommunications company. Since then Selma has given birth to their second child. Tahir himself has started working in a large international pharmaceutical company. Since we first met, Tahir has become both a husband and a father. He has also become a more religious man who attempts to follow the Sunna of the prophet Muhammad by growing a beard and going on the *umrah* (the little pilgrimage) with his family. Today he is *murid* (follower) of a shaykh settled in North America and regularly meets some of his friends on Thursday evenings in order to listen to the on-line teaching of their shaykh and do *zikr* (remembrance of God).

This brief introduction to the previous history of Tahir and Selma is significant in order to understand the dilemma they face today, as they try to figure out whether or not Habib, Selma's younger brother and Tahir's brother-in-law, has been afflicted by *kala jaddu*.

An escalating family conflict

In retrospect, Tahir was by no means surprised that Habib, his brother-in-law, ended up in his current problematic situation, because 'he has always done things his own way'. Selma's parents had expected to arrange the marriage of their youngest son, Habib, themselves, but even before any candidates had been taken into consideration, Habib fell in love with Rubina, a young university student with an Afghan background, and declared that he wanted to propose to her. His parents were outraged by this premature decision and called a family meeting to discuss the critical situation it had caused. Habib was not invited, but Tahir was present as Selma's husband and as son-in-law of the patriarch calling the meeting. At the family meeting there been general agreement that Habib's move was unacceptable, as it jeopardised the reputation and honour of the family. Due to his previous volunteer work at various crisis-lines helping anonymous youngsters with severe family problems related to marriage arrangements, Tahir soon realised that the situation was getting out of control. He felt obliged to defend Habib, because he and Selma had been in a similar situation when they insisted on their love marriage against the will of the parents. So Tahir stood up for Habib and stated that, regardless of whether the family abandoned him or accepted his choice of Rubina, there would still be gossip about the family circulating in the community. It was already too late to change anything, so the most sensible solution would be to arrange a meeting with the Afghan family and offer them *rishta* as tradition demands. Tahir's suggestion was heatedly debated for a long time. Finally everyone agreed to follow his advice.

Now, the only problem was that neither Tahir nor Selma had any prior knowledge of Rubina or her family, besides the disturbing fact that she was 'a mortal enemy' *(dødsfjende)* of one of Selma's girlfriends. Tahir confronted his brother-in-law demanding to learn more about Rubina's background and family history, but apparently Habib knew very little, besides that he was hopelessly in love. Instead Tahir asked one of his male friends, who knew Rubina, to find out 'what she was like'. According to Tahir, the information he returned with was decidedly juicy gossip, and contained really disturbing stories.

Possessed of this knowledge about his brother-in-law's new fiancé, Tahir saw no possibility other than to confront Habib and tell him what he had heard. Habib became very upset, and insisted on knowing who had told Tahir these rumours and on meeting the person himself. So Tahir and Habib went to meet the friend, who once more had to relate the compromising rumours. Again Habib was furious, and accused Tahir and his friend of defaming Rubina. According to Tahir, Habib even visited the friend on a later occasion and threatened to hurt him if he continued to spread these rumours about his wife-to-be.

In order to legitimise his central part in this social drama, Tahir explained that he had only done his Islamic duty as a brother-in-law, informing Habib of the potential problems waiting for him in his planned marriage. Soon Rubina learned about the rumours and Tahir's role in the case, and it came to a big fight where she started crying. Since then Tahir and Habib have not been on speaking terms. Tahir considered staying away from the wedding, but decided to go anyway, so he would not expose the unravelling family conflict to the entire Pakistani community.

Meanwhile Selma and Habib's parents knew nothing of any of this. They believed that Tahir and Habib were really close because of the former's efforts to make everyone accept Habib's choice of marriage partner. Some time after the wedding, the parents invited Tahir, Selma, their children, Habib and Rubina to a family get-together on their return from a long holiday in Pakistan. When Habib learned that Tahir and Selma had been invited, he grabbed Rubina and left without a word.

Due to Habib's strong reactions, those around him have started to suspect that this might be a case of *kala jaddu*. Selma and her sisters are convinced that their younger brother has been subjected to some kind of evil influence from his new wife and her family. Tahir acknowledges all the signs, but nevertheless has his doubts.

First of all, Tahir describes Rubina as a 'spoiled girl' (*forkælet tøs*) and no less than 'a mistress in getting things done her way'. Apparently she can twist Habib around her little finger and make him do anything she commands. One example occurred before the wedding, when Rubina did not like the wedding dress her future parents-in-law had bought for her. Instead, she persuaded Habib to go to London and buy another one. According to Tahir, this proves that 'she pisses on the family' (*hun pisser på familien*). Another sign was that Habib apparently had started using many of the same words and expressions as his new wife. Once Tahir witnessed how Habib, while talking to his wife on his mobile phone during one of the numerous discussions with Tahir, went into some kind of trance. He just stood there expressionless, staring into space, listening to Rubina's voice. The episode supported the suspicion that Rubina had some kind of power over Habib.

Secondly, Rubina has an Afghan background, which in itself calls for some suspicion. A common explanation Pakistanis give for preferring endogamous marriages within the extended family is to get a *rishta* where you know the spouse and her family well and can be relatively sure that no skeletons will fall out of the closet after the marriage (see Chapter 3). Habib's choice of Rubina not only rejected the marriage preference of his family and kin, it also transgressed the boundaries of *zaat* fraternity and nationality. The differences between the two families were exposed in the planning of the wedding. Not only did Rubina's family expect several of their female Afghan guests to show up in revealing dresses, but they also wanted dancing at the *nikkah* (wedding ceremony), the part of the wedding celebrations hosted by the bride's family. Relating this, Tahir emphasised that he would under no circumstances let Selma dance at a semi-public event in front of strange men, and that several of the Pakistani guests felt very uncomfortable during the actual wedding celebrations.

The last but most incriminating evidence that this was a case of *kala jaddu* was that Habib started wearing a *ta'wiz*, an amulet infamous for its use in magic and sorcery. At least to Selma and her sisters, this proved that Habib was the victim of *kala jaddu* and explained why he blindly followed his new wife's orders rather than listening to them. So far, they have kept the knowledge of the amulet a secret because they know that their mother will 'freak out' when she learns that her son has started wearing a *ta'wiz*. Selma's mother is convinced of the power of *kala jaddu*.

The ambivalence of faith

A significant feature of Tahir's uncertainty is how he interprets the signs of *kala jaddu* in the social environment. As already stated, weighty evidence for the social diagnosis of sorcery is that Habib has been seen wearing a *ta'wiz*. But to complicate matters further, a *ta'wiz* is not only an object mediating malicious forces: it can also be an amulet or charm given by religious authorities such as a *pir* (saint) or an imam to protect people (Robson 1934; Werbner 2003; Ballard 2006). In this respect, the *ta'wiz* becomes an 'empty signifier' (cf. Laclau 1996) that can – and will – be interpreted differently according to position, power and interest in the social field.

Whereas Tahir and Selma suspected the *ta'wiz* was proof of Rubina's ability and power to control Habib, one could also suggest that Habib wears the charm as protection. Maybe he and Rubina fear that Tahir and Selma, or someone else in the family, are using illicit magic to try and break up their marriage and reintegrate Habib into the family. We will never know. In this respect the anthropologist shares the uncertainty of his interlocutors. Tahir and Selma will probably never have a definitive answer as to whether or not this is a case of *kala jaddu*. If the conflict with Habib and Rubina continues, they might find more evidence that substantiates the social diagnosis. And even if in time they manage to settle the conflict, the doubt will always be there – was it *kala jaddu*? And if so, who was responsible for it and what was the purpose?

The conflict with Habib is not the first time Tahir has been confronted with some of the more mystical dimensions of Islam. Just after he married Selma, he suffered dizzy spells for a long period. His doctor concluded that he was suffering from a virus. Nevertheless, his parents sent him to see a gifted elder Pakistani in the neighbouring city, 'a Sufi', who, besides working as a semi-skilled factory worker, also helped fellow countrymen with different kinds of problems.

Immediately after arriving, the man was able to list a number of episodes from Tahir's life, which proved to Tahir that this man was 'the real thing'. In order to get rid of his dizziness, Tahir was advised to say his five prayers daily and recite a certain *sura* from the Quran. Even though Tahir never explicitly said so, it seems plausible that his parents might have sent him to the 'Sufi' because they were worried about the specific illness that had struck their newly-wed son: they might have suspected Selma's family of causing the problem. No matter what, the episode illustrates how Tahir was already familiar with some of the more mystical aspects of Islam before his confrontation with Habib.

Another significant episode happened one evening when Tahir was hanging out with a group of male Pakistani friends. Suddenly one of the young men started moving around and talking with a strange voice in an unknown language. One of the other young men present explained that he sometimes behaved like this, and that the family believed it to be a *jinn* that entered his body from time to time. To help him, the group held their friend and calmed him down by reciting prayers. The episode taught them a lesson about the cultural-religious universe from which their families originate. Such an experience is very difficult to explain away afterwards.

According to Cecile Rubow (2000: 244), confrontations with ambiguous and bewildering religious experiences in our everyday lives form the basis for negotiation and contestation. Uncertainties over heterogeneous religious discourses, practices and experiences make up a constitutive process that urges us to reconsider already established views of the world. Tahir was confronted with several personal experiences that urged him to reconsider the limits and scope of Islam. Whereas it used to be relatively easy for him, one of the emerging Pakistani elite engaged in the proactive Islam movement, to repudiate superstitious elders' stories of occult attacks, he now had to make sense of numerous personal experiences that pointed in that very same direction.

Incompatible belief systems

As Pakistani migrants settled in Denmark, they began reconstructing the social, cultural and religious universes they knew from back home. As an unexpected consequence of the settlement process, other aspects of local Punjabi life followed as well. Pnina Werbner explains:

> As migrants have travelled to the West so too have their afflictions and the harmful spirits associated with them. The global reach of Sufism is, it seems, also the global reach of *jinns, jaddu* and other malevolent influences (2003: 223).

Living for decades in a European urban setting has not made occult forces disappear. On the contrary, there seems to be a renewed interest in spiritual matters and a growing market for Copenhagen-based 'helpers' whom migrants can consult in order to find out if they themselves or someone in their close family has been struck by *kala jaddu*. Furthermore, the large number of Pakistani spouses recruited from extended kinship networks in the 1980s and 1990s (see Chapter 3) and the continued engagement in the transnational social field stretching between Pakistan and Denmark have contributed to bringing the ideas and practices of 'popular Islam' into the everyday lives of second-generation Pakistanis in Denmark. The current de- and re-territorialisation (Appadurai 1996) of religious imaginaries affects common notions of time and space. The previous *temporal separation* between the 'cultural mentality' of the first generation and the religious revitalisation of the second generation, and the *spatial separation* between Danish middle-class life and the enchanted universe of rural Pakistani villages are no longer there. Instead, second-generation Pakistani Muslims experience being haunted by 'cultural' phenomena that interfere with their everyday family lives.

These encounters between different realities and rationalities constitute a matrix which people must pragmatically try to make sense of in their changing social environments. As noted in the previous chapter, Katherine Pratt Ewing (1997) has suggested the notion of 'shifting selves' in order to explain how interlocutors relate to multiple and in many respects incompatible systems of belief (see also the Introduction). From his fieldwork on Bali, Fredrik Barth finds a very similar coexistence of numerous knowledge traditions that, like 'streams', flow together and constitute 'the complex culture and society of Bali' (1989: 131). As a consequence of this historical constitution of the Balinese world:

> People participate in multiple, more or less discrepant, universes of discourse; they construct different, partial and simultaneous worlds in which they move; their cultural construction of reality springs not from one source and is not of one piece (Barth 1989: 130).

In one of my interviews, Zagib, a second-generation medical student, explained how he had developed a similar strategy to cope with the supposedly contradictory realities of his private and professional lives. Attending medical school at the university, he is dedicated to clinical explanations and a secular scientific rationality. Nonetheless, when he does voluntary work for the national Joint Council of Muslims (*Muslimernes Fællesråd*) in his spare time, he tends to become a dedicated Muslim absorbed in the religious orthodoxy of Islam. Finally he gave expression to what he called 'the Pakistani part of him', which includes all the cultural values and traditions he cherishes in the local Danish branch of the Barelwi-inspired transnational religious organisation of Idara Minhaj Ul-Quran. In his continued efforts to make sense of his life as a second-generation Pakistani Muslim in Denmark, and one who will soon become a medical doctor, Zaqib therefore navigates between three overlapping, and in many respects contradictory, frameworks: (1) scientific rationality, (2) Islamic orthodoxy and (3) his identity configuration as a Pakistani originating from a village in Punjab.

The ways in which Zaqib deals with conflicting belief systems in his everyday life resemble the findings of a study by Santi Rozario (2009), where she describes a Bangladeshi couple in Britain looking for a diagnosis and a possible cure for their sick child. In this search, there is no sharp dividing line between *daktari* (medical) and *upri* (supernatural) problems, and the family oscillates between quite different modes of explanation in their search for a diagnosis and possible treatment for their son (Rozario 2009).

Returning to Tahir, these examples shed light on some of his problems in trying to figure out what has happened to Habib. Tahir doubts that Habib is afflicted by *kala jaddu*. He does not question sorcery as an indisputable part of Islam, but considers that Selma and her sisters reached the social diagnosis of *kala jaddu* too quickly. Instead, he tends towards his first impression, that it is more likely the heated love affair that has changed Habib. In this respect, Tahir is in line with many other second-generation Pakistanis who reject *kala jaddu* as 'escapism', as just a culturally accepted way to deal with family conflicts without actually taking responsibility for them. To present *kala jaddu* as escapism is to take a certain privileged analytical position in which concrete experiences of occult interference are explained away within a socio-psychological framework. However, because the existence of sorcery and *jinn*s is confirmed in both the Quran and the *hadith*, they form part of the orthodox Islamic tradition and cannot be ignored (see discussions in Chapter 9).

Tahir is also willing to comply with the diagnosis of *kala jaddu* in social settings dominated by Pakistanis or fellow Muslims who are expected to understand his dilemma. I base this on the fact that Tahir and Selma contacted a trusted imam in Denmark and related the whole story to him in order to clarify whether or not this could be a case of *kala jaddu*. The imam had no absolute answer, but explained that, if this was the case, then the best thing they could do for Habib would be to fulfil their religious obligations and stay on the path of Islam by saying their prayers, reciting the names of God, fulfilling the obligation of *zakat*, etc. Since only those who neglect their religious duties can be affected by *kala jaddu*, the best Tahir and Selma could do for Habib was to pray for him.

As he makes sense of the escalating family conflict, Tahir is switching between three more or less discrepant universes and constructions of reality. On the one hand, he positions himself as the rational intellectual who rejects *kala jaddu* altogether as a symptom of escapism. On the other hand, he takes the position of the pious Muslim, acknowledging the existence of occult attacks, but able to keep the evil forces at bay. He is nevertheless also pulled towards a third position, that of the cultural-religious universe he associates with simple life in Punjabi villages, where *kala jaddu* often interferes with everyday family lives. However, Tahir resists this third option, well aware that, if he goes along with the interpretation of Selma and her sisters and agrees that Habib has been targeted by *kala jaddu*, it will disrupt his self-image as a modern, educated and religious man. It would turn him into something he has striven for years not to be, making him 'a cultural person' and a believer in superstitious folk religion. That is very difficult for him to accept.

The changing religious landscape

The ambiguous local experiences and suspicions of *kala jaddu* should be situated within the broader historical context of the securitisation of Muslim immigrant families and the security/integration response of the Danish nation-state (see Chapter 1). Like many other second-generation Pakistanis, Tahir used to be involved in the movement of proactive Islam (Simonsen 2001). However, since September 11, critical national and global events have widened the developing cleavage and contributed to further marginalisation and suspicion of Muslim immigrants in the Danish public. In this historical process, several articulate spokespersons from Muslim organisations have found themselves in the headlines, accused of being extremists, supporters of the death penalty, homophobic, anti-Semitic, etc. As a result, the proactive Islam movement today seems more or less to have resigned, and religion is again confined to more private spheres. Instead, young Muslims may end up in fundamentalist groupings (e.g., Wahhabi or Salafi), where Islam is presented as a political project beyond the borders of the nation-state, or they may do like Tahir and begin to focus more on the inward-looking spiritual dimensions of Islam, for example, by joining a Sufi *tariqa* (order) and attending regular *zikr*. In this respect, the ongoing contestation of Muslims has contributed to limiting religious practices and beliefs to private spaces, beyond the gaze or reach of the Danish public and authorities.

Another element in the securitisation process has been restriction of foreign religious preachers' ability to enter Denmark and stay in the country. In an attempt to increase its control of mosques in Denmark and to counter religious fundamentalism (which is suspected of leading to 'home-grown terrorism'), in 2004 the Liberal-Conservative government introduced new rules under which foreign imams (and religious preachers in general) must obtain a so-called 'preacher-visa' (*forkynder visum*). It stated that the person concerned must not be an economic burden to Danish society, must not be regarded as a threat to public order, health or safety, and must have a relevant religious education (Kühle 2006: 185). Especially the latter criterion is affecting the inflow of foreign imams, because now only 'real' religious scholars are allowed entry. Simultaneously with this regulation 'from above', the increased professionalisation of religious communities and mosques in Denmark has also contributed to changing the religious landscape 'from below', as to some extent the different (Pakistani) mosques have started to compete for the most famous, pious and educated imam (see Chapter 2).

The new religious landscape that has been created by these two factors – the external securitisation of migration and internal competition – seems to have changed the function of the imam and the mosque. Formerly, migrants could approach the imam when they found themselves in the middle of a family crisis they more or less explicitly suspected of being caused by *kala jaddu*; they could expect to have their concerns taken seriously and to be offered different religious technologies such as *dam* (blowing on water),⸱ *ta'wiz* (an amulet) or *wasifa* (specific prayers) in order to deal with their problem. Today they risk being ridiculed if they turn to the imam with these kinds of concerns; some interlocutors even relate that one risks being yelled at publicly and being humiliated as superstitious if one brings these kinds of concerns out in the open. One example is the local Danish branch of the transnational organisation Idara Minhaj Ul-Quran, where members are instructed that ordinary people should not worry about *kala jaddu*, as it only happens to extraordinary people like a shaykh or the Prophet Muhammad. Instead of the previous therapeutic consultations and conversations, where their problems and worries were recognised, members are now referred to a self-help manual provided by the Minhaj Ul-Quran leader, Tahir Ul-Qadri, on how problems can be dealt with by various prayers.

This example supports the general picture of educated imams and of increasingly professional religious organisations, which have become to some extent distanced from the everyday lives and problems of families in the migrant community. They no longer share the widespread belief in the kismetic dimensions of Islam, where people seek help in order to turn adversity in its tracks and deal with unfortunate events in their everyday family lives (cf. Ballard 1999). As a result of this lack of recognition, a new market of different private helpers has gained significance in the hidden public sphere of the Pakistani Muslim community. For instance, Noman, one of these helpers, who in his mid-twenties was gifted with *izn*, the power to help and heal his fellow Muslim brothers and sisters, claims that he receives several visitors from Idara Minhaj Ul-Quran who are looking for more than a self-help manual by way of spiritual guidance and protection from *jinns*, *nazar* and *kala jaddu*.

The changing morphology of the religious landscape exemplifies how the ongoing national securitisation of migration may have many unforeseen local consequences.

The re-enchantment of middle-class life

The process of making sense of life is not separate from the symbolic world in which people live, but is rather constitutive of it. Encounters with cultural phenomena such as *kala jaddu* often have a destructive–productive outcome, where Pakistani Muslims afterwards must try to make sense of the rubble and leftovers of relationships and moral orders that have been redefined or have disappeared altogether.

The extended account of Tahir illustrates how members of the second generation are today confronted with some of the same mystical phenomena they used to blame their parents for believing in. As they marry, have children and establish their own households, they are confronted with a range of urgent existential questions, over and above the moral expectations and obligations connected to family life. Tahir's conflict with Habib and his subsequent negotiation with the signs and suspicions of *kala jaddu* were the result of his transition from being a 'young man' to becoming an 'adult', a significant character within the family system as husband, father and brother-in-law. In this respect, the suggested analytical move from a focus on 'generation' to 'life-trajectory' enables us to approach the changes that migrants go through during individual life courses and common family cycles.

My suggestion that Tahir has ended up in an ontological cocktail (cf. Rubow 2000: 244) – one in which he has to navigate between the three distinct positions of rational science, orthodox Islam and the cultural-religious Punjabi universe – may leave the impression of a split personality. However, that would be to miss the point. On the contrary, I suggest that Tahir's dialogue, negotiation and ongoing testing of the frameworks offered by his postcolonial repertoire is a more common way to deal with the mystical events that appear in one's life. Even those who claim not to believe in *kala jaddu* have to come up with some counter-strategies if they suddenly find themselves in the middle of family conflicts or life crises that are suspected to be the result of sorcery.

In his ongoing struggles to sort out his religious beliefs and practices, Tahir has come to represent the second generation of well-educated Pakistani Muslims who find themselves being compelled to return to Islam as they experience that they themselves, or someone in their nearby surroundings, are being targeted by sorcery. These experiences not only challenge their perception of themselves as an elite that, due to social mobility, has definitively distanced itself from the backward 'village mentality' of their parents; it also confronts them with all the idiosyncrasies of the Punjabi cultural-religious universe that their families left behind decades ago. Despite second-generation Pakistanis' successful upward mobility and middle-class aspirations, the past has returned with a vengeance. Paradoxically, the current suspicions of *kala jaddu*, combined with the gradual acceptance of the undercurrent of ideas and practices referred to as 'popular Islam', have not only enlarged the cultural-religious repertoire of second-generation Pakistanis, but also reduced the distance between the first and second generations.

Conclusion: destructive–productive sorcery

In this and the previous chapter, I have argued that suspicions of *kala jaddu* are important among Pakistani migrants in Denmark as a way of reorganising family relations within local and transnational networks. The current preoccupation with *kala jaddu* should not be interpreted as a return to, or a reinvention of, tradition. Rather, it should be viewed as a thoroughly modern response to the growing uncertainties and insecurities that Pakistani migrants face as a result not only of changing ideas of what it means to be and to do family, but also of the eroding legitimacy of Muslim immigrants in Denmark discussed in some of the previous chapters.

An important argument regarding the reappearance of modern magical practices concerns their disjunction from the past combined with the radical reconfiguration of the ideas and practices of the past in terms of the circumstances of the present (Kapferer 2003: 19). Owing to the limited literature on *kala jaddu*, it is not possible to follow the trajectory of this phenomenon in time and space. There are no written sources that can validate whether there are more or fewer anxieties and suspicions of *kala jaddu* today than there were ten, twenty or thirty years ago in the Pakistani migrant community. But as ideas and suspicions of *kala jaddu* belong to the kismetic dimension of religious life, and are an integral part of the historically constituted identity repertoire of post-colonial migrants, they have most likely been there all along. In his historical study of the Bakweri in Cameroon, Edwin Ardener suggests that witchcraft may be subject to fashions, as beliefs are readjusted over time in response to the changing social and economic conditions of the local society (Ardener 1970: 141). Bruce Kapferer states that sorcery is characterised by its labile and volatile character, its capacity to metamorphose and maintain relevance to any situation and to the changing circumstances of situations (1997: 21). These conclusions support contemporary assertions that occult economies are forever changing, alive to the basic rhythms of our world over the *longue durée* (Moore and Sanders 2001: 11). Likewise, although *kala jaddu* has long been a marginal discourse in family affairs, the emerging crisis of the family institution has made suspicions of sorcery gain importance within the migrant community. One feature of *kala jaddu* that is definitely new in the migratory context is the range of the destructive–productive forces that are at work within the transnational social field that is stretched out between Pakistan and Denmark.

In his study of witchcraft in post-apartheid South Africa, Adam Ashforth finds striking similarities between the traditional diagnosis of witchcraft and the current medical diagnosis of HIV/AIDS. In this respect, the epidemic of HIV/AIDS also becomes an epidemic of witchcraft (2004: 142). The actual medical symptoms, like coughing, diarrhoea, wasting and so on, resonate with ailments that healers have identified for generations as resulting from witchcraft (2004: 148). Ashforth ends up reaching the provocative conclusion that:

> One might almost say that if AIDS did not exist, the witches would have to invent it. Thus, as the number of cases increases, so must the number and power of witches. As the number and power of the witches increase, so grows the need for protection. And in the face of evil wrought by malicious individuals, the desire for justice grows (Ashforth 2004: 152).

Along similar lines, I suggest that if there were no such thing as *kala jaddu*, it would have to be invented in order to conceptualise and deal with the growing problems, anxieties and uncertainties that Pakistani migrants are currently confronted with as a result of current upheavals in the family institution. However, South Asian Islam does contain elaborate ideas about the character and scope of *kala jaddu* – as well as of numerous other occult phenomena – and does provide detailed instructions to potential victims on how to counter malicious attacks. The notion of *kala jaddu* does not have to be invented, because it already constitutes a part of the post-colonial repertoire; it is a framework of indeterminate meaning that migrants can mobilise, draw on or end up in when they try to make sense out of escalating family conflicts and the renegotiation of what it implies to be and do family.

Still, contemporary rumours and suspicions of *kala jaddu* in local and transnational Pakistani families are not merely functional outcomes of family crisis and upheaval; they also work the other way around, and generate crises in themselves. As the case of the doubtful Tahir illustrates, *kala jaddu* constitutes a potentiality that generates suspicions that have to be taken seriously. In this respect, the notion of *kala jaddu* is not just a reflection of domestic conflicts or family crisis; it also generates problems and conflicts itself. This dual character constitutes one element of the destructive–productive forces of local and transnational suspicions of sorcery, where existing intimate relationships fall apart and families are reorganised; but it is also a process where new vertical and horizontal family formations and moral orders begin to take shape.

Conclusion

Family upheaval

This study has examined the negotiation of relatedness, identity and belonging in Pakistani migrant families from four different angles: intergenerational mobility and community competition; the institution of marriage; the contested notion of homelands; and the occurrence and suspicions of sorcery and affliction. The open and flexible agenda of this approach has enabled me to move with the flow of my interlocutors and their concerns, instead of being restricted to a predefined analytical framework of 'cohesion' or 'integration', as is common in more policy-oriented research. All four perspectives illustrate the destructive–productive constitution of the migrant family, where neglected responsibilities, obligations and trust lead not only to broken relationships, but also, and inevitably, to the innovative creation of new ones. In this process, however, the aging first generation of migrants, who often lack the desire, ability or energy to adapt to the changing circumstances and environment, are most likely to end up as losers. The migration project, which from the very beginning was about family improvement, seems to have been exceedingly successful. Today many families have achieved more than the young Pakistani women and men probably ever imagined or dreamed of in terms of social mobility, material possessions and economic security when they left Pakistan and settled in Denmark. Nevertheless, despite the obvious gains, women and men in both first and second generations also to some extent agree that they have lost something invaluable along the way. In this concluding chapter, I will take a step back in order to address the subtle, complex interconnections between, on the one hand, renegotiated family relations and images of identity and belonging in Denmark, Sweden or Pakistan, and on the other, the wider historical and political contexts in which they occur. In this way, this final chapter points to possible links between the micro-politics of family life and the macro-politics of national and international events, globalisation and modernity.

Relatedness as an approach to transnational migration studies

Applying the notion of relatedness to the study of dynamics in Pakistani migrant families contributes to contemporary migration research, as it emphasises that local families and transnational kinship networks only exist as long as they are enacted and reproduced. The concept of relatedness turns attention away from the ascribed family constituted by genetic connections, blood and 'the order of nature', and instead urges us to focus on the social transactions and local negotiations of moral orders out of which families, as well as notions of identity and belonging, are defined and redefined. It is these ongoing inter- and intra-familial negotiations that inevitably will lead to changes in and of the family institution. The notion of relatedness directs attention to the ongoing production of vertical and horizontal family relations, and as such both complicates and enriches contemporary academic discussions of transnational or global families.

Life-course transitions and family cycles are inevitably associated with upheaval, but these processes tend to become even more significant in the context of migration, where established ideas about family relations, obligations and expectations have to be renegotiated in new settings and frameworks. To summarise and elaborate on my previous discussion of the negotiation of relatedness in Pakistani migrant families, I first discuss relatedness as family-making in vertical and horizontal family relations, and then relatedness as belonging to Pakistan and to Denmark. In doing so, I use the distinction introduced in the Introduction between the vertical (local) family relations that are constituted by intergenerational relations, and the horizontal (transnational) family relations involving networks of relatives and *biraderi* members in Pakistan.

Relatedness as family-making: the vertical relations

New generations often constitute a challenge to the existing moral orders of what it means to be and to do family. Not only do different generational cohorts inhabit different 'locations in history' (Mannheim 1972 [1952]: 289); within the context of migration, they also embody different values and skills, due to their upbringing and socialisation in different places. Furthermore, the upward mobility enjoyed by the second generation creates a distance between parents, who in many cases have worked all their lives as non- or semi-skilled workers in Denmark, and children, who have become highly educated professionals. Given these intergenerational differences, it is hardly surprising that ideas and morality concerning what it means to be and to do family are being contested and renegotiated in many migrant families. In this process, the institution of marriage and the tradition of patrilocality are two specific sites where intergenerational differences become salient. The first generation's preference for arranged transnational marriages – seen as a means to reinvest in relationships with people, places and imagined communities in Pakistan – are being replaced by local love marriages, initiated by the second generation without the help, guidance or approval of their parents or extended families. Many newly-wed couples furthermore neglect the generalised reciprocity implied in the tradition of patrilocality when they establish independent households. Those in the better educated second generation tend to prioritise their careers, their friends and their children, which leaves little time and energy for taking care of aging parents. Such self-fashioning is concerned with individual trajectories, and constitutes a means to escape from excessive family restrictions and obligations: in other words, it is a subtle rebellion against the traditional family system. Meanwhile, those who do comply with the preferences of parents and wider family, and actually marry a spouse from Pakistan, often have to leave their families and social networks behind in Denmark and resettle in Sweden. Either way, the meaning and content of vertical family relations have to be redefined.

These intergenerational struggles result in new emerging moral orders and family formations. In this destructive–productive process, there are inevitably winners and losers. Some head successfully for the desired alternative 'family-scapes', identities and belongings of a middle-class life-style in the diaspora; others are left behind with the bits and pieces of what it used to be like to be and to do family. The rising second generation of Pakistanis are much better equipped to gain from these changes than their aging parents, partly because of their upbringing and general resources for life in Denmark, and partly because of their age. The future always belongs to the coming generations.

Relatedness as family-making: the horizontal relations

Horizontal transnational relations form a significant part of family history. The migrants who ended up in Denmark in the 1960s and 1970s left Pakistan in order to provide for their families. It has always been an important goal and an integral part of the family migration project to maintain and nurture horizontal family relations, but this can prove difficult for several reasons. First of all, because of the long separation, migrants experience a growing distance from the relatives they left behind in Pakistan almost forty years ago. Secondly, they find that the meaning and content of the horizontal transnational family relations and transactions are changing, and are being contested. Whereas migrants might try to cut down on remittances or the frequency of journeys to Pakistan, the family 'back home' often treats them solely as a means of access to the wealth of the West. Located as they are in Denmark, migrants have to accept that they may be cheated of rightful property and inheritance in Pakistan, or find that their house has been occupied by tenants – sometimes even family members – who refuse to move out. Contrarily, the family in Pakistan may see the migrants primarily as a means of obtaining financial resources, or as a way of getting their own sons or daughters to Denmark. As mentioned in Chapter 3, studies report of 'bogus' marriages, where South Asian men trick families into allowing them to marry their daughters, only to divorce them as soon as they acquire citizenship (Charsley 2006: 1170). In such circumstances, cherished horizontal family relations have become purely instrumental. This, in turn, generates suspicions and anxieties among migrants in Denmark that envious and jealous relatives in Pakistan may be trying to 'steal' from them by various kinds of occult attack.

Relatedness as place-making and belonging: Pakistan and Denmark

The problems of reproducing horizontal family relations substantiate the shared experience of migrants in Denmark that the homeland of Pakistan is disappearing. Today, Pakistan is primarily a theme in the dreams and imaginaries of the first generation; only to a much lesser extent is it a place where migrants could or would actually settle down permanently. After four decades in Denmark, migrants often have a hard time finding a place for themselves in the local social environment, family networks and place of origin when they do, infrequently, return to Pakistan. Those who do return more permanently often attempt to become part of the upper middle class in the major cities of Lahore, Islamabad or Karachi, where they can maintain a sufficient physical and social distance from needy and demanding relatives in the villages.

While migrants have highly ambivalent feelings towards Pakistan, often they do not find acceptance in Denmark. I have discussed how Muslim immigrants, including Pakistanis, are systematically subjected to critical debate in Danish public and political discourses and are excluded from being recognised as 'real' Danes. Pakistani immigrants are to some extent locked in a structural limbo in which they lack recognition both 'at home' in Pakistan and 'at home' in Denmark. In Pakistan, the horizontal extended family questions their presence, just as Danish majorities tend to do in Denmark. This lack of recognition – this feeling of not belonging in the world – is not necessarily a permanent condition, but a critical potential that frames social situations from time to time (and more and more often). This happens when, for instance, migrants experience being disqualified as 'real' Danes in political discourse, in the media or in day-to-day encounters with other Danes, or when their claims to belong to the transnational family or the local place of origin are ignored, neglected or contested. A current disturbing outcome of the migration process is that the claims of relatedness, ownership and belonging that migrants try to put forward are often not recognised by significant others. Migrants of all ages and both genders frequently attempt to find solace in alternative aspects of their post-colonial identity repertoire

– by being, for example, part of the global *umma* of fellow Muslims, a *murid* (follower) of a specific charismatic shaykh, or a devoted supporter of neo-fundamentalist transnational religious organisations.

Securitisation 'from above' = insecurity 'from below'

Although this book focuses on Pakistani migrant families, it also emphasises that these families are situated within a specific Danish context, where attitudes toward Muslim immigrants have changed dramatically in recent decades. The external historical and political contexts of Danish society must therefore be taken into consideration if we are to understand the internal dynamics of migrant families.

Chapter 1 discussed how political concerns regarding social cohesion and national integration that arose in the 1990s led to numerous legal initiatives in order to change specific aspects of immigrants' family lives that were considered problematic and basically 'un-Danish' (*udanske*). These integration policies resembled social engineering: immigrant families were urged, even compelled, to adopt Danish norms. These were rarely defined explicitly, but nonetheless the political strategy attempted to regulate the nutrition, dress, language, gender roles, family structures, housing and marriage practices of Muslim immigrants. In this period, the notion of 'integration' was conflated with 'assimilation'. The objective of the policy-makers was to reshape the immigrant family according to an ideal Danish (i.e. European) family model (see Grillo 2008: 16).

September 11 became the main trigger for a new national and international agenda, securitisation. The Danish immigration regime of 2002, discussed in Chapters 4 and 5, became a point of intersection between the two historical periods. In the name of integration, strict legislation attempted to alter the pattern and preference for transnational endogamous marriages, while, as a means of securitisation, it attempted to regulate the inflow of immigrants and thereby protect the Danish nation and territory from further Muslim transgressions.

Paradoxically, the ongoing national securitisation of migration has increased the experience of insecurity and uncertainty in immigrants' everyday lives. The fact that processes of securitisation generate insecurity reflects a basic point in the very constitution of the 'world risk society' (Beck 2002). I demonstrate how this happens very concretely when newly-wed couples, resettled in Sweden, are subjected to the dubious status of semi-legality. I have also suggested that a more general state of insecurity has become manifest in intimate interpersonal relationships as an unintended outcome of the intense gaze, public contestation and growing suspicion that Muslims in Denmark are currently exposed to and have to live with. In this respect, the uncertainty created by internal family cycles and community dynamics is reinforced by the external securitisation of the Danish welfare state in relation to the Muslim immigrant population. To push the conclusion a bit further, I suggest that there is a connection between the numerous measures of the security/integration-response introduced by politicians and policy-makers 'from above' and the emerging suspicions of sorcery that are felt, feared and experienced locally 'from below' in Pakistani families.

The ongoing process of securitisation creates and enlarges the gap between the immigrant minorities and majorities: a gap that can be termed a spiral of alienation or a developing dominant cleavage. The notion of a cleavage is not necessarily relevant all the time, but it constitutes a critical potential that can and will be mobilised when either minorities or majorities emphasise and enforce real or imagined differences between them. Currently, the dominant notion of Danishness (*danskhed*) is exclusive, and leaves little or no room for Danes with an immigrant background. In the current climate of ethno-nationalism and 'familism', the notion of Danishness constitutes an 'invisible fence' (Gullestad 2002b) that disqualifies certain groups with immigrant backgrounds from being recognised as 'real' Danes. This subtle exercise of power might work to reinforce shared notions of relatedness within the 'Danish family', but it only does so on behalf of the minority of 'not-quite-real' Danes. The result is a future scenario of Danish society where previous social imaginaries of national cohesion and integration have been replaced by the vision of a split society, divided between 'us' and 'them', Danes and Muslims. In this respect the security/integration-response that has dominated Danish society since September 11 works directly against the desired objectives of social cohesion and national integration.

However, recent developments suggest that the pendulum may be swinging back, and a new trajectory may be set for the future. First, the national elections of September 2011 brought to an end the ten years of the Liberal-Conservative government's absolute majority based on the support of the Danish People's Party. A centre-left government came to power in its place, with its own, presumably new agenda on immigrants, refugees, citizenship and family reunification. As this book goes to press, we are still waiting, however, to see actual substantial differences between the politics of the new and the previous governments. However, the global economic crisis has put the economy and the labour market at the top of the national political agenda. With the expansion of the economic crisis, a previous, more inclusive vocabulary of solidarity and mutual effort seems to have returned, which may cast immigrants and refugees as a neglected resource in the attempt to rescue the Danish economy and welfare state.

Secondly, a number of voices in the public debate, including Hans Jørgen Bonnichsen, former leader of PET (the intelligence service), have started to challenge the increasing tendency for surveillance and monitoring in Danish society that followed the anti-terror legislation introduced in the wake of September 11. For example, the authorities store 550 billion registrations of telecommunication and internet activities each year, amounting to approximately 100,000 pieces of information on every citizen in Denmark. If there is the political will to roll back parts of the anti-terror legislation, the current security/integration-response will obviously be reduced.

Finally, the terror attack in Norway on 22 July 2011, when the radical right-wing Anders Behring Breivik killed 77 people in Oslo and on the island of Utøya, had its own impact. In its own tragic way, the attack showed the public that terrorism is not the monopoly of Islamists. Breivik's manifesto, where he states his main motivation for the attack, also showed a deep-felt hatred towards Muslims, immigration and the multicultural society, including the politicians that support it (his reason for killing members of the youth organisation of the Norwegian Labour Party). It showed also that Breivik saw himself as a crusader, defending Christendom and the Norwegian nation. His rhetoric and fabulations are similar to discourses that circulated and were widely accepted in Danish public and political debates after 2001. Even in the Danish parliament, politicians have presented Muslim immigrants as invaders and themselves as a national resistance movement comparable to the one that fought the Nazi occupation during the Second World War (e.g., Kvaale 2011: 232–3). Breivik's terror act was a wake-up call, one that has initiated critical debates about the common sense of ethno-nationalism and cultural anxiety. In this respect it may have set the trajectory for a more inclusive political and national culture in the future.

Still, it should be emphasised that as this book goes to press, these are no more than indications of a possible future trajectory. No matter what, Danish society will probably not return to its state before 2001, because of the common and widespread conceptualisation of the Muslim population as potentially dangerous. Here the time dimension is also crucial; the upcoming generation of Danish Muslims have no other experiences and memories than that of being cast as *the usual suspects*. This will inevitably have its own impact.

Family upheaval and 'the diasporic condition'

The cases presented in this book show that many Pakistani migrant families in Denmark are in a state of turmoil as, due to intergenerational mobility and changes in the life cycle that have acquired particular salience in the specific social and historical contexts of Danish society, shared notions of relatedness and moral orders are being redefined. The securitisation of and legal interventions in numerous aspects of family life, along with the disturbing experience of neglected intergenerational obligations and a homeland that is fading away or being lost altogether, all contribute to the current upheaval.

An open question following from this line of argument is whether it was internal or external changes in migrant families that happened first. Is the family upheaval primarily a result of external political interventions, or did the internal changes to family intimacy begin long before? This question is not only difficult, if not impossible, to answer; it also seems to be the wrong question to ask in the first place. The object and ambition of this study have rather been to develop a historical perspective that can show how these *simultaneous* processes have challenged and/or reinforced each other over time and in different contexts. Just as it is impossible to give an adequate description and analysis of the internal dynamics of Pakistani families without taking the changing context of the Danish welfare state into consideration, it would be unsatisfactory to present a historical description of immigration and integration in the Danish context without discussing how the ongoing social engineering and securitisation affects the everyday lives of the 'immigrant other'. Instead of giving priority to one perspective, I have attempted to demonstrate the complex linkages between internal and external processes that have shaped migrant families and each other in different ways.

The case of the changing Pakistani migrant family is in no way exceptional. All over Europe, the forms, meanings and functions of the family institution are being challenged, contested and redefined. In this respect, the current fragility of relationships in Pakistani migrant families is merely an aspect of a more general 'family crisis', and as such an integral aspect of modernity itself (Grillo 2008; Carsten 2004), in which previously relatively stable institutions have become fluid (Bauman 2006, 2007). However, despite the wider transformation of the family institution, I suggest that the case of Pakistani family upheaval in Denmark is somewhat unique. Demographic changes, family cycles, dramatic upward social mobility and competition within the community, along with the ongoing securitisation and regulation of immigrants' everyday lives, have created a situation of general upheaval which manifests itself in intergenerational conflicts, broken relationships and suspicions of local and transnational sorcery. In this respect, Pakistani families in Denmark can be said to represent a specific variety of modernity.

But even if the case of Pakistani migrants in Denmark is unique, a broader comparative study might find that their situation just reflects more general aspects of the cultural fundamentalism, neo-racism, ethno-nationalism and securitisation that Muslim immigrants all over Europe are subjected to. There are most likely also interesting parallels to be drawn between the current situation of Pakistani families in Denmark and ethnographic studies from other parts of the world, where de-territorialised migrant families are experiencing high intergenerational mobility and are having to renegotiate moral orders and relatedness, thus creating a vulnerability that is articulated and negotiated by means of sorcery or witchcraft (*kala jaddu*, obeah, voodoo, juju, etc.). Such a future comparative project would be preoccupied with abstracting the principles that characterise the 'diasporic condition' of global migrant families on a much more general level.

Destructive–productive transitions and future horizons

My overall argument about family upheaval may seem pessimistic, even dystopian. The conclusions I end up with are influenced by my analytical focus on migrant families. If I had concentrated on, for example, educational mobility or entrepreneurship among second-generation Pakistanis in

Denmark, I would have ended up with a much more optimistic argument, through which the current changes in and of the Pakistani migrant community could have been framed as family creativity instead of family upheaval. However, my focus on the migrant family includes the two-sided destructive–productive process of intergenerational negotiations through which families, relationships and moral orders are produced and reproduced. I have chosen to focus on upheaval rather than creativity, to emphasise the fact that moral orders and common notions of relatedness have to be experienced as diminishing or lost before they can be restored or innovatively reinvented. By doing so, I remain true to my overall fieldwork experience that concerns and feelings of uncertainty and insecurity are much more salient among Pakistani immigrants than optimism and celebrations of creativity when it comes to the future prospects for the family institution.

Currently, Pakistani families are going through a historic period of demographic transition, as the aging first generation is about to be replaced by their descendants. During the next ten to fifteen years, the second generation will become the new elders of the Pakistani migrant community in Denmark; in contrast to their parents, however, they will in some respects be disconnected from Pakistan, as many have no close ties to relatives in Pakistan and do not own inalienable family land. They will have little or no childhood memories of their villages of origin, and many will in time be less proficient in Urdu or Punjabi, the languages of their ancestors. The second generation therefore do not have the same kind of formulaic truth (Giddens 1994: 63) – constituted by narratives, memories, anecdotes, sounds and smells, or knowledge of rituals and institutions like the *biraderi* or *zaat* – that today connects the first generation and links them to their shared past, upbringing and first-hand experiences in and of Pakistan. This unique embodied knowledge and memory will disappear when the first generation passes away. Instead, the second generation will relate to Pakistan in new ways, for instance, treating it as an imagined homeland, as in the case of the OPSA stage play (see Chapter 7), or as a momentary homeland, as happened with the intensive transnationalism following the Kashmir earthquake in 2005 (see Chapter 8). Both today and in the future, when the second generation reaches out to Pakistan, they will always do so from their current position, as having been born and raised in Denmark.

In the years to come, the segment of better educated, second-generation Pakistanis will aspire to become part of the emerging global middle class in the South Asian diaspora, consisting of the successful descendants of Pakistani, Indian and Bangladeshi first-generation migrants settled in Europe, North America or the Middle East. The new elites will most likely in many respects be transnationals like their parents, not necessarily in relation to distant relatives or a village of origin, but in relation to border-crossing networks of families like themselves that might have lost their connections with Pakistan (or India or Bangladesh) altogether, but instead have gained status and recognition as part of the new successful diasporic elite. Meanwhile, another segment among second-generation Pakistanis in Denmark will probably have no other option than to continue the uneven struggle for recognition, and to fight against the processes of alienation and securitisation they are subjected, to in Denmark. The two different trajectories of the maturing second generation (and the rising third generation) derive to some extent from the split into the two long-term family strategies – 'money' and 'education' – that was set in motion in the migrant community during the 1970s and 1980s, and that even today has a strong impact on everyday lives and future prospects.

Another urgent concern is whether or not Danish national kinship images will in time become more inclusive, so that Danish citizens with immigrant family backgrounds can become part of the imagined national community and be recognised as 'real' Danes, entitled to enjoy the benefits of the welfare state. In the current period of securitisation and national rearmament, however, there seems to be little hope in this regard. Meanwhile, second-generation Pakistanis will probably continue to settle in Sweden in order to obtain family reunification with spouses from Pakistan. The most resourceful marriage migrants will most likely find jobs and career opportunities in Sweden. Instead of returning to Denmark, they may decide to bring their parents and remaining family members to Sweden, so that they can have a new beginning together.

Finally, it is an open question what will happen when, a few years from now, the second generation of Pakistanis will have to negotiate family and gender relations all over again with their own teenage children. It is also an open question where – that is, in which national or international contexts or levels of society – the second generation will seek *rishtas* for their children, or what kind of real and symbolic mobility they will envisage in making these marriage arrangements, or whether the tradition of arranged marriages will disappear altogether, as current trends indicate. Only time and future research can answer these questions.

References

Abdel, M. 2000. *Mod min vilje*. Aarhus: CDR forlag.

Agamben, G. 2005. *State of Exception*. Chicago, IL: University of Chicago Press.

Ali, M. 2003. *Brick Lane*. London: Doubleday.

Ali, Y. 1992. 'Muslim women and the politics of ethnicity and culture in northern England', in G. Sahgal and N. Yuval-Davis (eds): *Refusing Holy Orders*. London: Virago Press, 101–123.

Al-Sha'rawi, S.M.M. 1995. *Magic and Envy – in the light of Qur'an and Sunna*. London: Dar Al Taqwa.

Alvi, A. 2007. 'India and the Muslim Punjab: a unified approach to South Asian kinship', *Journal of Royal Anthropological Institute* 13: 657–78.

Ameen, A.K.I. 2005. *The Jinn and Human Sickness: Remedies in the light of the Quran and Sunnah*. Riyadh: Darussalam.

Andersen, L.E. 2008. 'Den normaliserede terrorisme og partisanens teori', *Den Ny Verden. Tidsskift for Internationale Studier* 41(1): 55–72.

Anderson, M. 1998. 'Transnationale barndomme. Refleksioner over børnemigranter og identitet'. *Tidsskriftet Antropologi* 38: 107–16.

Andreassen, R. 2011. 'Burka og bryster. Debatter om tørklæder, tilgængelighed, ligestilling og nationalitet', in I. Degn and K.M. Søholm (eds): *Tørklædet som tegn: Tilsløring og demokrati i en globaliseret verden*. Aarhus: Aarhus Universitetsforlag, 80–98.

Anwar, M. 1979. *The Myth of Return*. London: Heinemann.

Appadurai, A. 1996. *Modernity at Large. Cultural Dimnsions of Globalization*. Minneapolis, MN: University of Minnesota Press.

Ardener, E. 1970. 'Witchcraft, economics and the continuity of belief', in M. Douglas (ed.): *Witchcraft Confessions and Accusations*. London: Tavistock, 141–60.

Ashforth, A. 2004. 'AIDS and witchcraft in post-apartheid South Africa', in V. Das and D. Poole (eds): *Anthropology in the Margins of the State*. Santa Fee, NM: School of American Research Press, 141–64.

Atkinson, R. 1998. *The Life Story Interview*. Sage University Paper Series on Qualitative Research Methods, Vol. 44. Thousand Oaks, CA: Sage.

Bajaj, K. and H.S. Laursen. 1988. *Pakistanske Kvinder i Danmark – deres baggrund og tilpasning til det danske samfund*. Esbjerg: Sydjysk Universitetsforlag.

Ballard, R. 1987. 'The political economy of migration: Pakistan, Britain and the Middle East', in J. Eades (ed.): *Migrant, Workers, and the Social Order*. ASA Monographs No. 26. London: Tavistock, 17–41.

Ballard, R. 1990. 'Migration and kinship: The differential effect of marriage rule on the processes of Punjabi migration to Britain', in C. Clarke, C. Peach and S. Vertovec (eds): *South Asians Overseas*. Cambridge: Cambridge University Press, 219–49.

Ballard, R. 1994. 'The emergence of Desh Pardesh', in R. Ballard (ed.): *Desh Pardesh. South Asian Presence in Britain*. Delhi: D.K. Publishing Corporation, 1–34.

Ballard, R. 1999. 'Panth, kismet, Dharm te Qaum: Continuity and change in four dimensions of Punjabi religion', in P. Singh and S.S. Thandi (eds): *Punjabi Identity in a Global Context*. Oxford: Oxford University Press, 7–37.

Ballard, R. 2003. 'A case of capital-rich underdevelopment: The paradoxical consequences of successful transnational entrepreneurship from Mirpur', *Contributions to Indian Sociology* 37(1–2): 49–81.

Ballard, R. 2006. 'Popular Islam in Northern Pakistan and its reconstruction in urban Britain', in J. Malik and J. Hinnels (eds): *Sufism in the West*. London and New York: Routledge, 160–86.

Ballard, R. 2008. 'Inside and outside: Contrasting perspectives on the dynamics of kinship and marriage in contemporary South Asian transnational networks', in R. Grillo (ed.): *The Family in Question: Immigrant and Ethnic Minorities in Multicultural Europe*. Amsterdam: Amsterdam University Press, 37–70.

Ballard, R. 2009. '*Madri and Padre Muzhub* in the Punjabi diaspora: a non-European perspective', paper presented at a seminar 'Global Families and Religious Practices', University of Copenhagen, 28–29 April.

Ballard, R. 2011. 'The re-establishment of meaning and purpose: *Madri and Padre Muzhub* in the Punjabi diaspora', in M. Rytter and K.F. Olwig (eds): *Mobile Bodies, Mobile Souls: Family, Religion and Migration in a Global World*. Aarhus: Aarhus University Press, 27–52.

Barth, F. 1989. 'The analysis of culture in complex societies', *Ethnos* 54 (3–4): 120–42.

Bauman, Z. 2006. *Flydende Modernitet*. København: Hans Reitzels Forlag.

Bauman, Z. 2007. *Liquid Times: Living in an Age of Uncertainty*. Cambridge: Polity Press.

Baumann, G. 1996. *Contesting Culture: Discourses of Identity in Multi-ethnic London*. Cambridge: Cambridge University Press.

Beck, U. 2002. 'The terrorist threat: World risk society revisited', *Theory, Culture & Society* 19(4): 39–55.

Beck-Gernsheim, E. 2006. 'Turkish brides: A look at the immigration debate in Germany', in Y.M. Bodemann (ed.): *Migration, Citizenship, Ethnos*. Gordonsville, VA: Palgrave Macmillan, 185–94.

Beck-Gernsheim, E. 2007. 'Transnational lives, transnational marriages: a review of the evidence from migrant communities in Europe', *Global Networks* 7(3): 271–88.

Berg, M. 1994. *Seldas andra bröllup*. Göteborg: Etnologiske föreningen i Västsverige.

Bledsoe, C.H. 2004. 'Reproduction at the margins: Migration and legitimacy in the New Europe', *Demographic Research*, Special Collection 3: 87–116.

Bleich, E. 2009. 'Muslims and the state in the post-9/11 West: Introduction', *Journal of Ethnic and Migration Studies* 35(3): 353–60.

Bolognani, M. 2007a. 'Islam, ethnography and politics: Methodological issues in researching amongst West Yorkshire Pakistanis in 2005', *International Journal of Social Research Methodology* 10(4): 279–93.

Bolognani, M. 2007b. 'The myth of return: Dismissal, survival or revival? A Bradford example of transnationalism as a political instrument', *Journal of Ethnic and Migration Studies* 33(1): 59–76.

Bourdieu, P. 1997. *Af praktiske grunde: Omkring teorien om menneskelig handlen*. København: Hans Reitzels Forlag.

Bourdieu, P. 2000. *Pascalian Meditations*. Cambridge: Polity Press.

Bourdieu, P. and L.J.D. Wacquant. 2001. *Refleksiv Sociologi – mål og midler*. København: Hans Reitzels Forlag.

Bredal, A. 1999. *Arrangerte ekteskab og tvangsekteskab i Norden*. Tema Nord 1999:604, Nordisk Ministerråd.

Bredal, A. 2006. '"Vi er jo familie". Arrangerte ekteskab, autonomi og fellesskab blant unge norsk-asiater', Doktorafhandling, Institut for Samfunnsforskning. Unipax 2006.

Bryceson, D. and U. Vuorela (eds) 2002. *The Transnational Family: New European Frontiers and Global Networks*. Oxford: Berg.

Callan, A. 2007. '"What else do we Bengalis do?" Sorcery, overseas migration, and the new inequalities in Sylhet, Bangladesh', *Journal of the Royal Anthropological Institute* 13, 331–43.

Carstairs, G.M. 1983. *Death of a Witch: A Village in North India 1950–1981*. London: Hutchinson.

Carsten, J. 1995. 'The substance of kinship and the heat of the hearth: Feeding, personhood and relatedness among Malays in Pulau Langkawi', *American Ethnologist* 22(2): 223–41.

Carsten, J. (ed.) 2000. *Cultures of Relatedness: New Approaches to the Study of Kinship*. Cambridge: Cambridge University Press.

Carsten, J. 2004. *After Kinship*. Cambridge: Cambridge University Press.

Carsten, J. 2007. 'Introduction: Ghosts of memory', in J. Carsten (ed.): *Ghosts of Memory: Essays on Remembrance and Relatedness*. Malden, MA: Blackwell Publishing, 1–34.

Cesari, J. 2010. 'Securitization of Islam in Europe', in J. Cesari (ed.): *Muslims in the West after 9/11: Religion, Politics and Law*. London: Routledge, 9–27.

Chamberlain, M. and S. Leydesdorff. 2004. 'Transnational families: Memories and narratives', in *Global Networks* 4(3): 227–41.

Charsley, K. 2005. 'Unhappy husbands: Masculinity and migration in transnational Pakistani marriages', *Journal of the Royal Anthropological Institute* 11(1): 85–105.

Charsley, K. 2006. 'Risk and ritual: The protection of British Pakistani women in transnational marriage', *Journal of Ethnic and Migration Studies* 32(7): 1169–87.

Charsley, K. 2007. 'Risk, trust, gender and transnational cousin marriage among Bitish Pakistanis', *Ethnic and Racial Studies* 30(6): 1117–31.

Charsley, K. and A. Shaw 2006. 'South Asian transnational marriages in comparative perspective', *Global Networks* 6(4): 331–44.

Chock, P.P. 1987. 'The irony of stereotypes: Towards an anthropology of ethnicity', *Cultural Anthropology* 2(3): 347–68.

Christiansen, C.C. 2011. 'Islamisk mode og stilmæssige strategier', in M.H. Pedersen and M. Rytter (eds): *Islam og muslimer i Danmark. Religion, identitet og sikkerhed efter 11. september 2001*. København: Museum Tusculanums Forlag, 219–43.

Clifford, J. 1986. 'Introduction: Partial truths', in J. Clifford and G. Marcus (eds): *Writing Culture, the Poetics and Politics of Ethnography*. Berkeley, CA: University of California Press, 1–26.

Clifford, J. and G. Marcus (eds) 1986. *Writing Culture, the Poetics and Politics of Ethnography*. Berkeley, CA: University of California Press.

Cole, J. and L. Thomas (eds) 2009. *Love in Africa*. Chicago, IL: University of Chicago Press.

Collier, J. 1997. *From Duty to Desire: Remaking Families in a Spanish Village*. Princeton, NJ: Princeton University Press.

Comaroff, J. and J. Comaroff. 1999. 'Occult economies and the violence of abstraction: Notes from the South African postcolony', *American Ethnologist* 26(2): 297–303.

Constable, N. (ed.) 2004. *Cross-Border Marriages: Gender and Mobility in Transnational Asia*. Philadelphia, PA: University of Pennsylvania Press.

Crone, M. and M. Harrow. 2010. 'Homegrown terrorism in the West, 1989–2008', *DIIS Working Paper* 2010:30.

Dahya, B. 1974. 'The nature of Pakistani ethnicity in industrial cities in Britain', in A. Cohen (ed.): *Urban Ethnicity*. ASA 12; London: Tavistock Publications, 77–118.

Das, V. 1995. *Critical Events: An Anthropological Perspective on Contemporary India*. New Delhi: Oxford University Press.

Deveci, A. 2004. *Tvang*. København: Aschehoug.

Donnan, H. 1988. *Marriage among Muslims – Preference and Choice in Northern Pakistan*. Delhi: Hindustan Publishing.

Donnan, H. 1997a. 'Family and household in Pakistan', in H. Donnan and F. Selier (eds): *Family and Gender in Pakistan: Domestic Organization in a Muslim Society*. New Delhi: Hindustan Publishing, 1–24.

Donnan, H. 1997b. 'Return migration and female-headed households in rural Punjab', in H. Donnan and F. Selier (eds): *Family and Gender in Pakistan: Domestic Organization in a Muslim Society*. New Delhi: Hindustan Publishing, 110–31.

Douglas, M. 1966. *Purity and Danger – An Analysis of the Concepts of Pollution and Taboo*. London and New York: Ark Paperbacks.

Eastmond, M. and L. Åkesson (eds) 2007. *Globala Familjer: Transnationall migration and släktskap*. Göteborg: Gidlunds.

Edwards, J. and M. Strathern 2000. 'Including our own', in J. Carsten (ed.): *Cultures of Relatedness: New Approaches to the Study of Kinship*. Cambridge: Cambridge University Press, 149–66.

Eglar, Z. 1960. *A Punjabi Village in Pakistan*. New York: Columbia University Press.

Ejrnæs, M. 2002. 'Etniske minoriteters tilpasning til livet i Danmark – forholdet mellem majoritetssamfundet og etniske minotiteter'. *AMID Working Papers* 18/2002.

Erdemir, A. and E. Vasta. 2007. 'Differentiating irregularity and solidarity: Turkish immigrants at work in London', *COMPAS Working Papers no. 42*, University of Oxford.

Eriksen, T.H. 1997. 'The nation as a human being – a metaphor in a mid-life crisis? Notes on the imminent collapse of Norwegian national identity', in K.F. Olwig and K. Hastrup (eds): *Siting Culture: The Shifting Anthropological Object*. London: Routhledge, 103–22.

Evans, T.M.S. and D. Handelman (eds) 2006. *The Manchester School: Practice and Ethnographic Praxis in Anthropology*. New York and Oxford: Berghahn.

Evans-Pritchard, E.E. 1976 [1937]. *Witchcraft, Oracles and Magic among the Azande*. Oxford: Clarendon Press.

Ewing, K.P. 1997. *Arguing Sainthood: Modernity, Psychoanalysis, and Islam*. Durham, NC: Duke University Press.

Ewing, K.P. 2008. 'Introduction', in K.P. Ewing (ed.): *Being and Belonging: Muslims in the US since 9/11*. New York: Russell Sage Foundation, 1–11.

Faist, T. 2006. 'The migration-security nexus: International migration and security before and after 9/11', in Y.M. Bodemann (ed.): *Migration, Citizenship, Ethnos*. Gordonsville, VA: Palgrave Macmillan, 103–19.

Fenger-Grøn, C. and M. Grøndahl. 2004. *Flygtningenes Danmarkshistorie 1954–2004*. Aarhus: Aarhus Universitetsforlag.

Foner, N. 1997. 'The immigrant family: Cultural legacies and cultural changes', *International Migration Review* 31(4): 961–74.

Foucault, M. 1988. 'Technologies of the self', in L. Martin, H.H. Gutman and P.H. Hutton (eds): *Technologies of the Self. A Seminar with Michel Foucault*. Amherst, MA: University of Massachusetts Press, 16–49.

Gad, U. 2011. 'Muslimer som trussel: identitet, sikkerhed og modforanstaltninger', in M.H. Pedersen and M. Rytter (eds): *Islam og Muslimer i Danmark: Religion, identitet og sikkerhed efter 11. september 2001*. København: Museum Tusculanums Forlag, 61–88.

Gardner, K. 1993. 'Desh-Bidesh: Sylheti images of home and away', *Man, New Series* 28(1): 1–15.

Gardner, K. 1995. *Global Migrants, Local lives: Migration and Transformation in Rural Bangladesh*. Oxford: Oxford University Press.

Gardner, K. 2002. *Age, Narrative and Migration: The Life Course and Life Histories of Bengali Elders in London*. Oxford: Berg.

Gardner, K. and F. Osella. 2003. 'Migration, modernity and social transformation on South Asia: an overview', *Contributions to Indian Sociology* 37(1&2): v–xxviii.

Geaves, R. 2006. 'Learning the lessons from the neo-revivalist and Wahabi movements: The counterattack of the new sufi movements in UK', in J. Malik and J. Hinnels (eds): *Sufism in the West*. London and New York: Routledge, 142–59.

Geaves, R. and T. Gabriel. 2004. 'Introduction', in R. Geaves, T. Gabriel, Y. Haddad and J.I. Smith (eds): *Islam & The West Post 9/11*. Aldershot: Ashgate, 1–12.

Geertz, C. 1988. *Works and Lives: The Anthropologist as an Author*. Stanford, CA: Stanford University Press.

Genova, N.P. de. 2002. 'Migrant "illegality" and deportability in everyday life', *Annual Review of Anthropology* 31: 419–47.

Geschiere, P. 1997. *The Modernity of Witchcraft: Politics and the Occult in Postcolonial Africa*. Charlottesville, VA: University of Virginia Press.

Giddens, A. 1991. *Modernitet og Selvidentitet. Selvet og samfundet under sen-moderniteten*. København: Hans Reitzels Forlag.

Giddens, A. 1992. *The Transformation of Intimacy: Sexuality, Love and Eroticism in Modern Societies*. Cambridge: Polity Press.

Giddens, A. 1994. 'Living in a post-traditional society', in U. Beck, A. Giddens and S. Lash (eds): *Reflexive Modernization: Politics, Tradition and Aesthetics in a Modern Social Order*. Cambridge: Polity Press, 56–109.

Gluckman, M. 1940. *Analysis of a Social Situation in Modern Zululand*. Bantu Studies XIV.

Gluckman, M. 1963. 'Papers in honor of Melville J. Herskovits: Gossip and scandal', *Current Anthropology* 4(3): 307–16.

Gluckman, M. 2006 [1961]. 'Ethnographic data in British social anthropology', in T.M.S. Evans and D. Handelman (eds): *The Manchester School: Practice and Ethnographic Praxis in Anthropology*. New York and Oxford: Berghahn Books, 13–22.

Goffman, E. 1959. *The Presentation of Self in Everyday Life*. New York: Doubleday.

Grillo, R.D. 2003. 'Cultural essentialism and cultural anxiety', *Anthropological Theory* 3(2): 157–73.

Grillo, R.D. 2004. 'Islam and transnationalism'. *Journal of Ethnic and Migration Studies* 30(5): 861–78.

Grillo, R.D. 2008. 'The family in dispute: Insiders and outsiders', in R. Grillo (ed.): *The Family in Question: Immigrant and Ethnic Minorities in Multicultural Europe*. Amsterdam: Amsterdam University Press, 15–35.

Gullestad, M. 2002a. *Det Norske – sett med nye øyne*. Oslo: Universitetsforlaget.

Gullestad, M. 2002b. 'Invisible fences: Egalitarianism, nationalism and racism', *Journal of the Royal Anthropological Institute* 8(1): 45–63.

Gullestad, M. 2006. *Plausible Prejudice: Everyday Experiences and Social Images of Nation, Culture, and Race*. Olso: Universitetsforlaget.

Gundelach, P. 2002. *Det er Dansk*. København: Hans Reitzels Forlag.

Gupta, A. and J. Ferguson. 1997. 'Discipline and practice: "The field" as site, method, and location in anthropology', in A. Gupta and J. Ferguson (eds): *Anthropological Locations: Bounderies and Grounds of a Field Science*. Berkeley, CA: University of California Press, 1–46.

Hage, G. 2003. *Against Paranoid Nationalism: Searching for Hope in a Shrinking World*. Melbourne: Pluto Press Australia.

Haraway, D. 1991. *Simians, Cyborgs and Women: The Reinvention of Nature*. London: Free Association Books.

Harriss, K. and A. Shaw. 2009. 'Kinship obligations, gender and the life-course: Rewriting migration from Pakistan to Britain', in V. Kalra (eds): *Pakistani Diasporas: Culture, Conflict and Change*. Karachi: Oxford University Press, 105–28.

Harvey, D. 1989. *The Condition of Postmodernity: An Enquiry into the Origins of Cultural Change*. Oxford: Blackwell.

Hastrup, K. 1995. *A Passage to Anthropology: Between Experience and Theory*. New York: Routledge.

Hastrup, K. and K.F. Olwig. 1997. 'Introduction', in K.F. Olwig and K. Hastrup (eds): *Siting Culture: The Shifting Anthropological Object*. London and New York: Routledge, 1–16.

Hedetoft, U. 2006. 'Divergens eller Konsekvens? Perspektiver i den dansk–svenske sammenstilling', in U. Hedetoft, B. Petersson and L. Sturfelt (eds): *Bortom Stereotyperna? Indvandrare och integration i Danmark och Sverige*. Göteborg: Makadam, 390–407.

Heide-Jørgensen, V. 1996. *Allahs piger – 8 indvandrerpiger fortæller om livet og kærligheden*. Aarhus: Aschehoug.

Hermansen, M. 2005. 'Dimensions of Islamic religious healing in America', in L. Barens and S. Sered (eds): *Religion and Healing in America*. New York: Oxford University Press, 407–22.

Hervik, P. (ed.) 1999. *Den Generende Forskellighed – danske svar på den stigende multikulturalisme*. København: Hans Reitzels Forlag.

Hervik, P. 2004. 'The Danish cultural world of unbridgeable differences', *Ethnos* 69(2): 247–67.

Hervik, P. 2011. *The Annoying Difference: The Emergence of Danish Neonationalism, Neoracism, and Populism in the Post-1989 World*. New York and Oxford: Berghahn Books.

Hervik, P. and M. Rytter. 2004. 'Med ægteskab i fokus', in B. Olsen, M.V. Liisberg and M. Kjærum (eds): *Ægtefællesammenføring i Danmark*. Udredning nr. 1. Institut for menneskerettigheder, 131–60.

Herzfeld, M. 1997. *Cultural Intimacy: Social Poetics in the Nation-State*. New York and London: Routledge.

Hirsch, J. and H. Wardlow (eds) 2006. *Modern Loves: The Anthropology of Romantic Courtship and Companionate Marriage*. Ann Arbor, MI: University of Michigan Press.

Hjarnø, J. 2000. 'Indvandrere som selverhvervende – en sammenlignende analyse af udbredelsen af selverhverv hos danske pakistanere, tyrkere og eksjugoslavere', *Dansk Sociologi* 3/2000, 95–112.

Holland, D. and M. Cole. 1995. 'Between discourse and schema: Reformulating a cultural-historical approach to culture and mind', *Anthropology & Education Quarterly* 26(4): 475–90.

Holland, D., D. Skinner, W. Lachiotte Jr. and C. Cain. 1998. *Identity and Agency in Cultural Worlds*. Cambridge, MA: Harvard University Press.

Holm, A. and A.S. Fabricius. 2008. *Transnationalisme på sigt – en undersøgelse af transnational aktivitet blandt efterkommere af pakistanske indvandrere i Danmark*. Speciale ved Roskilde Universitetscenter.

Holmen, A. 2002. 'Betydningen af sprog, tosprogethed og sprogligt bårne kulturformer for integrationsprocesserne', *AMID Working Papers no. 23*.

Howell, S. 2001. 'Self-conscious kinship: Some contested values in Norwegian transnational adoption', in S. Franklin and S. Mckinnon (eds): *Relative Values: Rethinking Kinship*. Durham, NC: Duke University Press, 203–223.

Howell, S. 2003. 'Kinning: The creation of life trajectories in transnational adoptive families', *Journal of the Royal Anthropological Institute* 9: 465–84.

Hummelgaard, H., L. Husted, H.S. Nielsen, M. Rosholm and N. Smith. 2002. *Uddannelse og arbejde for andengenerationsindvandrere*. Copenhagen: AKF Forlaget.

Hunter, M. 2009. 'Providing love: Sex and exchange in twentieth-century South Africa', in J. Cole and L. Thomas (eds): *Love in Africa*. Chicago, IL: University of Chicago Press, 135–55.

Huntington, S.P. 2006 [1993]. *Civilisationernes sammenstød – mod en ny verdensorden*. København: People's Press.

Hussain, M. 2003. 'Diskurs om islam i medier og politik', in M. Sheikh, F. Alev, B. Baig and N. Malik (eds): *Islam i bevægelse*. København: Akademisk Forlag, 199–229.

Ignatieff, M. 1993. *Blood and Belonging: Journeys into the New Nationalism*. London: BBC Books.

Jacobsen, B.D. 2004. 'Tilknytningskravet og forbuddet mod racediskrimination', in B. Olsen, M.V. Liisberg and M. Kjærum (eds): *Ægtefællesammenføring i Danmark*. Udredning no. 1. Institut for menneskerettigheder, 104–25.

Jacobson, J. 1997. 'Religion and ethnicity: Dual and alternative sources of identity among young British Pakistanis', *Ethnic and Racial Studies* 20: 238–56.

Jacobson, J. 1998. *Islam in Transition: Religion and Identity among British Pakistani Youth*. London: Routledge.

Jakobsen, J.S. 2011. 'Præmisser for dialog efter 11. september 2001. Gülen-bevægelsen i danske offentlige sfærer', in M.H. Pedersen and M. Rytter (eds): *Islam og Muslimer i Danmark: Religion, identitet og sikkerhed efter 11. september 2001*. København: Museum Tusculanums Forlag, 245–68.

Jensen, T.G. 2008. 'To be "Danish", becoming "Muslim": Contestations of national identity?', *Journal of Ethnic and Migration Studies* 34(3): 389–409.

Jensen, T.G. 2011. 'Omvendelse til islam. Kulturelle forestillinger om (u)renhed og fare', in M.H. Pedersen and M. Rytter (eds): *Islam og Muslimer i Danmark: Religion, identitet og sikkerhed efter 11. september 2001.* København: Museum Tusculanums Forlag, 143–66.

Johansen, K-L. 2002. *Muslimske stemmer: Religiøs forandring blandt unge muslimer i Danmark.* Viborg: Akademisk Forlag A/S.

Jöhncke, S. 2011. 'Integrating Denmark: The welfare state as national(ist) accomplishment', in K.F. Olwig and K. Paerregaard (eds): *The Question of Integration: Immigration, Exclusion and the Danish Nation State.* Cambridge: Cambridge Scholars Publishing, 30–53.

Jöhncke, S., M.N. Svendsen and S. Whyte. 2004. 'Løsningsmodeller: Sociale teknologier som antropologisk arbejdsfelt', in K. Hastrup (ed.): *Viden om Verden.* København: Hans Reitzels Forlag, 385–408.

Johnson-Hanks, J. 2002. 'On the limits of life stages in ethnography: Toward a theory of vital conjunctures', *American Anthropologist* 104(3): 865–80.

Johnson-Hanks, J. 2006. *Uncertain Honour: Modern Motherhood in an African Crisis.* Chicago, IL: University of Chicago Press.

Jørgensen, S. 2011. 'Sharia og dødsstraf: Et indblik i komplekse troværdighedsbetingelser', in M.H. Pedersen and M. Rytter (eds): *Islam og muslimer i Danmark. Religion, identitet og sikkerhed efter 11. september 2001.* København: Museum Tusculanums Forlag, 189–218.

Kalra, V. 2000. *From Textile Mills to Taxi Ranks: Experiences of Migration, Labour and Social Change.* Burlington, VA: Ashgate Publishing.

Kapferer, B. 1997. *The Feast of the Sorcerer: Practices of Consciousness and Power.* Chicago, IL: University of Chicago Press.

Kapferer, B. 2003. 'Introduction: Outside all reason – magic, sorcery and epistemology in anthropology', in B. Kapferer (ed.): *Beyond Rationalism: Sorcery, Magic and Ritual in Contemporary Realities.* New York and Oxford: Berghahn Books, 1–30.

Kapferer, B. 2010. 'Comments', *Cultural Anthropology* 51(2): 211–12.

Khader, N. 1996. *Ære og Skam. Det islamiske familie- og livsmønster fra undfangelse til grav.* Valby: Borgen.

Khan, N. 2006. 'Of children and Jinn: An inquiry into an unexpected friendship during uncertain times', *Cultural Anthropology* 21(2): 234–64.

Khawaja, I. 2011. 'Blikkene: Muslimskhedens synlighed, kropsliggørelse og forhandling', in M.H. Pedersen and M. Rytter (eds): *Islam og muslimer i Danmark. Religion, identitet og sikkerhed efter 11 september 2001.* København: Museum Tusculanums Forlag, 269–91.

Kibria, N. 2008. 'The "new Islam" and Bangladeshi youth in Britain and the US', *Ethnic and Racial Studies* 31(2): 243–66.

Kickbusch, J. 2001. *Kærlighed med stort M – Muslimske drenge og unge mænd om kærlighed, kærester og ægteskab.* Aarhus: CDR Forlag.

King, R. 2000. 'Generalizations from the history of return migration', in B. Gosh (ed.): *Return Migration: Journey of Hope or Despair?* Geneva: UN and IOM, 7–55.

Klausen, J. 2009. *The Cartoons that Shook the World.* New Haven, CT: Yale University Press

Kleist, N. 2006. 'Danmark to ansigter: Somali-danskeres oplevelser af stille integration og diskrimination', in M.H. Pedersen and M. Rytter (eds): *Den stille integration.* København, C.A. Reitzels Forlag, 118–42.

Knudsen, A. 1996. *Her går det godt – send flere penge.* København: Gyldendal.

Koefoed, L. and K. Simonsen. 2010. *'Den fremmede!'*, *byen og nationen – om livet som etnisk minoritet*. Fredriksberg: Roskilde Universitets Forlag.

Kofman, E. 2004. 'Family-related migration: A critical review of European studies', *Journal of Ethnic and Migration Studies* 30(2): 243–62.

Koser, K. 2010. 'Dimensions and dynamics of irregular migration', *Population, Space and Place* 16: 181–93.

Kublitz, A. 2010. 'The cartoon controversy: Creating Muslims in a Danish setting', *Social Analysis* 54(3): 107–25.

Kühle, L. 2006. *Moskeer i Danmark, islam og muslimske bedesteder*. Højbjerg: Univers.

Kühle, L. 2011. 'Radikalisering: ekstremisme eller vækkelse? En undersøgelse af aarhusianske muslimers holdninger', in M.H. Pedersen and M. Rytter (eds): *Islam og muslimer i Danmark. Religion, identitet og sikkerhed efter 11. september 2001*. København: Museum Tusculanums Forlag, 89–114.

Kvaale, K. 2011. 'Something begotten in the state of Denmark? Immigrants, territorialized culture, and the Danes as indigenous people', *Anthropological Theory* 11(2): 223–55.

Laclau, E. 1996. 'Why do empty signifiers matter to politics?', in *Emancipation(s)*. London: Verso, 36–46.

Lakoff, G. and M. Johnson. 1980. *Metaphors We Live By*. Chicago, IL: University of Chicago Press.

Larsen, M. 2000. *Elsker – elsker ikke: Om kærlighed og arrangerede ægteskaber*. Aarhus: CDF Forlag.

Laustsen, C.B. and O. Wæver 2000. 'In defence of religion: Sacred referent objects for securitization', *Millennium: Journal of International Studies* 29(3): 705–39.

Lefebvre, A. 1999. *Kinship, Honour and Money in Rural Pakistan: Subsistence Economy and the Effects of Internal Migration*. Nordic Institute of Asian Studies, No. 78. Richmond: Curzon Press.

Levitt, P. and N. Glick Schiller. 2004. 'Conceptualizing simultaneity: A translocal social field perspective on society', *International Migration Review* 38(145): 1002–39.

Lewis, P. 1994. 'Being Muslim and being British: The dynamics of Islamic reconstruction in Bradford', in R. Ballard (ed.): *Desh Pardesh: The South Asian presence in Britain*. Delhi: D.K. Publishing Corporation, 58–87.

Lewis, P. 2002. *Islamic Britain – Religion, Politics and Identity among British Muslims*. New York: I.B. Tauris.

Liisberg, M.V. 2004. 'Regler og administrativ praksis for ægtefællesammenføring', in B.K. Olsen, M.V. Liisberg and M. Kjærum (eds): *Ægtefællesammenføring i Danmark*. Udredning nr. 1. Institut for menneskerettigheder, 16–45.

Lindekilde, L., P. Mouritsen and R. Zapata-Barrero. 2009. 'The Muhammad cartoons controversy in comparative perspective', *Ethnicities* 9(3): 291–313.

Linde-Laursen, A. 2003. 'Regional integration: processer og paradokser', in I. Adriansen and P.O. Christiansen (eds): *Forskellige Mennesker? Regionale forskelle og kulturelle særtræk*. Ebeltoft: Forlaget Skipperhoved, 185–204.

Lyon, S. 1999. 'Gujars and Gujarism: Simple quaum versus network activism', Paper written in Bhalot, Punjab, Pakistan.

Macmillan, H. 1995. 'Return of the Malungwana drift: Max Gluckman, the Zulu nation and the common society', *African Affairs* 94: 39–65.

Madsen, D. 2002. *Kan tvang være en æressag? Idekatalog til en dansk indsats mod tvangsægteskaber*. København: Videnscenter for ligestilling.

Mahler, S. 1998. 'Theoretical and empirical contributions: Towards a research agenda for transnationalism', in M.P. Smith and L. Guarnizo (eds): *Transnationalism from Below*. New Brunswick, NJ: Transaction Publishers, 64–102.

Mamdani, M. 2002. 'Good Muslim, Bad Muslim: A political perspective on culture and terrorism', *American Anthropologist* 104(3): 766–75.

Mannheim, K. 1972 [1952]. 'The problem of generation', in K. Mannheim: *Essays on the Sociology of Knowledge*. London: Routledge & Kegan Paul, 276–320.

Marcus, G.E. 1995. 'Ethnography in/of the world system: Emergence of multi-sited ethnography', *Annual Review of Anthropology* 24: 95–117.

Mauss, M. 2001 [1924]. *Gaven – gaveudvekslingens form og logik i arkaiske samfund*. København: Forlaget Spektrum.

McLoughlin, S. 2009. 'Contesting Muslim pilgrimage: British-Pakistani identities, sacred journeys to Makkah and Madinah, and the global postmodern', in V. Kalra (ed.): *Pakistani Diasporas: Culture, Conflict and Change*. Karachi: Oxford University Press, 233–66.

McLoughlin, S. and V. Kalra. 1999. 'Wish you were(n't) here: Discrepant representations of Mirpur in narratives of migration, diaspora and tourism', in J. Hutnyk and R. Kaur (eds): *Travel-Worlds: Journeys in Contemporary Cultural Politics*. London: Zed Books, 120–36.

Mehdi, R. 2008. 'Supernatural means to affect the outcome of family disputes in courts: The case of Muslim Pakistanis in Denmark', in R. Mehdi, H. Petersen, E.R. Sand and G.R. Woodman (eds): *Law and Religion in Multicultural Societies*. København: DJØF forlagene, 197–216.

Mian, S.L. 2007. *Ambivalence, Care and Intergenerational Relations. The Case of Elderly Pakistani Immigrants in Denmark*. Masters Dissertation, Department of Sociology, University of Copenhagen.

Mitchell, C. 2006 [1983]. 'Case and situational analysis', in T.M.S. Evens and D. Handelman (eds): *The Manchester School: Practice and Ethnographic Praxis in Anthropology*. New York and Oxford: Berghahn Books, 23–42.

Mikkelsen, F., M. Fenger-Grøndahl and T. Shakoor. 2010. *I Danmark er jeg født ... Etniske minoritetsunge i bevægelse*. København: Center for Ungdomsforskning, Trygfonden og Frydenlund.

Moen, B. 2002. *Når hjemme er et annet sted: Omsorg for elder med minoritetsetnisk bakgrunn*. Norsk institutt for forskning om oppvekst, velferd og aldring. Rapport 8/02.

Moen, B. 2008. *Tilhørighetens balance: Norsk-pakistanske kvinners hverdagsliv i transnasjonale familier*. Doktoravhandling, Socialantropologisk institutt, Universitetet i Oslo.

Mohammad-Arif, A. 2009. 'Pakistanis in the United States: From integration to alienation?', in V. Kalra (ed.): *Pakistani Diasporas: Culture, Conflict, and Change*. Karachi: Oxford University Press, 316–34.

Moldenhawer, B. 2005. 'Transnational migrant communities and education strategies among Pakistani youngsters in Denmark', *Journal of Ethnic and Migration Studies* 31: 51–78.

Mølgaard, M. and P. Lindblad. 1995. 'Aging and immigrants: Their condition and expectation to old age', in *Multiculturalism in the Nordic Societies*. Nordisk Ministerråd.

Møller, A.S. 2007. *Ghazala – et æresdrab i Danmark*. Århus: Siesta.

Moore, H.L. and T. Sanders. 2001. 'Magical interpretations and material realities: An introduction', in H.L. Moore and T. Sanders (eds): *Magical Interpretations, Material Realities: Modernity, Witchcraft and the Occult in Postcolonial Africa*. London: Routledge, 1–26.

Mørck, Y. 1998. *Bindestregsdanskere – fortællinger om køn, generationer og etnicitet*. København: Forlaget Sociologi.

Najam, A. 2006. *Portrait of the Giving Community, Philanthropy by the Pakistani-American Diaspora*. Cambridge, MA: Harvard University Press.

Nielsen, J. 2004. *Muslims in Western Europe*. Edinburgh: Edinburgh University Press.

Olsen, B.K., M.V. Liisberg and M. Kjærum (eds) 2004. *Ægtefællesammenføring i Danmark*. Udredning nr. 1. Institut for Menneskerettigheder.

Olwig, K.F. 1998. 'Børn i vestindiske familienetværk. Fire livshistorier fra Nevis', *Tidsskriftet Antropologi* 38: 117–32.

Olwig, K.F. 2007. *Caribbean Journeys: An Ethnography of Migration and Home in Three Family Networks*. Durham, NC: Duke University Press.

Olwig, K.F. and K. Paerregaard (eds) 2011. *The Question of Integration: Immigration, Exclusion and the Danish Nation State*. Cambridge: Cambridge Scholars Publishing.

Olwig, K.F. and N.N. Sørensen. 2002. 'Mobile livelihoods: Making a living in the world', in N.N. Sørensen and K.F. Olwig (eds): *Work and Migration: Life and Livelihoods in a Globalized World*. London: Routledge, 1–20.

Osmani, N. 2000. *Forbandede Ære*. Aarhus: CDR Forlag.

Østberg, S. 2003. *Muslim i Norge: religion og hverdagsliv blant unge norsk-pakistanere*. Oslo: Universitetsforlaget.

Østergaard, B. 2007. *Indvandrerne i Danmarks Historie: Kultur- og religionsmøder*. Odense: Syddansk Universitetsforlag.

Paine, R. 1967. 'What is gossip about? An alternative hypothesis', in *Man*, New Series, 2(2): 278–85.

Papanek, H. 1973. 'Purdah: Separate worlds and symbolic shelter', *Comparative Studies in Society and History* 15(3): 289–325.

Peacock, J.L. and D.C. Holland. 1993. 'The narrated self: Life stories in process', *Ethos* 21(4): 367–83.

Pedersen, M. 2009. *Practices of Belonging: Ritual Performances and the Making of Place and Relatedness among Iraqi Women in Copenhagen*. Ph.D. series no. 52. Department of Anthropology, University of Copenhagen.

Pedersen, M.H. and M. Rytter (eds) 2006. *Den stille integration: Nye fortællinger om at høre til i Danmark*. København: C.A. Reitzels Forlag.

Pedersen, M.H. and M. Rytter (eds) 2011. *Islam og Muslimer i Danmark: Religion, identitet og sikkerhed efter 11. september 2001*. København: Museum Tusculanums Forlag.

Pittelkow, R. 2002. *Efter 11. september: Vesten og islam*. København: Lindhardt og Ringhof.

Poole, D. and V. Das (eds) 2005. *Anthropology in the Margins of the State*. Santa Fe, MN: School of American Research Press.

Preis, A-B.S. (ed.) 1998. *Kan vi leve sammen? – Integration mellem politik og praksis*. Viborg: Munksgaard.

Qadeer, M.A. 2007. *Pakistan: Social and Cultural Transformations in a Muslim Nation*. London and New York: Routledge.

Quraishy, B. 1999. *Fra Punjab til Vesterbro: det pakistanske samfund i Danmark.* København: Forlaget Etnisk Debatforum.

Rapport 1, 2006. *Bro, Bostad, Bil och Kärlek – ökar flyttströmmen från Danmark til Skåne.* Udfærdiget i samarbejde mellem Malmö stad, Migrationsverket, Skåneregion, Skatteverket og Öresundskommiteen.

Rapport 2, 2004. *Innflyttningar från Danmark.* Udarbejdet af Helene Hedebris for Skatteverkets rättsenhet. Available at: http://www.skatteverket.se

Rasanayagam, J. 2006. 'Healing with spirits and the formation of Moslem selfhood in post-Soviet Uzbekistan', *Journal of the Royal Anthropological Institute* 12: 377–93.

Rashid, R. 2000. *Et løft af sløret.* København: Gyldendal.

Rashid, R. 2006. *Du lovede, vi skulle hjem.* København: People's Press.

Rashid, R. and J.H. Højbjerg. 2003. *Bag om sløret.* København: People's Press.

Rehman, S. and V. Kalra. 2006. 'Transnationalism from below: Initial responses by British Kashmiris to the South Asia earthquake of 2005', *Contemporary South Asia* 15(3): 309–23.

Rezaei, S. 2002. 'Indvandrerejede virksomheder'. *AMID Working Papers* 8/2002.

Robson, J. 1934. 'Magic cures in popular Islam', *The Muslim World* 24: 33–43.

Roy, O. 2004. *Globalized Islam: The Search for a New Ummah.* New York: Columbia University Press.

Rozario, S. 2009. 'Allah is the scientist of the scientists: Modern medicine and religious healing among British Bangladeshis', *Culture and Religion* 10(2): 177–99.

Rubow, C. 2000. *Hverdagslivet teologi. Folkereligiøsitet i danske verdner.* København: Forlaget Anis.

Rudie, I. 2001. 'Om kohorter og kulturelle generasjoner: Noen refleksjoner om livsløbsanalyse som heuristisk redskap', *Norsk Antropologisk Tidsskrift* 12(1–2): 94–102.

Ruhs, M. and B. Anderson. 2010. 'Semi-compliance and illegality in migrant labour markets: An analysis of migrants, employers and the state in UK', *Population, Space and Place* 16: 195–211.

Rushdie, S. 1992. *Fantasiens hjemlande: Essays og kritik 1981–1991.* Århus: Samleren.

Rytter, M. 2003a. *Lige Gift: en antropologisk undersøgelse af arrangerede ægteskaber blandt pakistanere i Danmark.* Masters Thesis no. 261. Department of Anthropology, University of Copenhagen.

Rytter, M. 2003b. 'Islam i bevægelser', in M. Sheikh, F. Alev, B. Baig and N. Malik (eds): *Islam i Bevægelse.* København: Akademisk Forlag A/S, 137–59.

Rytter, M. 2005. 'Til døden os skiller ... eller forener. Oplevelser af hjem og tilhørsforhold blandt pakistanere i Danmark', *Social kritik* 99: 42–49.

Rytter, M. 2006. 'Ægteskabelig integration: pakistanske og danske arrangerede ægteskaber', in M.H. Pedersen and M. Rytter (eds): *Den stille integration. Nye fortællinger om at høre til i Danmark.* København: C.A. Reitzels Forlag, 18–43.

Rytter, M. and K.F. Olwig (eds) 2011. *Mobile Bodies, Mobile Souls: Family, Religion and Migration in a Global World.* Aarhus: Aarhus University Press.

Sachs, L. 1983. *Evil Eye or Bacteria: Tukish Migrant Women and Swedish Health Care.* Stockholm Studies in Social Anthropology no. 12. University of Stockholm.

Said, E. 2003 [1978]. *Orientalism.* London: Penguin Books.

Samad, Y. and J. Eade. 1996. *Community Perceptions of Forced Marriage.* Report for the Community Liaison Unit (CLU). www.fco.gov.uk/files/kfile.clureport.pdf

Sanjek, R. 1996. 'Intermarriage and the future of races in the United States', in S. Gregory and R. Sanjek (eds): *Race*. New Brunswick, NJ: Rutgers University Press, 103–30.

Sareen, M. 2003. *Når kærlighed bliver tvang: Generationskonflikter og tvangsægteskaber i Danmark*. København: People's Press.

Sayad, A. 2004. *The Suffering of the Immigrant*. Cambridge: Polity Press.

Schlytter, A. 2004. *Rätten att Själv Få Välja: Arrangeade Äktenskap, Kön och Socialt Arbete*. Studentlitteratur AB, Sverige.

Schmidt, G. 2002. *Tidsanvendelse blandt pakistanere, tyrkere og somaliere – et integrationsperspektiv*. København: Socialforskningsinstituttet 02:28.

Schmidt, G. 2004. 'Islamic identity formation among young Muslims: The case of Denmark, Sweden and the United States', *Journal of Muslim Minority Affairs* 24:1, 31–45.

Schmidt, G. 2007. *Muslim i Danmark – Muslim i Verden: En analyse af muslimske ungdomsforeninger og muslimsk identitet i årene op til Muhammad-krisen*. Uppsala: Universitetstryckeriet.

Schmidt, G. 2011. 'Law and identity: Transnational arranged marriages and the boundaries of Danishness', *Journal of Ethnic and Migration Studies* 37(2): 257–76.

Schmidt, G. and V. Jakobsen. 2000. *20 år i Danmark – en undersøgelse af nydanskeres situation og erfaringer*. København: Socialforskningsinstituttet.

Schmidt, G. and V. Jakobsen. 2004. *Pardannelse blandt etniske minoriteter i Danmark*. København: Socialforsknings Instituttet.

Schmidt, G., A. Liversage, B.K. Graversen, T.G. Jensen and V. Jakobsen. 2009. *Ændrede familiesammenføringsregler. Hvad har de nye regler betydet for pardannelsesmønstret blandt etniske minoriteter?* København: SFI – Det nationale forskningscenter for velfærd 09:28.

Schneider, D.M. 1980 [1968]. *American Kinship: A Cultural Account*. Chicago, IL: University of Chicago Press.

Schneider, D.M. 1977. 'Kinship, nationality, and religion in American culture: Toward a definition of kinship', in J. Dolgin, D.S. Kemnitzer and D. Schneider (eds): *Symbolic Anthropology: A Reader in the Study of Symbols and Meaning*. New York: Columbia University Press, 63–71.

Schuster, L. and J. Solomos. 2004. 'Race, immigration and asylum: New Labour's agenda and its consequences', *Ethnicities* 4(2), 267–300.

Schwartz, J. 1985. *Reluctant Hosts. Denmark's Reception of Guest Workers*. Kultursociologiske skrifter, no. 21. København: Akademisk Forlag.

Schwartz, J. 1990. 'On the representation of immigrants in Denmark: A retrospective', in F. Røgilds (ed.): *Every Cloud has a Silver Lining*. Copenhagen: Akademisk Forlag, 42–52.

Schwartz, J. (ed.) 1998. *Et midlertidigt liv: bosniske flygtninge i de nordiske lande*. Nordisk Ministerråd. Nord 1998:9.

Shakoor, T. 2004. *Imellem diaspora og Islam – et studie af en pakistansk friskole i København*. Kandidatspeciale i religionssociologi, Københavns Universitet.

Shakoor, T. and R.W. Riis. 2007. *Tryghed blandt unge nydanskere*. Lyngby: Trygfonden.

Shaw, A. 2000 [1988]. *Kinship and Continuity: Pakistani Families in Britain*. Amsterdam: Harwood Academic Publishers.

Shaw, A. 2001. 'Kinship, cultural preference and immigration: Consanguineous marriage among British Pakistanis', *Journal of the Royal Anthropological Institute* 7: 315–34.

Shaw, A. 2004. 'British Pakistani elderly without children: An invisible minority', in P. Kreager and E. Schöder-Butterfill (eds): *Aging without Children: European and Asian Perspectives*. Oxford: Berghahn Books, 198–222.

Shaw, A. and C. Charsley. 2006. 'Rishtas: Adding emotions to strategy in understanding of British Pakistani transnational marriages', *Global Networks* 6(4): 405–21.

Simonsen, J.B. 2001. *Det Retfærdige Samfund: Om Islam, Muslimer og Etik*. Viborg: Samleren.

Sinclair, K. 2008. 'Globale drømme, nationale virkeligheder. Hizb ut-Tahrir i Danmark og Storbritannien anno 2008', *Den Ny Verden: Tidsskrift for internationale studier* 41(1): 9–18.

Skjoldager, M. 2009. *Truslen indefra. De danske terrorister*. Latvia: Lindhardt og Ringhof.

Smedal, O.H. 2001. 'Innledning: Modeller, fenomener og realiteter', in S. Howell and M. Melhuus (eds): *Blod – tykkere enn vann? Betydninger af slektskap i Norge*. Bergen: Fagbokforlaget, 9–44.

Smith, L.H. 1996. *Indvandrere med egen forretning. En kultur analytisk undersøgelse af selverhvervende indvandrere i København og deres livsformer*. Esbjerg: Sydjysk Universitets Forlag.

Soares, B. and F. Osella. 2009. 'Islam, politics, anthropology', *Journal of the Royal Anthropological Institute* 15, special issue: 1–23.

Sørensen, N.N. 2005. 'Den globale familie – opløsning eller transnationalisering af familien?', *Tidsskriftet Sociologi* 1/16: 71–89.

Sørhaug, T. 1996. *Fornuftens Fantasier: Antropologiske essays om moderne livsformer*. Oslo: Universitetsforlaget.

Spooner, B. 1970. 'The evil eye in the Middle East', in M. Douglas (ed.): *Witchcraft Confessions and Accusations*. London: Tavistock, 311–19.

Stage, C. 2011. *Tegningekrisen – som mediebegivenhed og danskhedskamp*. Aarhus: Aarhus Universitetsforlag.

Stefansson, A.H. 2003. *Under my own sky? The cultural dynamics of refugee return and (re)integration in Post-war Sarajevo*. Ph.D.-rækken no. 25. Department of Anthropology, University of Copenhagen.

Stolcke, V. 1995. 'Talking culture: New boundaries, new rhetorics of exclusion in Europe', *Current Anthropology* 36(1): 1–24.

Strathern, M. 1981. *Kinship at the Core, An Anthropology of Elmdon, a Village in North-West Essex in the Nineteen-Sixties*. Cambridge: Cambridge University Press.

Svane, E. 2002. *Sibel*. København: Ekstra Badets forlag.

Taylor, C. 2004. *Modern Social Imaginaries*. Durham, NC: Duke University Press.

The Government's Action Plan for 2003–2005 on Forced, Quasi-forced and Arranged Marriages. 2003. The Danish Government, 15 August 2003. www.nyidanmark. dk/NR/rdonlyres/05ED3816.../forced_marriages.pdf

Thomsen, C.B. 2006. *Den Falske Melodi. En personlig og kritisk skildring af regeringens stramninger på udlændingeområdet*. København: Politikens Forlag.

Varley, E. 2008. *Belaboured Lives: An Ethnography of Muslim Women's Pregnancy & Childbirth Practices in Pakistan's Embattled, Multi-Sectarian Northern Areas*. Doctoral Thesis: Department of Anthropology, University of Toronto.

Veer, P. van der 2001. 'Transnational Religion', Paper given at the conference on Transnational Migration: Comparative Perspectives. Princeton University, 30 June–1 July.

Walle, T.M. 2004. 'Virginity vs. decency: Continuity and change in Pakistani men's perception of sexuality and women', in R. Chopra, C. Osella and F. Osella (eds): *South Asian Masculinities*. New Delhi: Kali, 96–130.

Werbner, P. 1990. *The Migration Process: Capital, Gifts and Offerings among British Pakistanis*. New York: Berg.

Werbner, P. 1999. 'Global pathways: Working class cosmopolitans and the creation of transnational ethnic worlds', *Social Anthropology* 7(1): 17–35.

Werbner, P. 2002. *Imagined Diasporas among Manchester Muslims – the Public Performance of Pakistani Transnational Identity Politics*. Santa Fe, NM: School of American Research Press.

Werbner, P. 2003. *Pilgrims of Love: The Anthropology of a Global Sufi Cult*. London: Hurst and Company.

Werbner, P. 2004. 'The predicament of diaspora and millennial Islam: Reflections on September 11, 2001', *Ethnicities* 4(4): 451–76.

Werbner, P. 2009. 'Revisiting the UK Muslim diasporic public sphere at a time of terror: From local (benign) invisible spaces to seditious conspiratorial spaces and the "failure of multiculturalism" discourse', *South Asian Diaspora* 1(1): 19–45.

Werbner, P. and H. Basu (eds) 1998. *Embodying Charisma: Modernity, Locality and the Performance of Emotion in Sufi Cults*. London: Routledge.

Whyte, S.R. 1997. *Questioning Misfortune: The Pragmatics of Uncertainty in Eastern Uganda*. Cambridge: Cambridge University Press.

Whyte, S.R., A. Erdmute and S. Geest. 2008. 'Generational connections and conflicts in Africa: An introduction', in E. Alber, S. Geest and S.R. Whyte (eds): *Generations in Africa: Connections and Conflicts*. Berlin: LIT Verlag, 1–27.

Whyte, Z. 2011. 'Asyl, ish'allah. Tro og mistro i det danske asylsystem', in M.H. Pedersen and M. Rytter (eds): *Islam og muslimer i Danmark. Religion, identitet og sikkerhed efter 11. september 2001*. København: Museum Tusculanums Forlag, 115–40.

Wikan, U. 1995. *Mot en ny norsk underklasse – indvandrere, kultur og integrasjon*. Oslo: Gyldendal Norsk Forlag.

Wikan, U. 2002. *Generous Betrayal – Politics of Culture in the New Europe*. Chicago, IL: University of Chicago Press.

Wikan, U. 2003. *For Ærens Skyld. Ære og Drab, Fadime en sag til eftertanke*. København: Gyldendal.

Wimmer, A. and N. Glick Schiller. 2003. 'Methodological nationalism, the social sciences, and the study of migration: An essay in historical epistemology', *International Migration Review* 37(3): 576–610.

Glossary

Barakat: blessing, spiritual power

Barat: groom's 'party' at a wedding

Barelwi: name of the religious movement in South Asia originated from the city of Bareilly in Uttar Pardesh, India, whose members venerate Sufi saints and shrines

Bazar: marketplace

Bhut: a ghost or spirit that haunts graveyards and other dangerous places

Biraderi: classificatory brotherhood

Burqa: specific dress covering the entire body. Associated with women in Afghanistan

Churail: the ghost of a woman who dies during pregnancy or in the forty-day seclusion after childbirth

Dam: literally, breath. A ritual in which a *Pir* bestows the blessing of someone by blowing on the person or on water that the person afterwards can drink

Darbar: saint's shrine, lodge

Deobandi: religious movement founded in the city of Deoband, sought to use the Islamic law as a bulwark against the inroads of non-Islamic influences

Desh: home, homeland

Dua: prayer, supplication made by an individual addressed to God

Dupatta: headscarf

Eid: Islamic festival

Gora: white man

Hadith: tradition describing the sayings and actions of the Prophet Muhammad

Hafiz: being able to recite the Quran by heart

Hajj: the pilgrimage to Mecca, one of the five pillars in Islam

Halal: permitted

Haram: forbidden

Hijab: veil

Hijra: the emigration of Prophet Muhammad and his followers from Mecca to Medina

Iftar: end of the daily fast in the month of Ramadan

Izn: the gift of *barakat*, divine abilities to help and heal others

Izzet: honour

Jinn: non-human beings, created by God from smokeless fire. Mentioned in the Quran along with humans and angels

Kafir: non-believer, non-Muslim

Kala jaddu: black magic, sorcery

Kammi: artisan, low caste

Khandan: household, family

Khatmi-Quran: readings of the entire Quran

Mehndi: henna party

Mohajir: refugees that came to Pakistan from India after partition

Murid: follower of a *Shaykh* or *Pir*

Nazar: the evil eye, unintentional witchcraft

Nikkah: wedding ceremony
Pardesh: at home abroad
Pir: saint, spiritual guide
Purdah: veil, codex for interaction between women and men
Ramadan: month of the fast
Rishta: marriage connection, proposal
Sahaba: the first companions of Prophet Muhammad
Sahih: true
Salafi: a doctrine of political Islam, Islamism
Shadi: marriage
Shalwar Kameez: traditional Pakistani dress, loose trousers and a long shirt/blouse
Sharia: body of Muslim jurisprudential law, including the Quran and *hadith*, along
    with later interpretations.
Shaykh: head of a Sufi order, *Pir*, honorific title
Shia: major Muslim religious stream, which starts from the belief in leadership rights
    of Ali, the Prophet's son-in-law
Shirk: infidelity, blasphemy through idolatry, assigning partners to God
Sunna: a practice or saying of the Prophet Muhammad that serves as a model for
    behaviour
Sunni: major Islamic religious stream, the majority of Muslims worldwide, which
    accepts the authority of the Prophet's historical successors
Sura: verse of the Quran
Tariqa: a Sufi 'path' or order
Ta'wiz: amulet
Ulama: scholars of Islamic law
Umma: the global fraternity of Muslims
Umrah: the little hajj to Mecca
Wahhabi: doctrine of political Islam, forbid all expressions of popular Islam
Wali: friend of God, see also *Pir* or *Shaykh*
Walima: wedding reception hosted by the groom's family
Wasifa: specific prayers
Zaat: caste, clan, occupational rank, ethnic identity
Zakat: alms, a religious duty to Muslims
Zamindar: segment of landowning castes
Zikr: remembrance of God

Index